The
Dream Team

The ones who shall rule and reign in
The Coming Kingdom of God

BRO. SHANE VAUGHN

Distributed by: The Apostolic Church of God ©

DISCLAIMER

The *Apostolic Church of God©* is in no way affiliated with the various Christian organizations called Church of God; *ex; Cleveland, Anderson, Worldwide, United, Philadelphia, Living* and various others. We use the term **Church of God** because it is the only biblical term for Gods' Church. We use the term **Apostolic** because the true Church of God recognizes the teachings of the Apostles of Christ as the foundation of the church and we strive to obey their teachings.
Overcomers International Outreach is the evangelistic outreach ministry of the author and incorporates all the Publications, telecast, musical recordings and various outreaches of Evangelist. Shane Vaughn.

The Dream Team

THOU HAST REDEEMED US AND MADE US KINGS AND PRIEST UNTO OUR GOD AND WE SHALL REIGN OVER THE EARTH!

REV 5:10

NOTE FROM THE AUTHOR:

THE REVELATIONS CONTAINED IN THIS BOOK SAVED MY LIFE! I WAS ADDICTED, BOUND AND TORMENTED FOR NEARLY FORTY YEARS UNTIL I CAME TO UNDERSTAND THE REAL PURPOSE FOR MY LIFE. I wrote this book to help bring clarity to the subject of the *Coming Kingdom of God*.

Without a correct understanding of your future role in the Kingdom of God that you are now preparing for in this life; you will live this life without the vision necessary to prepare yourself for your ultimate role in the future Government of God. The passion for this book and this study has come from my own life experiences.

After a lifetime of struggling with a hidden addiction; I have come to realize that the message that I present to you in this book is the most important message that God has ever revealed to me; it has literally saved my life and enhanced my walk with God. I can only pray that it does the same for you. If you are struggling with continual sin; strongholds in your own life you must come to understand the truths contained in this book. You were born to walk in holiness and this book will show you why!

When I come to realize after a year of continual study of the scriptures that I had never been taught my true purpose in life; I was sorely disappointed. Even after reading the famed book *"Purpose Driven Life"* something was still missing. Finally, I realized what it was! **My purpose for this life is only understood if I understand my purpose in the next life and that is where all other books on the market have failed.**

YOU ARE ABOUT TO DISCOVER MAYBE FOR THE VERY FIRST TIME WHAT YOUR *"REAL PURPOSE DRIVEN LIFE"* REALLY IS. I assure you that if you take the time to peruse these pages, you will never be the same. I do not say that with redundancy. It is my testimony that I have finally been able to overcome a lifetime of hidden sin and addictions only after receiving this revelations in these pages. You must read every page!

After running from the call of God on my life; after choosing my ways instead of God's ways; after controlling my own life; I met face to face with God's divine discipline. In His loving kindness He pulled me away from everyone that I loved for three solid years into the Louisiana prison system and there is where He saved me from myself. I wasn't a train wreck waiting to happen, I was a wrecked train! I lost everything; a seventeen year marriage, three wonderful sons, a great career and most importantly a lifetime of ministry because I could not overcome sin in my personal life. But TODAY I have it all back plus more!

This revelation came to me of the *Coming Kingdom of God* in the solitude of a lonely cell when God Himself invited me to join His *"Dream Team"* and since that time *(by the grace of God)* I have been able to enjoy a more overcoming life. I wish to share the same with you! Please, study the scriptures with me; you are about to find out why you are saved, why the struggle is worth it and why you have been called into God's holy church. Be prepared; it has nothing to do with Heaven nor Hell . . . it all has to do with the *Coming Kingdom of God* and your role in that government.

Dedication & Thanks

*The writings of this book are preserved for posterity and
lovingly dedicated to my children;*
NICHOLAS TYLER , ANDREW CHANDLER , & BRANHAM ALEXANDER SHANE:

You guys are my reason for living, my reason for never giving up and for finally making the much needed changes in my life. I pray that the writings of this book will open your own eyes to the importance of living according to God's ways.

Let the lessons learned from my life be an example for each of you my sons; Fall in love with Jesus, obey God's laws, go to the house of God, teach my grandchildren these truth, pay His tithe, remember His Sabbath, honor your mother and father with the lives that you live and always keep your faith in the cross, empty tomb and soon coming of the Lord Jesus Christ.

Each of you have been handed a legacy without price. Your great, great grandmother is a product of the early American revival that was poured out at Azusa street; your grandmother was a product of the great healing revival of the early part of the 20th century. Your father and mother were both children of Pentecost and blessed to see the mighty outpourings of God Spirit upon the earth during the latter rains of our age.

However, if I understand Bible prophecy correctly by the time your children read this book; there will hardly be any true, living faith left upon the earth. However, I challenge you to make sure that horrible lot doesn't befall our family. Always honor the legacy of faith handed to you and strive to enter into the glorious kingdom of God. I plan to meet you there, each of you. I love you all!

MENU OF CHAPTERS

CREDITS

Special acknowledgements belong to the following ministries for the information that I have gleaned from their teachings. While the Holy Spirit introduced these truths to me He also led me to the writings of the following ministries. Their publications has lent me the scriptural teachings that helped to advance my understanding of the Coming Kingdom of God.

The Apostolic Church of God
The United Church of God
The Living Church of God
The Restored Church of God
Voice of God Recordings
New Hope Revival Ministries

What is The Dream Team?
- You and God in perfect harmony -

THE PROLOGUE

As we begin this journey and this Bible study we need to clarify some terminology. Without a clarification of terms and semantics you will find the following study difficult to follow; The first word on our agenda is the word "***Kingdom***" more specifically the "***Kingdom of God***" or the "***Kingdom of Heaven***".

Since you and I now live in a time of human history without many true examples of earthly kingdoms or true monarchies; it is difficult for our western and self-governing minds to grasp the meaning of such an archaic and outdated word as ***kingdom***. As Westerners we are void of understanding when it comes to anything related to kingship and kingdoms. As a result of our ignorance of this meaning we are unable to fully comprehend the meaning of God's kingdom. So, I would encourage you in this Bible study to replace the word *kingdom* in your mind with the synonym for kingdom, which is ***Government***. Perhaps the changing of the word will impress upon your mind the fuller meaning of the actual word, ***Kingdom***.

> **A KINGDOM IS SIMPLY A GOVERNMENT**

A kingdom is nothing more or less than a government. A Kingdom is made up of and includes the ministers or the cabinet of the King and also the people under the authority of a King.

Allow me to create a scenario for you; If you were somehow granted your own kingdom today wouldn't you have your own utopian ideas of what plans you would like to implement in your kingdom? What would your "Dream Kingdom" consist of? Good health for everyone; perhaps parks and playgrounds for all children to enjoy; a perfect and splendid environment for every citizen? Perchance you would desire a Kingdom where everyone is cultured in the arts or educated in the sciences. Whatever your grandiose plans are they cannot be implemented by you alone, you will first need a government or a team.

You will require a cabinet of ministers that have earned your trust and these people will lay aside all of their own personal agendas to serve your ideals and to serve your plans among the people. Your cabinet or government has only one job: to bring into reality among the population of your kingdom the ideals of your mind. They are to be trusted above all people, they are your ministers. You only chose them for your cabinet positions after they came highly recommended because of their loyalty and faithfulness. You watched them complete their previous jobs with previous employers with absolute loyalty and obedience. You chose them because you knew that they were not so stuck on themselves that they couldn't become absorbed in your dreams.

Your desire for these chosen members of your government is for your mind to become their mind; your thoughts their thoughts; they should live only to implement your governmental policies. Any employer will tell you that the best employee is the one who needs not be told anything because they understand the employer's methods and thoughts completely and they faithfully do things the employer's way.

Theses members of your new government that you have chosen after much observation from a previous job will begin their new job by educating the masses. They will bring your curriculum, your ways into the schools and begin training young minds into your ways. They will cause people in your kingdom to see the beauty of your plans and therefore cause your subjects to desire the results of your plans.

DETAILS OF A DREAM

A dream without a team will always remain a dream! Every great dreamer must find a team of people that believes in his dream; this team must become completely inculcated with this dream in order to bring it to pass especially if that dream is dealing with masses of people.

> **A DREAM WITHOUT A TEAM WILL ALWAYS REMAIN ONLY A DREAM**

Henry Ford dreamed about his automobile but he needed a team to build those automobiles.

Steve Jobs had the Apple dream but he had to find a team who became so absorbed in the thoughts and dreams of *Steve Jobs* that they themselves began to see apples everywhere they looked.

If someone hadn't become part of *Dr. Martin Luther King's* dream it would have forever remained his dream rather than becoming "***our dream***". If he had "*looked over the mountain and seen the Promised Land*" alone then today many of us might still be living in a backwards world. However, he had a team of colleagues and trusted ministers who began to preach his message to their neighbors and congregations and the dream seeped into the minds of the masses and as a result the message of peace began permeating the public mind-set and the end of that story need not be explained.

I had a dream to write this book, I remember well sitting alone with my thoughts about the subject of "*The Ultimate Dream Team*" while driving down the highway or relaxing with my beautiful children at home and these chapters that I'm now writing lived only in my mind. Before I shared this dream with a publisher, editor, proofreader and marketing professional I had nothing but a dream. However, now you're holding the manifestation of a dream in your hands, only because my dream found a team! I could dream the dream but I do not own a printing press nor do I have the grammatical skills necessary to arrange this book into its completed form. However, someone else who believes in my message can bring my dream and place it in your hands.

GOD HAS A DREAM

God has a dream! God has a sovereign and illustrious desire for His earth. The Eternal *Yahweh* of heaven existed before time immemorial and lived alone with His dreams or His thoughts. The very name of *Yahweh* simply means "*the Self-Existing one.*" In those thoughts of *The Eternal One* was a utopian planet called earth; a place of rapturous bliss where he would birth spiritual sons and daughters that would reign and rule over the earth and the universe with him; they would beautify, dress and care for this earth and enjoy eternal lives in such a paradise. This planet was so beautiful and picturesque that when created even the angels in heaven rejoiced upon its completion[1]. It seems quite evident and tenable in my mind that if a planet that we refer to as heaven previously existed before the creation of earth and if indeed it was more beautiful and glorious than the

1 *JOB 38:7*

earth and if those angels were already living in this pre-existent heaven then quite sensibly there would have been no cause for such great angelic rejoicing and elation; but rather disappointment. If heaven was indeed superior in comparison to the earth then surely the angels would have wept over such an inferior creation rather than "***shout for joy***." Evidently, God must have really outdone himself with the creation of earth with her snow-capped majestic mountains, her fields of golden grain; heavenly harbors of pristine water and her divinely designed streams of solitude and trees of tapestry.

Just as earthly sovereigns or kings delight in giving their throne *(their government, their kingdom)* to their descendents who make up their natural blood family, so does Yahweh, the eternal King. He created in His image a man to reign on his throne, Adam and Adams' sons. This book will prove in forthcoming chapters that Satan was already reigning on God's throne on this earth before the creation of Adam and for this very reason the first Adam was created to rightfully and legally dethrone Satan; he was to actually "***subdue it and have dominion***" [1] In studying these few words in Genesis you will find in the original Hebrew words that this entire thought of subduing and dominion is actually the idea of subjugating, conquering, dethroning and bringing under control. This is what the first Adam was created to do; he was to qualify by his obedience to God to bring Satan under his dominion and control. Sadly, the opposite became the facts of our lives. Where the first Adam failed, the second Adam *(Jesus Christ)* succeeded. God always has a Plan B!

Simply look at the royal families of earth and their histories. Anytime a stranger invades and takes over the family throne from the legally reigning family there will be generations of constant warfare until the rightful heir is enthroned again. In like manner Satan took over God's government on this earth and God allowed it to be so because he saw a greater outcome which you and I shall soon see the full proof of in the coming Kingdom age.

According to all biblical genealogies, Adam was called the Son of God. [2] This simply means that all of Adam's sons would have indeed been Son(s) of God and therefore all of them would have been in God's royal family ruling over and forever enjoying the wealth of the earth. In this reign and in this Kingdom there would be nothing but God's peace, tranquility, joy and righteousness.

WHY ARE THE DREAMS OF GOD AS OF YET UNFULFILLED?

Scripture gives us glimpses into Gods dream for the earth, especially found in the book of Isaiah. No one would ever "*hurt in all of God's holy mountain*". [3] Rather than living the selfish and Satanic life of "*get*" all people would live the heavenly and righteous life of "*give*". The *law of the jungle* would no longer prevail, the law of *survival of the fittest* would find no place in God's dream. The laws of chance would be replaced with the laws of faith and perfection. There would be no anger, no politics and no division on His earth. Even the animals would be at peace; lions and lambs playing together. [4] In God's dream the babies would play with the serpents and the adders and the parents would have no fear of harm as the serpents would be gentle and never strike anyone *(ISAIAH 11:8)*. There

1 *GEN 1:26 & 28*

2 *LUKE 3:38*
3 *ISAIAH 11:9*
4 *ISAIAH 11:6*

would be no one that ever broke Gods *law of liberty* and His *law of love* because those laws would be a natural part of every mans character.[1] The *Ten Commandments* would simply become a given, a lifestyle for everyone without a second thought; God's eternal law would be the law of the land. In God's dream every weapon on earth; every sword would be melted and turned into farming instruments or plowshares *(ISAIAH 2:4)*. No one would ever go hungry, no child would ever cry from abuse. No drunken father would ever mistreat his wife and children. The creditors would never take your home away.[2]

The forces of nature would operate perfectly with no disastrous storms but rather there would be even rainfall or underground mist over the entire earth as its needed. There would be no deserts on God's earth but instead those deserts would blossom like a rose filled with soft streams and teeming with life *(ISAIAH 35:1)*. In this dream no one would ever steal from his neighbor and no one would ever break up a blissful, idyllic and harmonious home because of adultery. Sexually transmitted diseases would be unheard of in this dream because no one would be committing fornication. No one would ever go bankrupt because none would be desirous of what his neighbor had and therefore there would be no need for debt.

Not one person would ever have mental breakdowns from the stress of overworking because in Gods dream, men and women and children would rest completely every Sabbath or seventh day, refreshing their souls with worship and relaxation. In God's dream all the rivers and streams would be healed and food would be plentiful.[3] The earth would be beautified and made a complete paradise of parks and utopian scenes as every man, woman, boy and girl took special pride in the beauty of earth and together they continued "***dressing***" the earth.

According to Isaiah every person would have their own beautiful home, their own tree to rest under and they would never lose their cherished and beautified property[4]. Every person would help to make the earth even more beautiful as they realized that this earth is the inheritance of the saints. "***Blessed are the meek for they shall inherit the earth***"[5] Did you ever speculate as to why no minister can really explain that one and very simple teaching of Christ? Because they've been convinced that God is through with the earth and moving us all to another planet or place called heaven.

I've barely touched upon some of the scriptural details of God's dream. . . **Alas, it was only a dream!**

Why was it only a dream rather than a fulfillment in reality? Why is this dream of God as of yet, unfulfilled? Why does Jesus pray this prayer "***Father, let your dreams (will) be as fulfilled on earth as they are in the heaven***" Because quite simply; <u>God never had a team on the earth to implement His dream!</u> In the heavens, in the spiritual dimensions He has a team; two-thirds of his angels remain on His team in complete harmony with His eternal laws, they love His ways, they trust Him and He trust them. The scriptures tell us that these angels "***hearken to the voice of his Word***."[6] We're also told that they are "***Spirit Ministers that serve him and his creation.***"[7]

1 *JER 31:34*
2 *MICAH 4:4*
3 *EZE 47:9*

4 *MICAH 4:4*
5 *MATT 5:5*
6 *PSALMS 103:20*
7 *PSALMS 104:4*

Likewise, He created Adam and Eve as prospective members of his earthly dream team; they were told to dress the earth, beautify it, fill it up again with people and enjoy it; they were designed to bring God's dream to pass. Ideally, they also would learn God's *laws of liberty* from Him personally each day in the cool of the evening; sitting with him in a garden called Eden on a planet called earth. Here it was; the hope of *His Holiness* that these free-moral agents would see the joy of the angels who didn't join in the Luciferous rebellion and also walk in the same obedience. These members of his team would soon be faced with a choice after being taught by God himself at the *First Church of Eden.* They would be given the opportunity eventually to receive eternal life, a natural result of total obedience to the Word and/or Laws of God which are in fact the trees or source of life.

Jesus was and is the *Tree of Life* because He is the Word of God and in His lifetime He kept perfectly, the laws of God. Sadly, our first parents, Adam and Eve chose as we all did on our earthly sojourn to join the team of self-rule rather than God's rule, they chose democracy instead of theocracy, they had their own dreams.

Adam and his Eve chose to determine for themselves with their own knowledge what was good and what was evil. They chose the source of self-knowledge rather than obedience to a sovereign King. After all, they probably reasoned in their minds as we all have; who gave God the right to decide what was good or evil for them or us? Didn't God realize that all truth is relevant as the philosophers of our day teach and that there are no such things as outdated absolutes given by a mad monarch? They themselves would use their own power of reasoning to determine if adultery was good or evil or if stealing was good or evil. In their convoluted minds such as our own, sometimes stealing might even be justified. Perhaps if adultery makes me feel better about myself and my sexuality then perhaps it's not always evil. After all, isn't this life about me finding happiness? Don't my opinions matter? Isn't it time that I live for myself and forget what any and everyone else thinks? Isn't it my turn at the proverbial pie and isn't it someone else's turn to be mistreated and used and abused? Also, maybe it's better to rest one day a month or on the first day of the week rather than the seventh[1], they decided we will decide these issues of good and evil for ourselves. Because of their human deductions and reasoning they failed in establishing God's throne of righteousness on the earth. They failed to overthrow Satan's government legally; therefore, today it remains only a dream in the mind of God. Today, the King of this world, the God of this age continues to be as it has been since the beginning; Lucifer himself. Adam failed to change this fact as he was created to do. So now only one of his legally born sons, what scripture calls a near-kinsman could legally obtain the throne that Adam failed to apprehend. Of course that Son did come and his name was Jesus. However, as this book will teach you, Jesus did NOT seize the throne of Satan at his first coming, that joyous duty is reserved for his second coming. The Lamb came to love, the Lion comes to conquer.

> **GOD HAS BEEN PAINTED WITH COLORS OF CRUELTY ON EASELS OF EVIL AND CANVAS OF CORRUPTION**

1 *Exo 20:10*

The accusations against God

So many people sadly accuse God of the horrors of our planet. I hear people daily ask the proverbial question of *Why.* With a broken heart I listen to news commentators describe the latest natural disasters as *Acts of God.* Why does God allow such horrible things on earth? They scream their accusatorial ribaldry; their faithless questions masked so deceptively in the shawls of sincerity and the coats of concern. With demonic directives they cast their contumelious words into the cosmic mind-set of mankind; through books, television and conversations. It saddens my soul because God has planted in my converted mind and millions of others; He has planted in my spirit and millions of others **His dream** and His overflowing love for humanity.

When you have been saturated with Gods Holy Spirit and you have felt His heartbeat of love and known His ways of mercy and grace you cannot help but have hope for humanity. What they accuse my awesome and loving God of is so far from His desires for humanity. No wonder humanity hates her sovereign and holy God; He has been painted with colors of cruelty on easels of evil and on a canvas of corruption. If you are redeemed today dear friend then you are part of that team that God is uniquely putting together by the drawing of the Holy Spirit wherewith He can install his "*spirit mind*" or His dreams into your spirit which is your mind[1]. God desires to replace your character with His, your mind with His, your dreams with His and you selfishness

with his selflessness. Until you become a baptized[2] member of his sacred church which is the *"mother of us all"* then you are clueless of His love for people and until that changes you cannot truly have a godly compassion on the masses of lost people. You must love what Jesus loves . . .broken people.

After this Baptism you will see God's desire for every soul; you will become associated with His pain and also His hopes as you become an intercessor for humanity and for the dwellers of earth. Only after this baptism will you truly hate the results of sin and only then will you be moved to pray for every sick person and every addicted person and every bound person. Members of the *Dream Team* have hope, oh yes! We have hope because we have seen by the Spirit that a better day is coming; a better government; a better King is coming to the earth. We have hope and therefore we pray, we believe, we persevere to be counted worthy of earths coming King. I believe it was the Apostle Paul who wrote the church this admonition "***let this same mind that was in Christ be in you***."[3]

For *The Dream Team* there is no fear of tomorrow, we face today with no alarm because we have seen tomorrow through the eyes of the Prophets; we have heard the happy songs of tomorrows children; we have seen the drying of every weeping eye; we have smelled the coffee of tomorrows morning and whatever it takes, no matter how great the sacrifice or how continental the cost; we will be **more than saved** ! We will be counted worthy to rule and reign, we will overcome! Yes, we will fight against the hold of sin; we will become the enemies of flesh and the rewards thereof. We now have a reason to overcome;

1 *The mind and the spirit are one and the same.*

2 *Physically and spiritually*
3 *Phil 2:5*

we must overcome because according to the beloved Apostle John; only those who overcome will sit in Christ government or on his throne.[1] Only a few will overcome and be chosen for God's government or kingdom. Only a few will "*take the kingdom by force*". The goal of this book is to cause you to reach for more than salvation; reach for the higher calling; the *Overcomers* calling. Only those who can hear the Eagles scream will ever make it on The Dream Team because only those who fly with eagles can hear the eagles scream.

THE VERY FIRST MEMBER OF THE DREAM TEAM

How glorious to watch the life of Christ; He had God's dream. He was the first member of God's *Dream Team;* He understood Gods plans for man. He is in fact the "***firstborn of many brethren***"[2] ; He was the first of many members to join this *Dream Team* but I assure you and I assure Satan that many more "*brethren*" are coming; we are simply waiting for the "*redemption of our bodies*" when we will be born again in the resurrection of the dead and therewith add our membership with Christ and together with Him form the great government of Zion; making up the great *Family of God* or *God's Family*, or the *God Family*, whichever phrase you choose, they each one all declare the same valid truth.

Simply watch Christ in action; He healed all manner of diseases, He raised the dead, He wanted man to enjoy life. When Christ turned water into wine it was only so that man could enjoy the fun and the joys of this life. Christ loved to see workers

being rewarded for their labor; He made sure that the fishermen's nets were always overflowing with fish. He stopped natural disasters from destroying creation when He spoke peace to even the storms. Christ loved education and He loved a free thinking mind. Don't we find Him astounding the elders with His education? God loves education and He wants all of the earth educated. To truly see Gods dream for His earth you must look at the only earthly man that ever truly shared His dream and that man is Jesus Christ.

We know how much God loves the innocent children by the scriptural accounts of Jesus playing with and giving attention to the children. Yet, men of this world would have you to believe that God allows children to be abused and to die with diseases and to starve in Africa and when I hear these perversions of truth, I simply want a megaphone so that I can scream to the whole world – **Not true! Not true!**

God loves the children and it's proven in the fact that Jesus healed all the children He prayed for. God has assigned angels to every child and oh how He longs for the day when not another child will be born under the administration of Satan's government with its decrees of death, doom and destruction. God's dream for you, God's dream for the earth is seen in Christ! What was the only thing that Christ ever showed contempt for on this earth? Satan, disease, injustice, insanity, greediness, hypocrisy and unrighteousness!

For those of us who have been predestined and elected to receive the call of the Holy Spirit in the church age; for those precious and chosen few, there is a transplanting of the mind that is taking place in our Spirits as God is writing His laws, His dreams,

---

1 *Rev 3:21*
2 *Rom 8:29*

His ways and His plans upon our hearts. God is looking for a team who will see the beauty of His dream for all people and as a result of understanding the dreams of God they will begin while still living in mortal bodies on earth *"Training for Reigning and Schooling for Ruling"*.

This *Dream Team* will lose all these horrible images of God that modern man has created. They will not listen to nor entertain these atrocious accusations against God. Instead they will begin training in this lifetime by their absolute obedience to God and training for their role in His Majesties government and by doing so help to bring to pass Gods dream in the soon coming Kingdom Age. The rapidly approaching *Day of the Lord* will be a Golden age on earth when God's dreams will finally find reality. Right now in this Church Age only a few are being chosen because only a few are grasping the *Kingdom dream*. Only those who are allowing "***this mind to be in them***" have any inclination of their purpose for being saved.

While the majority of saved people are looking to escape this earth for a place called heaven, the *Dream Team* is preparing to take this earth for God and to implement His government and His rule and His righteousness for all eternity. While the traditional church is singing and dreaming about "*flying away*" the true A*postolic Church of God* is preparing to stay right here as the scriptures teach us and we are preparing to rule and reign. We are in fact preparing for this glorious Kingdom of God by proving our lives and our faithfulness in this lifetime. We are taking the small talent given to us by the good master and actually increasing our talent with our works, our obedience and in doing so we are earning authority in the future government of Jesus Christ upon this

earth. This book does not advocate nor adhere to the *Kingdom Now* message that is falsely filling the entire of Christianity. I will state emphatically and will prove by the scriptures in the forthcoming chapters that the Kingdom of God is not filling the earth at this time, in this age! Many people are making the same mistake as Augustine of Hippo[1]. He originated the teaching of the modern *Kingdom Now* doctrines during the 4th century.

As the modern, *seeker-sensitive* church grows weary of preaching about a coming King that seemingly is never returning; they have once again fallen back into false teaching and they simply advocate that in fact the King has already come and that the Kingdom is already here. Just as erroneous as the *Kingdom Now*[2] theology is; even more erroneous is the traditional teaching of the church that God's plan for man is to whisk him away to a planet called Heaven after his death to pluck on harps and spend a very, very long time basically gawking at the throne.

Is that really what all the suffering on earth is for? Is an eternal retirement home the real reward for the righteous? The truth will astound you as you read the undeniable and scriptural facts plainly printed in this book. You will be surprised in our study to find not one scripture[3] promised heaven as the reward of the believer; the only promise made to the overcoming believer is THE KINGDOM OF GOD. But, where is that Kingdom and what shall it be like? Here's a hint; it has nothing to do with streets of gold or gates of pearl[4] Let's begin our journey!

---

1 *The early Catholic Church Father*
2 *The teaching that the Kingdom of God is on the earth already*
3 *When read in proper context and with proper exegesis*
4 *This book will teach you what those symbols in Revelations chapter twenty-one actually represent*

What's the point

Chapter One

*Thy word. . .none of the wicked shall un-
derstand, but the wise shall understand.*
DANIEL 12:10

IS THERE A PURPOSE

WHY? WHY DO WE DO IT? **As Christian believers, why do we hang on so faithfully while enduring the trials that so many other "normal" people in our world do not seem to encounter?** Why do we drag ourselves and our children to church each and every Sabbath? Why do we faithfully have family devotionals; pray without ceasing and live such ridiculed and peculiar lives? Why in fact are we "saved", redeemed and filled with the Holy Spirit? What exactly is the point?

The typical answer to all of these questions is often given by well meaning people. However, their answers are basically a chorus of conundrums and confusion; answers of tradition and absurdity; leftover plates of paradoxes. These ministers are indeed true servants of God and this writing is not intended to ever convince you otherwise. However, these servants of God have become satisfied in their understanding of God and simply given their answers to the above questions without much thought but rather from what they have been taught. Over and over in Christian sermons, literature and talking points the same answers of antiquity are reheated and served as gourmet meals of truth.

I'm told that we go through all of these trials on earth to "*Go to Heaven*" and of course to avoid God's unbelievable and seemingly psychopathic eternal madness and wrath. My response is, Really? *Hmmm (my mind is contemplating this thought)*. I have heard these answers all my life, it's the same answers that I have given to scoffers and believers; they would

sincerely ask me; an ordained minister, the same questions. They honestly seek to know why anyone would choose to "*suffer for a season*" for Christ and His gospel rather than to enjoy the admitted pleasures of sin. If the only reason that man serves God is to escape hell and to go to heaven then this fully explains why a person could lose interest and abandon their walk with God after the fear of hell is abated and the hope of heaven; emotions within themselves, have subsided.

I mean, doesn't everyone want to go to heaven? Don't you want to go to heaven? Does anyone in their right mind really wish to purchase a ticket on the midnight train to hell? That's really the only reason we are enduring all of this suffering and ridicule as Christians, right? Aren't we all planning on retiring eternally to "h*eaven's retirement home*" and enjoying billions of years of a celestial *Disney World*? Don't we patiently endure all of these trials and testing's as we quietly wait for that quixotic cruise into the asteroid belt as we make rest stops at Mars, Venus, Pluto and Jupiter? Such has been the reasons given to us in our past and elementary understanding. However, as the ages come to a close, God is revealing more and more of His purposes and plans for His holy church.

GOD'S PLANS NEVER INCLUDED LOSING HIS CREATION!

LETS REALLY TALK ABOUT HEAVEN

Ok, so let's talk about heaven, that celestial home in the sky; that dreamy destination after we "*fly away*." After years of study and research I fail yet to find one scripture about the saints flying away to heaven. Rather, countless scriptures prove to us that the saints are going to rule this "heaven on earth" that is soon to be restored to it's original edenistc glory. Please pardon the use of my literary license as I put a voice to the hidden and secreted thoughts and the very questions that have quite possibly visited your own mind; but you were always to afraid to ask for fear of committing blasphemy or incurring the wrath of God or most important, not going to heaven.

HERE ARE THE QUESTIONS:

#1 - WHAT EXACTLY WILL YOU AND I BE DOING FOR ONE HUNDRED GAZILLION YEARS OUT THERE FAR PAST THE MILKY WAY?

I mean, I can only sit in my mansion for so long and I doubt there will be internet or cable or radio up there. So, what will I be doing? I mean, heaven to me is cooking in my kitchen and giving a huge feast for my friends. But, since we will be floating spirits and not have bodies then there is no need to eat; so there goes my heaven. I suppose that I could then go fishing in the crystal river for a couple hundred years but then what do we do with all the fish?

#2 - WHAT DOES GOD PLAN TO DO WITH ALL OF MY "SAVED ENEMIES"

Truthfully, I actually have no desire to be stuck with my "saved enemies" for umpteen years? *(oh, come on now, don't act like you don't have any)* If they didn't like me down here what's going to make them like my up there? Of course my traditional and sincere Christian teachers would have me to believe that I could always, if bored, go and visit the transcen-

dent and awe-inspiring throne room and worship with the angels for a couple of million years.

#3 - ANOTHER QUESTION; WHY DOES GOD NEED ME TO DO WHAT THE ANGELS ALREADY DO, WORSHIP HIM?

I mean the antagonist and agnostic must wonder; is God really that self-serving to need my worship for all eternity? He already has a quadrant of angels around the clock worshipping him, does he not?

#4 - SO, AFTER I'VE NOW RUN OUT OF THINGS TO DO IN HEAVEN…. WHAT'S NEXT?

#5 - ALSO, HERE'S ANOTHER THOUGHT! WHAT WILL STOP SOME OF US FROM DOING WHAT LUCIFER DID IN HEAVEN; ACTUALLY TURNING AGAINST GOD IN REBELLION AND CAUSING ANOTHER CATASTROPHE IN HEAVEN?

I mean, after all, it seems to me like after walking the street of gold and seeing all the gates of pearl that a few folks could become bored at sightseeing and galactic tourism and actually begin acting out their boredom and in their tediousness somehow turn heaven into a gossip center; causing drama in the dream world.

OK, so I have unloaded upon you, my reader, a cacophony of oblique thoughts in this first chapter. Actually, I have probably expressed what your intelligence and human reasoning have whispered into the dark caverns of your repressed thinking. However, all questions are not bad! There is no sin in questioning as long as you truly seek truth and biblical answers. We should never allow our questions to become a magnet for controversy nor as a way to secretly express our rebellious natures under the guise and sinister cover of "sincere questions". This is a hard lesson that I had to learn through many years of inadvertently causing controversy with my thoughts and questions. I have learned the hard way that most people will never be as grateful for your revelations as you are. There is nothing wrong with these people; they are simply at a different place than you are, respect that! Most people see your *outside of the box* revelations as "*fanaticism*". So, take a hint from me; only share these things with those whom God sends to you. In other words, some people are at different places on their journey with God and their minds somehow block out and reject anything outside of their current stage of revelation. You will only frustrate them with your continued, although earnest desire to show them these glorious truths. I have found that the best way to share these thoughts is only when you are asked for your opinion. The Holy Spirit will always send someone that you can invest these revelations into and they will receive it if the timing is right. Remember that many times, you yourself were not ready to accept the revelations that you later came to accept at the time they were first offered to you, timing is pivotal!

Many times it's the Spirit of God Himself that is placing these *outside the box* questions into your mind; only to draw you into the "*Search for Truth*." However, many leaders in Christendom will despise and spurn you for failing to accept canned and traditional answers, they will throw the word "orthodox" and "unorthodox" around like it's a golden football on the field of the faithful. To qualify for heresy to them, one must simply disagree with the edicts of the Catholic counsels. . Your sincere search for truth will sometimes be labeled as rebellion, unfortunately. You will finally yield under the pressure of "*fitting in*" and being "*accepted*" and you will accept those answers that they give you as truth even though your mind is scream-

ing that "*something isn't adding up*".

If two plus two doesn't equal four then something is wrong! Many of the answers given to you up until this point in your life about the hereafter is in fact a gross miscalculation that your mind has always recognized but you had no one to give you the answers. The Word of God is clear and only demands for your diligent study of its pages and therein you will always find the answers. A great prophet said "*Every biblical question has a biblical answer*".[1]

TWO PLUS TWO NEVER EQUALS THREE

Any answer that comes from God will always make deep spiritual sense; not necessarily to your carnal mind but always to your converted spirit,[2] there will always be a witness as to the logical reasoning of the scriptures. Two plus two will never equal three with God. Your intelligence isn't your enemy! God gave you that intelligence and aptitude to seek after the answers; to challenge false religion and to know the truth. If you are depending upon anyone else to lead you into all truth beside the holy spirit of God; such as your spiritual mentor, your parents or your friends; then you will only have the amount of truth that God has entrusted unto them. **However, unto you God is willing to reveal as much as you are willing to learn.** Study for thyself!

Allow me to tell you right now what is going to happen to many of you that read this first chapter.

> # IF TWO PLUS TWO DOESN'T EQUAL FOUR THEN SOMETHING IS VERY WRONG!

1 William Branham, The Masterpiece, Los Angeles, Ca, 1963

You will not make it past these primordial pages of introduction. The reason is simple; you are fully persuaded of your personal or of your own family's religious traditions. You are not desirous of anything that would place you outside of that familiar and comfortable box and I completely understand that.

However, someone who reads these words will hear the ring of truth; the bells of breakthrough will chime into the alleys and the clandestine lanes of your life; you will be forced to stare truth in the face, to study the scripture and then finally to give a prayer of thanksgiving to God for having loved you enough to bring you further into His mind, His purposes, His understandings and the revelation of His plans. So many Christians claim an ardent desire to know Gods will and yet reject any further revelation of His will that doesn't fit into their Baptist, Pentecostal, Apostolic, Catholic, Protestant or even their non-denominational boxes.

WHAT THEN?

So, back to the subject of heaven! When you and I draw our last breath and we shall, what then? Honestly, pause and take a reading recess and ask yourself that question internally… What then? Will we all be whisked away to some distant planet called Heaven? Is that Gods ultimate plan for us? If so, then another question presents its pestilent head; if going to heaven is God's plan for believers, why not just take us there at the point of repentance and salvation? Why even leave us on this earth if this earth is indeed not God's predestined place for us? Why leave us here after the moment of conversion, simply remove us to the home He has supposedly prepared for believers.

Is God is so disappointed in his perfect creation called Earth and the one hundred and fifty-five billion people who have lived and died on this globe that he's simply going to snatch away a couple million of us and move us to an eternal *Disney World* in the sky and give up on all of the rest of this creation; and for all eternity wish that he had done a better job of keeping what he created? Do you really believe this? I beg you to ask yourself, do you **REALLY** believe that? Well, the vast majority of Christianity is in your company if you do. They believe that an elect few, maybe a million or so out of 155,000,000,0000 (*yes, that's billion*) who have lived since Adam will be raptured out of here and saved while God basically accepts defeat, washes His hands in His tears of regret and send Satan and those billions into an eternal inferno for them to boil as long as God lives.

Sadly, this was my belief all of my life. This was my mind set and I didn't even realize that with such a mind-set I was in fact serving a defeated and a seemingly subjugated God. God defeated, you ask? Absolutely, if God loses ninety percent of His creation to Satan and if He cannot save nor keep them; then in fact He has lost his creation! Satan wins and God is lucky to get a few for all eternity. There is one word for this version of Christian Theology……. Hogwash!

Imagine you having created a masterpiece of some type and although you had the ability to create the masterpiece you actually made no provisions to preserve your creation. As a result the major part of that creation is lost for eternity; what would that make you? A failure! Are you willing to acknowledge this about yourself? Then you must also accept the same notion about God?

I emphatically declare that I do not serve an incapable, inept or a defeated God. The Almighty creator; The Eternal One; Yahweh[1] neither slumbers nor sleeps. His plans are impeccably and immaculately perfect and those spotless plans never included losing what He created! I render to you this conclusion; **God will never allow the majority of his creation to be lost.** He has provided a way to bring them back to Himself! He will get them back; He will save them by gentleness or by divine discipline, whatever means are necessary.

In the proceeding scripture you will find Gods greatest desire and I am of the persuasion that God normally gets his way!

I Tim 2:4
God desires for all men to be saved and come to the knowledge of the truth.

Only after reading this book or any other book with the same understanding of scriptures will the question of HOW He's going to do this be answered. The HOW includes YOU! If you think that you have a ministry here and now just wait until this book shows you your eternal ministry!

I pleadingly and respectfully request of you; after giving this book a fair-minded reading to **Perish the Thought!** Perish these childish and traditional ideas and elucidations. Perish such worthless paradigms and accept fully the truth. Here is the truth… **God is going to save the majority of his creation** and He has a marvelous plan for doing so and IF YOU ARE BEING CONVERTED…. You are in that plan.

1 *Yahweh is the original name of Israels God*

You are concretely the most pivotal part of His plan. The salvation of the vast majority of Adams children *(humanity)* is going to happen through you.

Heb 12: 23
But ye are ......the church of the firstborn!

If we are the firstborn group of people that is to be born into the Kingdom of God, the firstborn church, then I must beg you to answer; who will make up the *"nextborn"* or *"second-born"* group of people? These answers are forthcoming in this book.

You are the *"Firstfruit Company"* or more plainly the *"First Harvest"*. Paul refers to The Church, those called-out and elected believers; those members of his *Dream Team* saved in this span of time *(the Church Age)* he calls us the First Fruits! However, if there is indeed such a thing as *"First Fruits"* that only indicates to me that there must be *"More Fruit"* because you cannot have a first if there isn't a second. So beloved, if you and I are the *"First Harvest"* as Paul so plainly describes us; does this not indicate a *"Second Harvest"*? My job was to write the book, your only job now is to answer the questions. I am not the teacher here, I'm the questioner! Your answers to my questions will teach us both. These question demand your answers, who indeed will be in the *"second harvest"* if indeed the church, the saved, the elect, the believers make up the *"first harvest"*?

GOD'S EARTH RESTORED

The restoration of Gods earth, the return of His legally owned property to Him is going to happen because of your salvation during the Church age[1]. The re-turning of Gods earth; the salvation of Adam's children; and the lifting of the curse are all part of your future job description.

Trust me, I'm simply teasing you now, it is not my intention to give neither scriptural references nor lengthy teachings in this chapter. However, should you decide to read this treatise, this exposition in its entirety, only then can I assure you that it will be revealed with clear scriptural support.

WE ARE IN THE CHURCH AGE -NOT- THE KINGDOM AGE

Because of the fact that during this age[2] you rebelled against Satan's government, you defected and chose God's government; because you believed His gospel and submitted to His laws even while living under the mesmerizing grasp of Satan's deceptive influences; because of that you are a precious and pivotal part of his future plans for planet earth. **God has learned to trust you during this earthly sojourn of yours as much as you have learned to trust him.** He knows that there is no rebellion to His laws in your character and just as "*a leopard cannot change his spots*," a man cannot change his character. This is the very reason He requires an earthly life for you before birthing you into your resurrected spiritual life.

Your character is developed in this life and your position in His coming kingdom will be granted by His knowing that you can be trusted with His Kingdom authority. True authority is never granted it can only be earned. Christ did not receive "*all author-*

1 *The present span of time in God's prophetic time line.*
2 *The church age*

ity in heaven and earth" as he so plainly declared until after His resurrection; not until after he earned that authority from the life lived here on earth in a mortal body. The only biblical guidelines for a man to hold legitimate authority, he must be "*in authority and under authority*." All that can be granted or demanded in relation to authority is dictatorial and doctrinarial power but never true and legitimate authority. True authority is only gleaned after you've been faithful in certain aspects of your life and or career.

The authority that shall be granted to you in the coming Kingdom will be the authority that you have earned in this life. You will be able to lead others during the *Coming Kingdom* and teach them to obey God's laws because you are in fact an authority on the subject after a lifetime of obedience. Only the Overcomers who learn complete obedience to God's laws in this lifetime will qualify for the *Dream Team,* His government.

In this life when it seems He had forsaken you, what did you do? When He didn't come through for you, what did you do? Did you still believe? Did you still pay Him His tithe, when He didn't pay your light bill? What did you do with every opportunity that He allowed Satan to give you to rebel against him? What did you do? Were you determined to obey the least of His commands? Did you keep His Sabbath holy? Did you love your neighbor as much as yourself? He has the record and you will be counted worthy of ruling with him in His government if indeed you have been faithful to Him even when it seemed He wasn't faithful to you. If you are a believer in Christ right now and you do not understand anything about *The Coming Kingdom (Government) of God* then you will cherish this book

WHAT AGE ARE WE LIVING IN?

Please note: This book is not advocating the doctrine commonly referred to as *Kingdom Now.* The teaching contained in these pages is totally different from those taught in modern *Kingdom Now* theology. We are not adherents of and are in fact polar opposites of the *Kingdom Now* message which teaches that Gods Kingdom is now filling the earth. They fail to understand as the Apostles failed to understand before Jesus corrected them, that the Kingdom of God is not on the earth at this time nor shall it be until the return of the King Himself. Neither is the Kingdom of God in our hearts nor it is *"within you"* as the *King James Version* of the Bible has so incorrectly and erroneously translated[1].

shape or form! His Church is currently on the earth as a clandestine occupying army *"Occupying until he comes"* under furtive cover waiting for the moment or the age when we shall rule, serve and heal the nations of the earth with Christ as His emissaries and the literal cabinet of his Jerusalem-based, global government. Until then, we are *The Apostolic Church of God*, we are initiated members of His *Dream Team;* we are the set apart *"First Fruit"*. **We are kings without our thrones, princes without our robes and heirs without our homes**. We are a despised few with an indescribable present and future responsibility.

Remember this well! We are now living in the Church Age **not** the Kingdom Age! The Kingdom Age will be the Golden Age[2] that you never hear preached about. In fact, the early church up to the 18th century preached constantly on the upcom-

WE ARE KINGS WITHOUT OUR THRONES; PRINCES WITHOUT OUR ROBES AND HEIRS WITHOUT OUR HOMES.

These sincere and well-meaning Christians have turned this literal, tangible and corporeal government of God into a surreal, dreamlike, fluffy and spiritual state-of-being rather than what it truly shall be; an earthly, material and world-ruling government. We are all living in Satan's government under his earthly administration; under the rule of man. This is NOT THE LORDS DAY. His day is coming, His Sabbath is coming to the earth but until then His Kingdom is NOT on the earth in any way,

ing Kingdom Age, it was a primary part of their sermons. However, in modern times the church has morphed its message. However, in the true Church of God, in those who desire to preach the Apostolic message of the Apostles, we are teaching as Jesus taught about a future and forthcoming literal, corporeal Kingdom; not a present spiritual or ethereal, otherworldly Kingdom! For herein rest the truth and the greatest understanding; Satan has somehow held this revelation from the Church of God for six-thousand *(6,000)* years. However, the time has come as millions of believers around the earth are awaken-

---

1 *This will be proven in forthcoming chapters*

2 *Sometimes referred to as the Millennium Reign*

ing to understand their role in the *Coming Kingdom of God* and that role has nothing to do with a distant place called heaven, it has nothing to do with neither streets of gold nor gates of pearl[1]. Rather, it has to do with peoples, nations; kingdoms and a place called Earth which shall soon become the Paradise of God and you beloved are going to make it all possible. If you could only imagine your importance then you would never again let sin reign in your mortal bodies. If you were cognizant of your eternal purpose you would begin preparing now for your role in Gods future government.

The entire earth, according to the Apostle Paul is begging and groaning for your new birth. The earth is groaning to be released from her curse, from her evil destructions, from her pollutions, from her death and whether you know it or not, you are going to make that happen!. You will not be able to read this book as a novel, it must be studied. In writing this book I have chosen to lay it out as a study guide rather than a book to simply be read. As you begin to read the scriptural references you will become one of the happiest people in the world as you begin to finally understand what the Church has failed to teach you. **You are not saved to go to heaven. You are not saved to escape hell. You are saved to begin qualifying and training for a life that you cannot imagine in a world that your mind cannot begin to comprehend**. That world will be ON THIS EARTH; the recreated and renewed earth and not in some mystical place called Heaven! Albeit, the re-created and renewed earth will be heavenly indeed and as such could rightfully be called Heaven. However, if we fail to realize that our heaven will be on

earth then we live with a false and uninformed hope rather than living with the reality of truth. Some well meaning people have accused me of taking away the *"Blessed Hope"* of the saints and my response is respectfully given; Would you rather have a *Blessed Hope* based on a lie or a Real Hope; a hope based upon the scriptures?

So, to answer the questions that served as the preamble and prelude of this chapter; Why, Why, Why . . . The purpose of the sanctified, Christian life is summed up best in the following phraseology; ***Training for Reigning and Schooling for Ruling!*** I challenge you to allow me to prove these statements by the scriptures before you draw your conclusions. May I present this one interesting side-note? There is not one scripture[2] in any of the books of prophecy about a place called heaven! In the gospels we find no sermons from Jesus about the saints going to heaven. None of the Pauline epistles promise heaven to the believer. Neither does John's famed book of Revelation nor any of the other New Testament books present such a claim. Not one time is the believer promised a home in heaven; Not once! Did you realize that the Bible never promises mansions in heaven? Sadly, the *King James Translators* used the word mansions in St. John 14:1 in a gross and repugnant error as this book along with other respected theological authorities will prove.

Discover this truth and inculcate yourself with this teaching and you will begin to notice that you finally have the power and most importantly the reason to begin living an overcoming, victorious life right now! If you truly understand that your current actions are deciding your future position in Gods government then all of a sudden you will begin your journey

1 *I will explain in detail the symbolical meaning of all those traditional thoughts of heaven as mentioned in Rev twenty-one (21) in forthcoming chapters, the truth will amaze you*

2 *When read in proper context and with proper exegesis*

From Mt. Calvary to Mt. Zion

Here is the danger of not understanding the true purpose of your salvation and why this book is so important to you. Ministers across the globe are inviting people to be saved and then they leave those new believers with absolutely no direction and no compass for their spiritual walk. These believers are now settled and happy to have salvation but they are clueless about the need to live an overcoming life of holiness. They have been taught that they were saved to go to heaven; now just sit back and relax until the rapture; enjoy the ride. However, these are the very ones who will not inherit the Kingdom of God. These are the very ones who might indeed be saved but they will not inherit any position in Gods future government on the earth; they will be counted unworthy to rule and reign in the next life because they failed to rule and reign over their own bodies in this life. Jesus said "*he that breaks the least of my commandments with be least in my government and he that keeps the least of my commandments will be greatest in my government*"

As a result these are the very ones who Jesus describes as having been so disappointed at the judgement and saying "*Lord, Lord we believed on you; Didn't we prophesy and preach and witness in your name; didn't we pray for the sick in your name*" However, these believers never KNEW Christ

THE PROGRAM OF GOD ENDS AT MT. ZION, NOT AT MT. CALVARY

and his true role as soon coming King. They know him as Savior, Healer and Deliverer but no one has taught them about his Kingship and his *Coming Kingdom* and sadly they walk around with their head to the clouds waiting for heaven. They never KNEW the details of their purpose for salvation and as a result they invested no works along with their faith; they believed the lie of the extremism of eternal security[1] and floated along just happy to be saved. They have fallen hook line and sinker for "*The finished work of the Cross*" doctrine; they truly believe that this whole program of God ended at Mt. Calvary. Sadly, no one has taught them that the program of God ends at Mt. Zion, not Mt. Calvary.

The journey from Calvary to Zion is a journey of conquering sin, it's a walk of *holiness unto the Lord*. Mt. Calvary is beautiful but Mt. Zion is the mountain of God's government and it's on Mt. Zion that the prophets all see the coming King standing with His chosen government. Only those who overcome their own flesh will ever come up to Mt. Zion. At Mt. Calvary you're accepted as you are but at Mt. Zion you're only accepted as He is, victorious! But no one is teaching the church about the true goal of all believers - Mt. Zion. Paul said that *we are come unto Mt. Zion*. These babies in Christ will be unaccepted in the government or Kingdom of God because they counted themselves as having apprehended salvation without any works and did not press toward the higher calling. This high calling will be judged not by faith but by works. Jesus said "*Behold I come quickly to judge every man according to his works.*" He told all the seven churches in Revelation "*I know they works.*" While modern preachers have lied with lullabies

1 *This doctrine has some valid points but can easily be abused and taken to its most extreme point*

called sermons to the modern masses and told them to "just believe"; God has been waiting for their works, for their actions to match their faith. God is watching and keeping a record. However, these poor, innocent saints of God are being lied to. They are clueless as to why they are saved. May everyone who reads these pages be warned! There is more to this story than you have been previously told. God is putting together a *Dream Team*, a government of overcoming saints who will stand with Him on Mt. Zion to usher in His Kingdom on this earth.

Ever wonder what that little scripture means ***"Judgment (or decisions) begin in the house (Family) of God"?*** [1] You are about to have that answer! As an appetizer, did you ever wonder what Jesus meant when he referred to "***the least and the greatest in my Kingdom"?*** [2] If we are all saved and God is no respecter of person then how can anyone be least and someone else greater? Didn't we all receive the same salvation? You owe it to yourself to find these answers in the Word of God! Did you ever wonder about that little verse in the New Testament ***"do you not know that the saints shall judge the world"?*** [3] Or what about this one "***Blessed are the meek for they shall inherit THE EARTH"?*** [4]

I pray that the eyes of your understanding shall be enlightened and that your heart will be as rapturous as mine when I first learned this truth. These trials; these heartaches; these life lessons are not to get you to heaven; they are to get you prepared! But, prepared for what? Your ears really have never heard nor have your eyes ever really seen what God TRULY

has prepared for you! Here's a hint, it's definitely not an eternal retirement. When this life is over, when this age has ended, Yahweh's [5] work of creation has just begun. However, this time He won't be creating alone. You see, creating is the family business. The Family of God, the sons of God will continue the family business, we are creators by trade and once we enter into that family at our resurrection, the work of creation will have just begun! According to Paul's writing; ***"All things in the galaxies and the earth will be put under our feet"*** [6] Tradition would have us believe that God will be relaxing in heaven for all eternity as we all sit around and sing *kumbaya* at that eternal Campmeeting in the sky! Not so; once a creator, always a creator! God and His sons will be creating worlds without end!

According to Isaiah ***"of the increase of his government, there shall be no end"*** [7] Do you have any idea what that verse is actually saying? Here's a hint – His government *(who will be his government? The Dream Team)* will ever be increasing, mounting, growing, rising, and expanding! Expanding where? Read the book!

What is a government

What exactly is a government? When our President in the United State of America is elected, we elect him but we do not elect his government. His government is those individuals who assist him in implementing his ideas, his laws and firmly fixing his authority throughout the whole of the United States.

1 I Peter 4:17
2 Matthew 5:19
3 I Cor 6:2
4 Matthew 5:5

5 The personal name of God in Hebrew
6 I Cor 15:27
7 Isa 9:7

Without a government, the Presidents ability to rule would be non-existent. A government is made up of people or ministers who work in perfect unity with the President or Head of State to make sure that his or her ideals become the implemented law of the land. When the Queen of England became queen, she immediately established her government or her ministers into all the necessary positions. These ministers include the *Prime Minister*, the *Minister of State* and the *Minister of Commerce, Taxation, Justice* and so forth. All these people make up or constitute her majesties government. Christ, the King of all kings will also have a world-wide earthly government when He steps from His role as Savior into His role as King and this government will be increasing throughout all of the Kingdom age, from galaxy to galaxy; there shall be no end.

Now, you are about to find out what you are being prepared for! Carnal minds will find no pleasure in these future chapters nor have I written this book for carnal minds. However for the person who is thirsty and hungry for answers about your eternal purpose I invite you to turn the next page and join me on the journey!

The Blueprints

Chapter Two

UNDERSTANDING THE AGES

HERE'S THE PROBLEM AND THE REASON THAT SO MANY MODERN CHRISTIANS CANNOT SEE THE FULL PLAN OF GOD FOR THE EARTH; they haven't looked at the blueprints! This is why everyone is falsely looking somewhere out in the galaxies to a place called heaven, simply because we fail in understanding that God's purpose for man is on this earth!

Gen 1:27, 28
God created man in his own image . . . God said unto them, Be fruitful, multiply and replenish the earth. Subdue and have dominion!

In Genesis chapter one we find in plain print and sacred writ the absolute, supreme, fixed, unquestionable and eternal plan for mankind. **God created man to rule and reign over the earth.** That plan didn't change over time; He didn't change His purpose for man; He never decided that we would like heaven better or that we would rule in heaven. There has never been a change of plans; He changes not. We were given the earth as our dominion or our dwelling place just as Lucifer and the fallen angels were originally given this earth to inhabit before their rebellion![1] Man was created for the earth not the heavens. We, the sons of Adam, failed in our mission on earth; to beautify it, to guard it, to enhance it and to subdue it. However, in our resurrected, immortal and spiritual bodies we will once again be given that opportunity. Heaven is God's dominion, the Earth is mans dominion. Get that

GOD CREATED MAN TO RULE OVER THE EARTH

ideal firmly planted into your world view. The Word of God tells us that after this life God will actually dwell with men, in mans domain. [2]

It would do us well to remember that heaven isn't a place; it's a dimension. Just as radio frequencies do not reside or inhabit a "place" but rather they reside in a dimension; a faster or higher dimension. So it is with the dimension of the Spirit of God or heaven. How foolish is the mind that thinks the eternal Spirit can be housed on a planet called heaven; just as His Spirit is omnipresent so is His dimension or His heaven. It *(heaven)* resides everywhere and anywhere, it should more properly be called the spiritual or unseen dimension rather than heaven. Howbeit, that otherworld is indeed heavenly but it is not a place as much as it is dimension. Our future has nothing to do with heaven or the unseen world. The Sons of God will usher in the atmosphere of heaven "*on earth as it is in heaven.*"

Rev 7:15
. . .and he that sitteth upon the throne shall dwell among men.

Where will God himself dwell after this age? He will establish his throne among men on the earth, among His resurrected, spiritually born children.

Rev 21:3
Behold, the tabernacle of God is with men and he shall dwell with them.

We are never promised to dwell with God in heaven. May I present you with a challenge? At this point I would like to point out that in all of my studies I have yet to find one promise of a place called heaven. Rather, we are promised that God will

1 *This will be proven in future chapters*

2 REV 21:3

dwell with us on the earth. He shall establish His throne in the New Jerusalem. He said in His Word; **Behold I come quickly and my rewards are with me!** [1] His rewards; which are the final gift of eternal life, heavenly life, righteousness, peace and joy are all coming to earth with Him. Do you realize that Jesus Christ even in his glorified state as King of Kings, is still a man? All future prophecies concerning Christ and His second coming in the Bible present Him as a man, albeit a God-man. [2] Why would God be preparing us another place to exist if He's already created the most perfect place in the entire universe, the earth?

If I'm building a home and I alone am fully aware of how I want that home to look when it's finished; then I alone am able to judge the progress being made on that home. Imagine if you should you decide to visit the construction site one day and when you arrive you see nothing but chaotic construction, then you might tell me "*Man, you got a mess out here*". But it's only a mess to you; it's only chaotic to you! To me, it's beautiful, it's in perfect order, and it's right on schedule. In your limited understanding and in your limited view by not having seen the blueprints then I can understand your shortsightedness and your premature judgment of my unfinished work. What looks like a collection of rubbish and a pile of junk with unfinished sheetrock and unpainted veneer is in fact one of the stages of development necessary for a beautiful home to come together. The only house that can come together in one day is a house that will fall with the first wind. God has a plan for His creation. When carnal minds look at that plan they can only see the current age, the current stage of Gods creation. Granted, if that's the

1 **Rev 22:12**
2 *A man born into the Family of God or the God Family*

Shane Vaughn

only eyes you're looking through, you will definitely have reason to believe that Gods creation is in chaos.

God's world is by all appearances on the verge of collapse; society is on the verge of total ruin. There is no world wide revival nor ever shall be again untl the Kingdom age; churches are losing memberships rather than gaining. Hurting humanity seems to be losing all interest in religion and the things of *Yahweh*, the Eternal God. While spiritualism and paganism is increasing, obedience to God and His laws are vaguely and hazily acknowledged. Morals and principles are at an all time low. Mankind for the first time in his history, in his saga of survival has the wherewithal to totally annihilate and eradicate his own kind with atomic bombs. In just one day all of humanity could be obliterated off of the face of the earth and no flesh would be saved or spared unless God intervenes and shortens his plan (*shorten the days*) before man is able to commit such folly.

Looking at the current stage of Gods building plan we would be hard pressed to see any purpose in the evils of this world. When we see people going hungry while a loving God could meet their needs, we definitely could call his work "a mess." When we see people bound by drugs and alcohol with no seeming hope, and families being destroyed, and sin running rampant, and nations destroying nations; with such sights we could all be justified in believing that the earth is indeed chaotic and no one is in control of this. We could prove this only without knowing His eternal plan; without that knowledge we could indeed conclude that God is unfair and uncaring. When storms kill thousands and earthquakes devastate communities and typhoons eradicate populations and separate families; when tears are flowing as rising rivers we could easily dismiss God's plan as cruel and we could even call it a failure. However, as Christians who are living in the Church age, we seem to forget that we are not the sum total of God's plan. We seem to forget about a little nation called Israel that still has a covenant with God. We seem to forget about another age yet to come, the Kingdom age which will have a total different purpose than our day has had. We seem to forget that we are a tiny part of his seven thousand *(7,000)* year plan.

GODS 7 DAY PLAN

Here's another little nugget that will be fully explained in this book; ever wonder why in every civilization on earth there is a seven day week? Why not eight days or five days? Why not different lengths for weeks in different societies? It has been proven from ancient discoveries of antiquity that the earliest civilizations such as the Sumerians and the Egyptians all held to a seven day week. Because, God's eternal plan for the ages of time is established in a Seven day or Seven Thousand year plan.[1] Every week that rolls around, nature is testifying to this fact and to the perpetuity and perfectness of Gods predestined plan for earth and man. Ever wonder why we go to church in a holy convocation and why we rest every Sabbath, every seventh day? Because it's a type and shadow, it's a weekly reminder to all the inhabitants of the earth of the coming Sabbath rest during that one-thousand year reign of Christ on the earth in the Seventh day or the Seven Thousandth year! The Seventh day or the seven thousandth year will be

IN THE KINGDOM AGE, ALL WILL COME TO CHRIST

"*The Lords Day*" when He will rule and govern this earth. Satan's government will be overthrown, he will be forced from his throne over the earth and for one whole day or one thousand years, the seventh day will be HOLY unto the Lord for all the inhabitants of the earth. There will be peace on earth at last; all wars will end; all hunger will cease; all enemies will be at peace as the Holy Spirit fills the earth with the knowledge of God's laws![2] Even nature is preaching the gospel every week, reminding us of God's Seven day plan!

In forgetting this we can adopt a very narrow minded understanding of scriptures by failing to see the magnanimity of his eternal plan. Whereas a house is built in stages or an office building is built story by story so is the eternal plan of God built age by age.

Namely:

1. The Angelic *(pre-creation)* age
2. The Antediluvian *(pre-flood)* age
3. The Patriarchal age
4. The Israel age, Laws and Prophets
5. The Dark age
6. The Church age
7. The Kingdom age

You must not fail to understand all these different epochs of time. All these different ages are all working together to build God's plan or God's house (family). You and I are not the entire story and as such we must look at Gods plan through the eyes of the ages for all of it to make sense. If you look at His

---

1 *We will give scriptural proof in future chapters*

2 Hab 2:14

plan with only the Church age[1] in mind then you will not be able to piece all of the pieces together. Indeed it will all be fragmented and nothing will truly make sense. Only questions will remain in your mind rather than answers.

For example: How does this make sense?
God devises a plan for a man to be saved in our age. **Here's the plan**: Man must hear the gospel, believe on Jesus Christ to be saved or he will die eternally. However, only those who are lucky enough to hear this message can benefit from it. Everyone else, the thirty-nine *(39)* percent of the earth who has never heard of His name or His message are basically without a prayer. Now, you tell me what kind of messed up plan is that? What happens to the man in this age that Satan has blinded his eyes and he simply CANNOT see the truth? What happens to the man that the Holy Spirit has never drawn to repentance?

Didn't Jesus say in one verse that he would draw *"all men" unto him*?[2] Yet, in another verse didn't Jesus also say that *"no man could come to him unless the Spirit draws them"*?[3] Isn't that a total incongruous contradiction? Of course it is, unless you have the master key that unlocks these mysteries, What is that master key? You don't understand the different ages in God's eternal plan. Jesus is definitely going to draw all men unto Him. However, that promise is for another age, an age yet to come; the Kingdom age.

In our age, the Church Age, He is only calling a predestined few, the elect. How could Jesus say that *"he would draw all men unto him"* in one breath

and then in another breath tell us that *"only a few would find the way to life"*?[4]

Simply put, IN THIS AGE, while Satan is still God of this world[5], only a few that's been called will come to him. Those few that He is calling now is being tried by fire and made worthy to assist in the *Coming Kingdom* with Christ; to actually sit and share in Christ throne or realm of authority. What a privilege it is; what a royal and regal calling that you and I have in this church age. We have been called to form His government, *His Dream Team*, to become His ministers not only in this age but in the age to come and into eternity and to assist Him in bringing in the second harvest; that greater harvest of souls in the greatest revival that the world has ever seen!

In the future Golden-Kingdom Age all will come to him! *"Every knee will then bow and every tongue will then confess that he is Lord,"*[6] not so in this age as you can look around and so easily see. All that God is concerning Himself with in this age is not the entirety of the world, only the Bride. He must first prepare a bride without spot or wrinkle. Once the Bride has been found, purchased and prepared then that bride shall join her groom for their honeymoon during the mellienium and together they shall do as husbands and wives do, they shall prodcuce multitudes of children, actually an entire world full of people shall be birthed into Gods family as a result of His union with His bride whom was prepared for the birthing of the nations in this age, the church age.

So, what happens to all of those in this Church

---

1 *The age you and I are now living in*
2 John 12:32
3 John 6:44

4 Matt 7:14
5 II Cor 4:4
6 Romans 14:11

Age whom the Spirit didn't draw to repentance? Are they eternally lost? Only if you believe that the age that we're now living in is God's only concern and that this is the only Day of Salvation and that we are the only part of his plan. However, if you can ever realize that we are one act in a seven act drama; only then can you make all the pieces of the puzzle fit together.

JOELS PROPHECY

This mistake of failing to see the *Coming Kingdom* Age has caused those of us in the Church age to apply all biblical prophecies to us and our age or our day rather than where they belong in the Golden-Kingdom age. For example; Joel's prophecy in chapter two of his book speaks of a coming revival, a coming restoration of what the locust and cankerworm had destroyed.

Joel 2:25
I will restore to you the years that the Locust hath eaten, the cankerworm, and the caterpillar and the palmerworm; my great army which I sent among you

Now, sadly those of us in this Church age who have been ignorant of the many ages involved in Gods dealings have failed to really read this prophecy in Joel. That prophecy has absolutely nothing to do with the Church age and yet every preacher claims this scripture as belonging in the Church age. However, if you will read that chapter more carefully you will see it is speaking absolutely about the Kingdom Age, the Millennium. The contextual setting for Joel 2:25 is found in the beginning of the selfsame chapter, Joel 2:1. Now read for understanding!

Joel 2:1
Blow the trumpet in Zion . . . . for the terrible Day of the Lord cometh! A day of darkness and gloominess. . .there has never been a day like it nor shall there ever be again.

Now you tell me, when are the promises of Joel 2:25 supposed to come to pass? Before reading my explanation, go back and read those two verses for yourself. Again, comparing verse 1 to verse 25 what span of time is being referred to by Joel? Notice verse 1 of Joel chapter 2 – **at the terrible Day of the Lord**. When is the awesome or terrible Day of the Lord? Why, its The Millennium, the Lords Day! It's at this day when Christ will intervene after that "*great army of the North*" has invaded Israel[1]. Now, as of yet, none of this has happened, it is yet to be fulfilled. This is what we call *future eschatology* rather than *realized eschatology*. However, unlearned and unsuspecting ministers have attributed this promise to the Church age and sadly so. They have gone so far as to use Joel's prophecy concerning the Kingdom age when the Holy Spirit is to be poured out upon the entire earth; they say that this happened on the Day of Pentecost but I declare to you that it did not! I will discuss this in detail in forthcoming chapters. Suffice it to say at this point; If Joel's prophecy concerning "*The Spirit being poured out upon all flesh*" happened at Pentecost then something has gone horribly wrong because "*all flesh*" is not filled with the Spirit and also the sun hasn't turned to darkness or the moon to blood as he also prophesied. Only with a correct understanding of "*The Ages*" can you fit Joel's prophecy where it belongs, in the Kingdom

1 *Probably Germany (ancient Assyria) or The revived Holy Roman Empire*

age. But didn't Peter mention Joel's prophecy when explaining the events of Pentecost? Of course he did, read this book to find out why he did and what immediate hope caused him to say such a thing!

During the *Coming Kingdom* age, in the Millennium or as the early church called it, the Golden age; everyone will be filled with the Holy Spirit; the greatest revival the world has ever known will take place during the Kingdom age. "***Every knee will bow and every tongue will confess***"[1] after Satan has been bound at the beginning of the Kingdom age and this earth is no longer being held by his deceptive sway[2]. At that time all the blindness will be removed from every eye as the God of this world, Satan, loses his hold upon humanity; they will now be able to truly hear the gospel message; that is when Joel's prophecy will come to pass. Immediately after "*that great northern army*" has been turned away; this is a direct prophecy of either Germany or the European Union coming against Israel in World War III and bringing great destruction upon The Land of Israel and God Himself is going to turn that Northern Army back and restore to Israel everything in the Millennium, the Kingdom Age. Then "***afterwards***", after this event takes place; then and only then will "*All Flesh*" receive the Holy Spirit of God. We *(the Church Age believers)* had a type of this, a shadow, a down payment, a small foretaste, a titillating appetizer on the Day of Pentecost but that prophesy will not find its ultimate fulfillment until the Lords Day, during the Millennium. We know that "*All flesh*" did not receive the Spirit at Pentecost, only three thousand did. Neither did "***the sun turn to darkness and the moon to blood***" as Joel prophesied would also happen on the Day of the Lord; that prophesy

is for the very soon coming Kingdom age. This is why it's so important that we understand all of the ages before us and the final age that will come after this age. Only then can we rightly divide the Word of God. Only then can we understand prophecy and understand our true purpose not only in this Church Age but also in the *Coming Kingdom* age.

THERE IS A REASON

So, as you prepare for the next chapters; remember well these words. . . Read the Blueprints! From Genesis to Revelation you will find bits and pieces; "***here a little and there a little***"[3] of the mysterious plans and celestial strategies of God, Almighty Yahweh. They, His plans are purposely hidden and veiled to the carnal mind but they are gloriously and liberally revealed unto babes such as you and I. To those of you who just like babes agree to know nothing on your own; only as the Spirit of God reveals them to you. If and when you realize that these blueprints for God's building or God's house include seven stories, seven chapters or seven ages then you will begin to see the whole picture or plan coming together. There is a reason that God hardly intervenes in the happenings of earth today. There is a reason that "*bad things happen to good people*" There is a reason that children are born with AIDS and die in poverty and hunger. There's a reason some prayers go unanswered. There is a reason that God doesn't stop the madness. There is a reason that our heavenly Father in his infinite wisdom allows us as children to learn from our own mistakes. The lessons learned will force us to recognize the folly of our own ways and cause us to desire His ways.   Now, let's discover those reasons . . .

1 Romans 14:11
2 Revelation 20:2

3 Isa 28:10

The Kingdom of God

Chapter Three

Then the eyes of the blind shall be opened, and the ears of the deaf shall be unstoppped. Then the lame shall leap like a deer and the tongue of the dumb sing. For waters shall burst forth in the wilderness, and streams in the desert

ISAIAH 35:5-6

Daniels interpretation

In Chapter two we presented Gods dreams and His desires to fill the entire earth with the knowledge of the Lord as the waters cover the earth[1]. Now, let's go further and look into the prophetic writings of that young gentleman from Jerusalem who now finds himself as a captive in Babylonian control. The setting takes place in Chapter two (2) of the book of Daniel. In this setting the King has had a troubling vision of a great statue. This statue is constructed of various kinds of metals and alloys *(please read the entire chapter)*. Daniel is called in unto the King to interpret this vision that has troubled the king. The Holy Spirit of God fills Daniel and gives him the interpretation.

> # GOD IS GOING TO FINALLY ESTABLISH HIS KINGDOM ON THE EARTH

It would do you well to note this chapter carefully and study these scriptural references; in the following verses you will see with your own eyes and your own understanding exactly what the Kingdom of God shall be and more importantly; where it shall be!

Let us note:
Daniel 2:39 – And after thee shall rise another Kingdom inferior to thee, and another third Kingdom of brass, which shall bear rule over all the earth.

Daniel is explaining to the King that his earthly Kingdom is about to fall and that other kingdoms are about to rise. Of course Daniel prophesies with pristine clarity and he sees with the perfection of eagle eyes as he looks into the future by the Spirit and actually foretells the exact rise and falls of all the major empires of the world. This book will not allow me the time nor space to deal with his prognostications. However, suffice it to say that *Alexander the Great* of Greece and Macedonia, *Ptolemy* of Egypt, *The Roman Empire* and all other world ruling empires are perfectly described even down to the dates of their rise and their falls. Daniels predictions are so perfect that many have tried to even say that he told these events after the fact since these predictions are so perfect. However, historians have proven by discoveries in antiquity that Daniel indeed scribed these prophecies long before their fulfillment.

The most important thing to note in the above scripture is the fact that Daniel is speaking of earthly kingdoms, physical and human kingdoms. Now, note carefully that as he is describing these earthly, physical kingdoms he all of a sudden beholds the coming Kingdom of God and he says concretely that the Kingdom of God is also an earthly, material kingdom on the earth and not in heaven.

Daniel 2:44 - And in the says of these kings shall the God of heaven set up a kingdom which shall never be destroyed: and the kingdom shall not be left to other people but it shall break in pieces and consume all of these kingdoms and it shall stand forever.

Now, how much more plain can this truth be made? Notice Daniels words carefully; "***In the days***

1 Isa 11:9

of these Kings" What kings? Earthly kings of the earth! In the realm of these earthly kings God is going to finally establish his Kingdom ON THE EARTH! Notice, this has nothing to do with heaven nor is heaven ever mentioned. However, the earth is where the Kingdom of God or the Kingdom of Heaven is going to be established. "*The Days of Those kings*" is a yet unfilfilled part of Daniels prophecy. Those kings are represenative of the restored Roman Empire which is being rebuilt before our very eyes in the embyonic form called the European Union which shall untimatly consist of ten nations. When Jesus came the first time He did not destroy any kingdoms of this world as this prophecy says would happen. He did not come the first time to accomplish this vision, this is an unrealized eschatological reality, a future event yet to happen.

Lest you be confused about the phrase *Kingdom of Heaven*; remember, Matthew's gospel is the only gospel that refers to the Kingdom of God as the *Kingdom of heaven*; all other gospels use the phrase *Kingdom of God*. However, the *Kingdom of Heaven* is not the Kingdom IN heaven, it is simply the Kingdom that is owned or governed from heaven. For example; The Bank of Mellon is not located in Mellon but rather it is owned by a man named Mellon. The word OF is indicative of ownership. I might be a citizen of Louisiana and not be living in Louisiana at the time. However, Louisiana is where I am from so in a a sense I am owned by Louisiana. However, I'm not IN Louisiana. A child OF God is not located IN God but rather I am the property of or the purchased posession of God. Likewise, the Kingdom of Heaven is the posession of God who resides in the heavenly dimension. So, the *Kingdom of Heaven* is by default the *Kingdom of God* since God created the heavens and the earth. Most scholarship also tells

us that Matthew was being true to Jewish form in his writings by using a phrase that represents God rather than saying "God" as the Jews considered the mention of His name as disrespectful to His name. We see this when Matthew says that Jesus "sits at the right hand of Power." All the other synoptist gospel writers say the "right hand of God." Matthews writing style here was very consistent with Jewish mentality.

In Daniels interpretation he is envisioning the Kingdom of God and he sees something very different than what you and I have been taught. He saw that one day in the future that God himself would come to earth and establish his government on the earth and *"consume all the earthly kingdoms"* Also, if you will remember in the teachings of Christ in the book of Matthew; He tells us that during the time of His Kingdom that he would gather the nations of the earth together and reward the nations who had been kind to Israel. Also,

Revelation 21:24 "the nations of the saved shall walk in the light of the New Jerusalem" it continues to say **"the kings of the earth shall bring their glory and honor into the city".**

Now, how will this happen if we are all in heaven? Nor did this happen when Jesus came and established the church; world leaders have never brought their honor, their finances into the church. These kings of the earth that shall bring their honour into the New Jerusalem[1] these kings shall be you and I as plainly shown in the book of Revelation;

Rev 5:10 "Thou hast made us unto our God Kings and Priest and we shall reign on the Earth"

1 *Which will be sitting where modern Jerusalem is now*

Plainly it is shown that these kings that shall come faithfully to the New Jerusalem to honor God will be the very ones that make up the empire of Christ. These kings are those whom He has placed over the nations at His coming and because we are His kings, under His royal empire, He can now rightfully be called King of kings; beloved, we are those kings that He shall be King over. Each of us will be ruling over municipalities and provinces and cities as we are counted worthy to reign with Christ.

Now, let's continue with Daniels inerpretation and you will begin to acknowlege that the scriptures are plain; the Kingdom of God will be established on the earth.

GOD IS NOT CALLING ALL MEN TO SALVATION IN THIS AGE

Now let us go to verse thirty-five (35) of the same Chapter in Daniel and notice something very startling. In this verse Daniel is interpreting the meaning of a little stone that this King had seen in his vision. Daniels tells the king that the "*little stone*" that he had dreamed of was in fact the Kingdom of God. He continues to elaborate and explain that this "*little stone*" would grow into a large mountain and this mountain was a symbol of a worldwide government. He makes it plain that the Kingdom of God[1], would start out small with only a few called out ones just a "*little stone*" but that eventually that "*little stone*" or that "*little flock*" would fill the entire earth and take over all of the Kingdoms of the earth. The last line of verse 35 states: **"and filled the whole earth"**

This is exactly how God's Kingdom is going to eventually fill the entire earth. In the Church Age that you and I live in it should be abundantly clear to any clear thinking person that indeed the Kingdom of God has not yet filled the earth in our age; otherwise we would be living in utopia. Simply look around; if the Kingdom of God is already here and being fulfilled in the Church as is so commonly taught; then sadly the Kingdom of God has been a colossal failure. The earth is growing more sinful every day. However, when Jesus came the first time He DID NOT come to set up His Kingdom at that time. He came to select his *Dream Team*, His yet-to-be trained government from among Satan's world; to bring in that *little stone* that precursor, that firstfruit type of His coming Kingdom as seen currently in this very small and despised group called, The Church. This is the very reason why He is only calling a few in the Church Age, He is not calling everyone. Right now in this age the Kingdom of God is in the form of a "*little stone*" or a "*little Church or Flock*." This little stone is supposed to be little because the "*First Harvest*" is always the small harvest. However, one day very soon, this *little stone* is going to grow into a large mountain during the Kingdom age. The Kingdom of God will cover the whole earth after he returns. Until then he has a "*little stone*" in the earth. However, this "*little stone*" will be the reason that the "*huge mountain*" finally comes!

THE SAINTS SHALL RULE GOD'S KINGDOM

It was not until that I read the following verse in Daniel that I became fully convinced that God's Kingdom shall not be established in the heavens but rather on the earth. Also, in the following verses I see

---

1 *The future, coming Kingdom of God*

without one shadow of doubt nor any need for further proof a clear and compelling scriptural reference that proves emphatically that when the saints are ressurected we are not going to heaven! We are going to be given control and given the governmental responsibilities of the Kingdom of God that we are now being trained for in the institution of the church. How blind we have been to not see these scriptures in the past. Now, please read these scriptures with spiritual understanding and prepare to be changed forever in your thinking;

Daniel 7:10 - A fiery stream issued and came forth from before him; thousand thousands ministered unto him and ten thousand times ten thousands stood before him; the judgement was set , and the books were opened.

Note carefully that we are beginning a study here into the "Judgement seat of Christ." Now, this is not the Great White Throne judgement which is the judgement of those who have not yet received the gospel. Rather, this is the judgement or seat of decisions concerning the worls of the saints of the Most High God while we lived on earth during our training in the church age. This judgement happens immediately after the first ressurection. This seat will not be to determine salvation. This seat of decisions will be to determine your position as "*least or greatest in the Kingdom*" or in the government of Christ UPON THE EARTH! It is at this judgement that every word you've spoken in this life will be evaluated to determine the intent of your heart and to determine your motives; whether they are were selfish motives or whether you have actually received the Dreams of God into your Spirit and received "the mind of Christ" into your mind.

This judgement as seen by Daniel will be your personal interview with the King as he begins placing into positions of authority all of those who caught his dreams for the earth and all of her citizens. It is here that your works, not your faith, will be judged. It is here that you will be evaluated (judged) for the deeds done in your body.

Rev. 22:12
Behold, I come quickly; and my reward is with me, to give every man according as <u>his work</u> shall be

The scene in Revelation 22:12 is the same scene as we find in Daniel Chapter Seven. This is the where judgement begins "In the house *(family)* of God" Notice carefully that once again we find that this judgement is a judgement of works. However, this subject of works has become a cursed word in today's modern and backslidden seeker-sensitive churches. They tell you to just believe and confess and enjoy the ride. How sadly mistaken they are; they are clueless of the coming judgements for both sinners and saints. You and I have a goal to reach, a government to attain unto, there is now a qualification period and we have been been woefully unprepared by the church and her teachings for this coming job interview with the King of kings. Truly there will be silence in heaven as well meaning Christians suffer loss at that great decision day that is soon to come. Only those who make up the "*first harvest*" or the "*Church of the Firstborn*" will be in this judgement.

Notice if you will in verse ten *(10)* that at this judgement, "*the books will be opened.*" Now, there is more than one book here and this is not the *Book of Life*. This verse is comparable with the account of the *Great White Throne* judgement in Revelation Chapter twenty-one (21). At both scenes in Daniel and in Revelation there are *"sets of books"* and then there is additionally the *"Book of Life"* So what are these books that will be opened? The word used here for books is the word *"biblia"* which has been translated in our language to the word "Bible." God will judge his saints with his Word; we will be judged by the instruction manual just as any employer judges or evaluates an employee; by referring to the employee manual. God will refer to his Word when we try to use the excuse of having never been taught by our church the importance of keeping His laws and doing *"works"* that are just as important as faith.

WORKS VS. FAITH

Oh how the modern church hates that word *"works"*! I assure you that one day you will wish someone had taught you about the importance of works, faithfulness, holiness and an overcoming lifestyle. Jesus said that "***everyone who hath forsaken houses and land, mother and father shall be rewarded in THIS LIFE and the life to come***"[1] The word *"life"* would have been better translated as *"age"*; it would read more correctly as *"in this age and the age to come."* This age is *"The Church Age"* and the age to come is *"The Kingdom Age."* The Protestant church and her founders, namely *Martin Luther* who founded the great reformation and the *"faith alone"* and *"Sola Scriptora"* mantra; they hold the word *"works"* with such contempt that Mr. Luther sadly called the New Testament, divinely inspired *Book of James*, he called that book *"An epistle of straw"* because of the emphasis it places on works. Mr. Luther birthed the mind-set of the *"Faith vs. Works"* rather than *"Faith and Works"* he set them against

1 Mark 10:29,30

each other instead of working with each other; this is the mind-set he firmly inculcated into the cradle of Protestantism; he felt that he needed to correct James, the brother of our Lord, and one of the saddest epithets of his life were his words that *"the Book of James was an epistle of straw."* How sad that such a man of God couldn't understand that works is not in competition with faith and neither are they enemies one to the other. Rather, they are married; Faith and works are interchangeable, one doesn't exist without the other. However, Mr. Luthers anger at the Catholic church and her unbalanced focus on works caused his mind to be biased against all forms of works and as such he and others will be responsible for failing to teach God's saints how very important "good works" are in the life of the maturing believer.

This is why the Holy Spirit will lead and guide you into all truth. If you have not been taught these truths as I hadn't been then I want you to take special note of how this book fell into your hands. You are seeing the scriptures, you are reading the very words that will face you at the judgement when the books or the *biblia* or the Bible will be opened to show you what you should have already known by the leading of the Holy Spirit.

Anytime greater truth is given to you, into the repository of your mind you then become custodian of those truths and therefore responsible for their content. You are without excuse when the Holy Spirit convicts you of error and draws you further and further into the mind of God and the ways of God.

Many time in my walk with God I have found myself almost asking God to please slow down on the added revelations and understanding because they do not bring more personal comfort into my life[1]. Actually, they require of me more sacrifice and more sanctification. Yet, I listen to television preachers and radio preachers and they all scream the same lazy message of easy believing with no works needed and no sacrifice needed and I feel out of sync with mainstream Christianity because this is not the message that the Holy Spirit is giving to me. While millions can seemingly just sign a card, shake a hand and make a confession and continue with their lives, uninterrupted by God; not so with me. He is constantly calling me deeper and deeper into more and more truth; more dedication, more commitment, more consecration and more understanding of Gods plan for his coming Kingdom.

For example: I personally have come to understand the importance of keeping all of Gods commandments; especially the fourth commandment concerning the Sabbath day. Now, granted many Christians do not feel the need to keep the Sabbath and I do not judge nor condemn you or them; However, in my own mind *I am fully persuaded*. So to me this is now a requirement in my walk with God. Should I refuse to keep His Sabbath then to me I would be walking in absolute rebellion and deemed unworthy of His future government. Now, perhaps to you He hasn't dealt with on that level concerning His Sabbath or the importance of tithing or anything else on that level. However, for me and for millions of others he has dealt with us in that regard and we are now responsible to walk in those understandings of God. Whereas had someone beside the Holy Spirit tried to teach me to keep the Sabbath I would have quickly explained to them that "*true believers keep the Sabbath everyday*" or that "*Jesus fulfilled the Sabbath and I don't have to keep it*" or

"*That's a Jewish law*"[2] but after two years of in-depth scriptural study of the Sabbath I have found that those responses that I had been taught to give by my church were in fact "*arguments of straw.*"

Allow me to explain more clearly: I was once employed with a company that held closely guarded secrets. Basically, anything that you knew was given to you on a "*need to know*" basis. Your understanding of the "*bigger picture*" was given to you in bits and pieces as your "*trust level*" increased from years of loyalty to the company. As you advanced you were given more and more knowledge of the inner workings of the company. No one really knew what the company actually "did." We only knew the level of knowledge needed at our level of trust and responsibility. However, upon becoming a manager in that company all of a sudden the picture become clear to me of what this company actually did. Why? Because I was now in a position that required me to know. This is exactly how the Kingdom of God is revealed unto us.

MYSTERIES OF THE KINGDOM

Do you remember when Jesus taught in parable to the crowds of people? Yet, the Bible says that "*to his disciples (students) he did not teach in parables.*" Jesus taught them plainly, why? Because they alone were being prepared to "***rule on twelve thrones over the tribes of Israel***" in his *Coming kingdom.* Therefore he said "i***t is not given unto them to know the mysteries of the Kingdom but it is given unto you.***" *Mrk 4:11.* In other words; Don't worry yourself about those people who are not receiving nor inter-

---

1 *Don't confuse the word comfort with joy - the revelations of God are my only joy but joy doesn't always equal comfort*

2 *Interestingly enough if the fourth commandment is a Jewish commandment then so are all the other nine*

ested in understanding more of God's truths; they will be judged according to their level of importance in God's Kingdom. However, you are being called into the trusted position of being a "*steward of the mysteries of God.*" So please don't ask the question "*Well, no one else that I know of is focusing on their works and no one else in my church is concerned about keeping the laws of God and his government; so why must I?*" Just as the grocery store clerk has no idea how much his employer pays for the wholesale price of sugar or tea or chicken or beans; so it is with those who have no desire to be obedient to the ways of God, they have no desire to know because they are clueless of the importance of their preparing to rule and to reign in an earthly government. They will not be asked as *John the Beloved* was to "*come up higher and see.*" Today God is calling for his *Dream Team* to "*know the mysteries of the Kingdom*" to "*know the plans, the mind, the will and the drams of God*" not only to know them but the become invested in them and to share in bringing them to pass in the earth.

THE TWO COMINGS OF CHRIST

Lets continue in our study:
Daniel 7:14 - There was given to him dominion, and glory, and a kingdom that all people, nations and languages, should serve him: his dominion is an everlasting dominion, which shall not pass away and his kingdom that which shall not be destroyed.

Now, it is of utmost importance that you understand that we are still at the throne in this scene

found in Daniel and this takes place at he second coming of Christ. I want to you notice explicitly that it is at the second coming *(Not the first coming of Christ)* that the Kingdom of God is actually given unto Christ. Now, why is this important? Because if you will remember that in the first chapter of this study I promised you to explain **why** that God allows "*bad things to happen to good people*" and I mentioned all those infamous "*Why questions*" . . . The time has now come in our study to answer those questions.

Most Christians are clueless as the purposes of the two comings of Christ. Why didn't he just come the first time and take care of the entire plan? Why was there a need for a first coming and an second coming? In the simplest of terms which I will explain in detail as we proceed: **Christ came the first time to qualify for the throne; he will come the second time to take the throne.** This is exactly why the Jews have been unable to accept our Christ as the Messiah. The prophets of the Old Testament presented a very different Messiah than the one that came to Jerusalem, or so it seemed. You must remember that the purpose of the Messiahs coming in the mind of the Jews was to restore the *Kingdom of God* on the earth. In this regard they are more knowledgeable of Gods plans for earth than most Christians who are dreaming about a place called heaven. The Messiah according to Isaiah's prophecies was coming to establish the Kingdom of God on earth and to bring peace on earth at last. However, in their eyes, Jesus did not fulfill this role and we can hardly blame them for realizing this. God deliberately blinded them to the ministry of Christ for purposes that we do not have time to discuss in this chapter. In fact, Jesus in his first coming did not fulfill the role of the Messiah nor was it his intentions to. He simply came to face the same serpent in the same garden that the "*first Adam*" faced and failed to destroy. Christ met that serpent on a mountain called Temptation and he chose the *Tree of Life* rather than human reasoning and self-righteousness. Upon choosing the Tree of Life which is the Laws and the Word of God he fulfilled all the Law and chose God's government rather than the serpents.

THE TWO ADAMS

To understand what you are about to be taught concerning the two comings of Christ you must fully understand who Christ was. He was the "*last Adam*" basically he was the clone of the "*first Adam.*" In other words, the *first Adam* was created just like Jesus, without human sperm and by miraculous creation directly from the hands of God, untainted by the serpent seed or by human sin. The only difference was that the "*second Adam*" was incubated in the womb of a woman for the purpose of being legally called "*the son of man.*" He only had to be incubated in a female womb to fulfill the required genealogy and be born into the house of David and also to fulfill the role of the kinsman redeemer for the sons of Adam. (*he had to be a legal son of David to sit on David's throne and a legal son of Adam to redeem Adam's sons.*) Otherwise, he could have been created without virgin birth and directly by the hands of God as the first Adam was. However, both men and I emphasize the word "men." Both men were called the "Son of God".

Luke 3:38
"*. . .and Adam, the Son of God*"

All of the genealogies call the first created Adam, *the Son of God*. Now, wasn't Jesus the only "*begotten*" Son of God? Indeed he was but you must understand what the word begotten means, it has been mistranslated by the *King James* translators. In most other scriptures that use the word "*begotten*" it is speaking of a "*conception or a conceiving*" but in John 3:16, the word "*begotten*" in that verse would have been better translated "*my uniquely born son*" The word "begotten" in this verse simply means "unique." While Jesus Christ was indeed uniquely born by virgin birth and the only one to ever be born in such a way; he was in fact NOT the only Son of God. Adam was the first Son of God and just like Jesus he was created uniquely without sin and without human instrumentality and just like Jesus Christ he was created for one purpose: "*To destroy the works of the devil.*" However, the first Son of God failed! Had he never sinned he would have been the "*acceptable son in whom God was well pleased.*"

> JESUS CHRIST WAS NOT AND IS NOT THE ONLY SON OF GOD

What works of the devil was Adam to destroy? Let us study further and find out. Only when you understand the two Adams and their purposes in the earth can we begin answering the questions of "Why" God allows such suffering on His earth.

Additionally before we continue with explaining the ministries and roles of these two Adams let me bring this one step further. **Jesus Christ was not and is not the only Son of God,** he was rather the only one born the way he was born. However, he was and is not God's only son. I present to you this glorious truth; In the resurrection of the dead when you and I are born again as spiritual sons rather than flesh and blood; when this corruption puts on incorruption and this mortal puts on immortality; a whole harvest of sons will be birthed. Jesus Christ was the "seed son" he was the first planting and the "*first sheaf of the first fruits.*" However, he was the ***firstborn among many brethren***" I declare to you that Jesus Christ is our elder brother and that one day very soon God's family, the royal family will be birthed onto the earth. Jesus was birthed first through the womb and finally born again through the tomb and one day you and I shall be born again and this time it will be through the tomb. Until that time, Paul says, "*the earth is groaning and waiting for the birth of the Sons of God*" Rom 8:19

The first Adam was the first Son of God, the scriptures say he was made "*a living soul.*" The reason he is called a "*living soul*" is because contrary to what the modern church teaches, souls can die; they are not eternal and they are not immortal and they are not separate from your body. *(My book entitled; The dead and the day after; fully explains what happens after death to the soul and the spirit)* Adam was called a "*living soul*" because he died and he did not live again even unto this day, he is dead. Therefore he is only a living soul. However, the "*second Adam*" is called a "*living Spirit.*" Now, why is this? Because, he became more than a living soul, he died as a soul dies but he was resurrected and born again into his spiritual body and therefore he received "*eternal life*" from God his father and thus is known as a "*Living Spirit.*" All of us that plan to be in the Kingdom of God must also become "*Living Spirits*" as God is referred to as the "*Father of Spirits*" not souls. Only those souls that receive eternal life will be "*living Spirits.*" All of those who will make up the Kingdom or Government of God will have to become immortal or spiritual as the scriptures teach us that "***Flesh***

and blood cannot receive the Kingdom of God." I Cor 15:50. Therefore if you plan to serve in Christ government you will also have to become more than a "*living soul*" as the first Adam was, you will have to become an eternal "*living Spirit.*" You will learn in forthcoming chapters that those who live and are born during the Kingdom age will all be mortals without eternal life until they are given eternal life. However, the saints of God who reign during the Kingdom age will indeed be immortal and have already been given eternal life.

Adam, the first Jesus, the first Son of God had a choice; obey God and live or obey Satan and die. Now, here is where I need your attention. Jesus was no more a Son of God than Adam was, he simply passed a test that Adam failed and as such was counted worthy to ascend to the Father. **Think about this**: What if Adam had obeyed God's eternal laws and what if he had depended wholly upon God and what if he replenished this earth the right way, the godly way and his descendents had all been born without the inherit disease of original sin? Would there have ever been a need for Jesus Christ? Of course not! Because, the first Son of God would have fulfilled the perfect laws of God just as the "*second Adam*" did and the entire earth would have been exactly as God intended it and his will or dreams would have been performed on earth for the last six thousand years and then you and I would not have to listen to all of these horrible accusations against God. We wouldn't have to answer these questions of "*Why does God allow bad things.*" The reason we wouldn't have to answer those questions is because we would all be living in God's Kingdom, in paradise and there would be no evil on this planet. There would be no sickness, no death, no heartache, no hunger, no poverty and no pain. All would be as God dreamed it, it would already be as it shall be in the Coming Kingdom age.

Here's where Adam actually failed; Before Adam came to this earth in Genesis there was many things that had happened on this earth prior to his coming. The scriptures gives us veiled clues into the *"pre-creation"* events. I will not claim to know what all happened as I was not here. However, I do know that the story did not start in Genesis and the *"re-creation"* account. There was much activity on the earth prior to Genesis 1:1. The *King James* translators actually did a horrendous job of translating Genesis 1:1 from the original Hebrew language and as a result we have looked like fools in the eyes of the scientist of this world as we have tried to declare that this earth is only six-thousand *(6,000)* years old. *Bro. William Branham* often said that *"science is not the enemy of God's word, it will always prove this Word."* For example; When science discovered that the earth was indeed round and not square as the church and science once believed, the Word of God held the answer the whole time when it told us about the "circle of the earth." Sadly, it took science to cause us to actually study Genesis 1:1 again and in fact upon this deeper study we have made some startling discoveries. God didn't create the heavens and the earth six-thousand *(6,000)* years ago, it was created possibly millions of years ago. Let us take a much closer look at these events.

BEFORE THE BEGINNING

Genesis 1:1
In the beginning God created the heavens and the earth.

When? When did God create the heaven(s) and the earth? **In the beginning!** However, when was the beginning? Scriptures do not tell us so we must remain silent on that subject. However, when we look at the original Hebrew words that Moses used to write this book by inspiration we find the truth. Let's look at the next verse which describes an event that took place *"after the beginning."* In your mind I want you to place distance between verse one and verse two because between the two verse, the time lapse between them is possibly millions of years.

Genesis 1:2
And the earth <u>was</u> without form and void. . .

The key that unlocks this mystery is found in the original Hebrew language and its meaning for the word "WAS" in verse two. The word "WAS" as underlined above is a gross mistranslation! It should have been translated as it was in all other scriptures as the word "became". For example let me show you another scripture where the same Hebrew word as used for "WAS" in verse two is correctly translated as *"Became."*

Gen 19:26
And his wife looked back and she <u>became</u> a pillar of salt.

Notice; the exact same Hebrew word is translated in this verse and many others as *"became"* rather than *"Was"*. In Genesis 1:2 the Hebrew word should have been translated *"the earth became without form and void"* rather than *"Was"*: it changes the meaning completely. Now, let's continue with Gen. 1:2 and

Shane Vaughn   *Page 47*

discover the true meaning of the rest of the verse, please follow along in your Bibles. *(By the way, most modern Bible translations have corrected these King James errors)*

Gen 1:2
. . . .without form and void

The Hebrew words for "*form*" and "*void*" are the words "*Tohu*" and "*Bohu*." They simply mean "*wasted*" and "*ruined or empty.*' Are you aware of God ever creating anything that was wasted, ruined and empty? Neither am I, his creations are all "good." So, how did his perfect creation of earth "*. . .became wasted and empty*" or "*without form and void*"? Scriptures tell us in other places such as Isaiah 24:1 that something caused the Lord to "*make the earth empty and waste.*" Something brought the wrath of God upon the "*pre-genesis" (before the beginning)* earth and God caused the earth to become empty and wasted. But what happened? We will find out, I assure you. Before we do let us look as the Prophet David as he plainly tells us what happened in Genesis 1:1.

Psalms 104:30
Thou sendest forth they Spirit and they are created and thou renewest the face of the earth.

What did God's Spirit do to the earth? Renewed it! Doesn't Genesis 1:3 tell us plainly that it was indeed the Spirit of God that breathed upon the waters? When this happened, God set all wrongs to right and began renewing the face of the earth. I ask you; Why did he tell Adam to re-plenish the earth instead of "plenishing" the earth? Because you can only re-plenish if something was there before you got there! Now, you will no longer have to wonder anymore about what happened to those dinosaurs?

They existed, absolutely and science tells us correctly what was always in the Word of God; that something cataclysmic destroyed those dinosaurs and we are about to find out what that cataclysmic event was. It would do us well to remember that we never have to be afraid of science, it's a gift from God to drive us back to the book and search for the answers that were always there. Before we do, let's read carefully what kind of earth God originally created; let's see if he created it "wasted, ruined and empty" and if he didn't create it that way then how did it become that way?

Isaiah 45:18
For thus saith the Lord that created the heaven(s); God himself that formed the earth and made it; he established it, he created it not in <u>vain</u>, he formed it <u>to be inhabited</u>: I am the Lord and there is none else.

Did the Spirit open your eyes? He didn't create the earth in VAIN. Please note that the word "*vain*" here is the exact same Hebrew word "*Tohu*" as used in Geneses 1:2 for the words "without form." Isaiah says that God did not create the earth in "*Tohu*" and yet men have taught that God created the earth in *Tohu*, without form and void. Absolutely not! He created it to be inhabited and we find in Geneses 1:2 that it has BECAME empty. What happened? I will tell you in a few short words "THE WORKS OF THE DEVIL" and it is this exact work that the first Adam was created to correct and when he failed then the *second Adam* qualified to correct this tragedy and very soon that *second Adam* is coming with all of his brothers to consume the kingdoms of this earth and to put to rights what Satan put to wrong!

How did Satan accomplish this great destruction

of Gods earth? Let's find out. Let me insert a note of caution here. We are about to delve into distant and galactic histories that no human being was alive to witness. Therefore, I can only depend upon the few glimpses that God gives us into these "pre-genesis" events. With that said; I simply present these scriptures for you to draw your own conclusions as to what actually happened before Genesis 1:1. I doubt there is anyone with a complete understanding of these events but nevertheless I share with you my limited understanding of the subject . Why even bother? Why delve so deep? Because, unless we understand what the "works of the devil" truly are then we cannot truly understand our ministry and our role in God's coming Kingdom. You and I are told by Paul that "Satan will be destroyed and placed under OUR FEET shortly." Without a proper understanding of the beginning you cannot appreciate Gods plan for the end. How is Satan going to be placed under OUR FEET if we are all going to heaven? Think about it!

We know from the book of Job that the angels existed long before the creation of the planet earth. God asked Job *"where were you when the earth was created and the Sons of God shouted for joy and the morning stars sang together"* The earth was such a beautiful paradise that evidently is surpassed their current habitation wherever it might have been. They rejoiced at the beauty of earth and sang together. Why would they have been so happy if they were not going to live on this earth? Follow me now closely, the angels had a very unique interest in the earth that caused them to rejoice over its creation. Let us look at some New Testament writings that give us further clues *(here a little and there a little)* into the *"pre-genesis"* account.

The inspired writer of the book of Jude gives this startling yet often overlooked insight into the origin of angels.

Jude 1:6
And the angels which kept not <u>their first estate</u>, but left <u>their own habitation</u>, he hath reserved in everlasting chains of darkness unto the day of judgement of the great day.

The angels had a home! A habitation is a home; an estate is a home. Where was Satan living before the book of Genesis? Where was his role of leadership in Gods government functioning? Could it have possibly been this planet called earth? Well, let me ask you - How did he get the title "Prince of this world" or "God of this world" if indeed he had not been given this earth as his planet to rule in God's kingdom? Evidently, he knew quite well that he had a legal claim to the earth because he told Jesus that *"the earth had been delivered to him"* (Luke 4:6) and therefore this is why he could give it to Christ if Christ would simply recognize Satan's legal title and his legal claim to the earth. Who delivered the earth to Satan? Who gave it to him? Only the owner, God himself could have given Lucifer this planet to inhabit. But Jude tells us that Satan and his angels evidently had bigger plans than just the earth, they were not satisfied with the realm of government God had given unto them and they wanted more and because of their rebellion to the government of God they have a judgement day coming where the legal title will be stripped from Satan.

Lets continue on before I teach you about the purpose of Christ first and second comings.

I Peter 3:19-20
By which he also went and preached unto Spir-

its in prison. Which sometimes were disobedient when once the longsuffering of God waited in the days of Noah . .

Notice carefully here that Jesus went and declared a message to these fallen angels in prison. *(Sadly, most Christian teachers claim that these Spirits in prison were dead saints in the grave; my book The Dead and the Day After will clarify these events for you)* These were disobedient angels that existed on the earth before and during the times of Noah. Now, you will notice that something horrible happened during the time of Noah. These rebellious angels that were roaming the earth (their legal home) they had sexual relations with women in Genesis Chapter 6 and giants were born from those unions. I want you to notice that the very reason that God sent the flood upon the earth was because of these ungodly sexual unions.

II Peter 2:4
For is God spared not the angels that sinned but cast them down to Tartarus (hell) and delivered them into chains of darkness to be reserved unto the judgement.

Where is Tartarus? God cast these rebellious angels back down to where they came from, their home (the earth) and we find them roaming to and fro during the days of Noah and they were continuing to wreak evil and havoc upon the earth. They are being held here until their judgement! At the second coming of Christ they will all be cast into eternal damnation but until then, they walk among us in total darkness and evil.

Please note that you cannot commit a sin without their being a law. Yet the Bible said that these angels sinned, so evidently they knew fully the laws of God while living on earth. When they chose Lucifer as their Sovereign rather than God then they chose to revolt and that revolt caused the earth to "*become ruined and empty*". This war threw the earth off of its axle and caused what science has proven, total destruction to earth in the form of an Ice age, all dinosaurs were destroyed at this point.

The revolt

Isaiah 14:12
How art thou fallen from heaven O Lucifer, son of the morning, how art thou cut down to the ground which didst weaken the nations.

Somehow Lucifer finds his way from earth into the heavens. Jude tells us that Lucifer leaves his intended estate or habitation or home. Now, Isaiah reveals to us that Lucifer has been cast out of the heavens. But notice carefully that before he was cast down from heaven he at one time had "weakened the nations." What nations would that be? Is it possible that it were the nations of angels that populated the earth before its destruction? Is this who built the mysterious Pyramids or the Stonehenge circle? I do not know but I do know this, they are humanly impossible to build! What nations existed at the time of this war in heaven? Again, is it possible that nations of angels existed on our earth prior to Genesis? Let's study more!

Isaiah 45:13
For thou hast said in thine heart, <u>I will ascend into</u> heaven, I will exalt my throne (government) above the angels of God; I will sit among the mount of the congregation in the sides of the north.

I will ascend! Ascend means to "go up." Where was Satan located at this pre-historic time that he would have to "ascend" in order to get into heaven? If he had to "ascend" to get into the heavenly dimension it is quite evident that he did not at that time live in the heavenly dimension, correct? You see, it's quite possible that Lucifer whom God had given this earth unto for his role in God's government, he was caught up in pride and as his angels built his ego he decided to overtake Gods government with his own. God's government of love and kindness and gentleness and holiness evidently became quite boring to Satan. He was so overtaken with his own agenda that he decided to wage war with the God of heaven. Of course, he lost and he was cast back down to his legal domain to continue ruling on his throne.

Ezekial 28:13

(speaking of Lucifer) **Thou sealest up the sum, full of wisdom and perfect in beauty. Thou hast been in Eden, the garden of God, every precious stone was they covering . . .I have set thee so, thou wast on the Holy mountain (government) of God**

Here is more scriptural proof of where Satan was actually located. He had been planted at the height of the government of God in Eden or on earth. The stones that covered him were indeed his medals or his regality of his position in Gods government. Notice that as long as he obeyed God's government, the earth was referred to as Eden, a paradise.

The earth belongs to the Lord, it is his footstool. However, he is a law abiding God and he gave this earth to Lucifer and established Lucifer's throne on this earth. There has been no one to subdue or defeat Satan and thereby legally replace him thus he remains on earths throne in control of earths government. So, God in his infinite wisdom designed a seven day plan wherewith he would legally remove Satan from the earth and Satan knows that his time of authority is short upon the earth. UNTIL someone could legally qualify to replace him and return Gods earth unto God along with all of its kidnapped citizens. Thank God someone has qualified for the Throne and that someone is now waiting for his government to qualify to reign with him. That someone is Christ and that government is YOU!

Now perhaps you are beginning to understand why the first Adams failure was so colossal. Had he simply chosen to obey the laws of God, the government of God and had he simply shown God that he could be trusted with the throne then this earth would never have seen the horror and destruction that has befallen her. Not one of babies would have died of AIDS, not one of her citizens would have gone to bed hungry. Greed would not have filled the hearts of her citizens. However, at this time dear reader; Satan is still the God of this age or this world and therefore it is completely hypocritical and ludicrous to ever blame Yahweh for the evils of Satan's world. Just look at Gods habitation where his angels reside with him if you want to see what earth was intended to be like; righteousness, peace and joy.

Didn't Christ defeat Satan at Calvary and didn't he take authority from Satan and didn't he de-throne Satan at that time; The answer is NO. Now you will begin to understand the purpose of the two comings of Christ. Sadly, even his disciples didn't understand the purpose of his first coming. It was not to establish his throne nor to redeem the earth from her curse. He came the first time to prove to his Father that he could choose the Tree of Life as a human and that he could Overcome the temptations of Satan and that he could be fully trusted to reign over the earth as her King. He came to pay the ransom price that justice demanded for the sins of mankind. He came to live God's laws, the Ten Commandments perfectly, he came to prove that indeed a man could obey God rather than self.

THE LORD OF THE SABBATH

However, he was not given his authority or his kingdom at Calvary, he was given his Kingdom at his resurrection and he will bring his Kingdom with him at his second coming. It is then and only then that he will de-throne Satan and BIND Satan for one day or one-thousand years *(With God, one day equals a thousand years according to the scriptures)* This one day will be Gods Sabbath rest, the last day of God's seven day redemption plan. During this one day or one-thousand years the rest that Paul speaks of in Hebrews 3 & 4 that "*still remaineth for the people of God*" will come to the earth. The struggle with sin and Satanic influences will end for all mankind. Rest from God will fill the earth as his Holy Spirit fills every man and everyone calls him *Lord*. This is why he is called the *Lord of the Sabbath* because the soon coming *"Day of the Lord"* will be the *"Sabbath Day"* of God's seven day plan; this is when the Lord Jesus will occupy Earths throne and it will no longer be the "Day of Man" but it will be a Sabbath Day on the earth and at last everyone will have the scales removed from their eyes including the Jews. No longer will God just be calling a few as he is in our age but he will then in that age draw all

> **EVEN WHEN THE CHURCH IS TIRED, SHE STILL CLINGS TO TRUTH!**

men unto him.

So, let us pick up now in Daniel and see what is actually happening with this Kingdom of God that shall fill the whole earth.

Daniel 7:14
There was given unto him a kingdom . . .

When was Christ given his authority and his kingdom? Not at his death on Mt. Calvary but rather after his resurrection and his kingdom is not given unto him until he returns as Daniels sees in this vision. When Christ returns with the angels and to receive his Dream Team, his saints, his government, this will be his coronation day.

Daniel 7:18
But the saints of the most High shall take the kingdom, and possess the kingdom forever, even for ever and ever

This scriptures shows us plainly that once Christ returns and his saints are resurrected to life that those saints, YOU AND I, will not be going to heaven but rather we will be given the KINGDOM OF GOD that Daniel so plainly states will "consume the governments of this earth" and we shall possess this kingdom and we shall rule OVER THE EARTH as the following verse so perfectly agrees with.

Rev 5:10
Thou hast made us Priest and Kings unto our God and we shall rule ON THE EARTH

Daniel 7:22

Until the Ancient of Days (Yahweh, God) came and judgment was given to the saints of the Most High and the time came that <u>the saints possessed the kingdom</u>

Allow me to explain; Judgement will be given for the saints first. We as the Family of God will be judged or interviewed or decided upon first. Then according to Daniel 7:22, immediately proceeding this first judgment we shall then be given our positions in God's government as kings serving with the King of all the kings and then the saints shall possess the kingdoms of the earth. Wow, that's all I can say. This is not about heaven, this is about this planet of earth! Do you see it? It's so plainly stated that it makes the mind wonder how we always missed it.

Daniel 7:22
And the kingdom and the dominion and the greatness of the kingdom <u>under the whole heaven</u> shall be given to <u>the people of the saints</u> of the Most High whose kingdoms is an everlasting kingdom and all dominions shall serve and obey him.

Did you notice those words? This kingdom shall consist of all the nations *"under heaven"* not *"in heaven"* and did you notice that all of the wonderful things *(the greatness)* of God's kingdom will be enjoyed by or given to *"all the people <u>OF THE SAINTS</u>."* The *"people of the saints"* are those people to whom you and I will be assigned to minister to and to serve in God's kingdom. They shall all, all the nations under the heavens shall all enjoy the greatness of Gods blessings and we shall bring this kingdom to them. This is the very reason that Paul stated that all of the inhabitants of the earth and the earth itself is groaning, they are pleading for and waiting for the day when the saints of God shall be born

again into their spiritual bodies and they shall have proven their lives and they shall take their rightful places in the government of God.

I Cor 6:2
Do you not know that the saints shall govern (judge) the world.

We are not promised to govern or judge in heaven but rather we are told that we will govern this world. This is the real "Blessed Hope" of the saints. This is the real and true biblical hope of the saints. No where in scriptures does God ever concern men with the heavens, our government shall be upon the Earth.

I Cor 6:2
Know ye not that we shall govern (judge) angels? How much more things that pertain to this life.

In this one verse Paul so beautifully gives us the answers to Why we are saved. We are called by God and saved in this age that we might overcome in this life. All of our overcoming is to prepare us for a trusted role in governing over humans and angels in the next life. This is why it's so important that we learn God's laws while here on earth because only those who keep his commandments will be counted worthy to partake in his government.

Rev 2:26
He that overcometh and keepeth <u>my works</u> until the end, to him will I give authority over <u>THE NATIONS.</u>

The nations, the nation, the nations! How much plainer must the scriptures me? For those who live an overcoming life; those who press toward the higher mark; those who live above the sways of sin; those who walk in obedience to God's eternal laws; they alone shall rule and reign in the government of Zion.

Rev 11:15
And the seventh angel sounded; and there were great voices in heaven, saying, The kingdoms of the world have become the kingdoms of our God.

The kingdoms of THIS WORLD!

Rev 12:17
And the dragon was wroth with the woman, and went to make war with the remnant of her seed, <u>which keep the commandments of God</u> and have the testimony of Jesus Christ.

Who is it in this verse that Satan is making war with on the earth? The Commandment keepers, *The Dream Team* and those who have the faith of Jesus Christ. You see there are two groups of people in the church that Satan can ignore. The "*Faith Only*" group who believes strictly in the "*finished work of the cross*" *(just how finished would that work be without an empty tomb and a soon coming King?)* and they make no effort to keep Gods laws. Then you have the "*Works Only*" group; they have no abiding faith in the Cross, their faith is in their own good works. These two groups are completely ignored in the counsel meetings of the Lords of darkness but that little group; the true *Apostolic Church of God* they are walking in Faith **and** Works. In Love **and** Law; according to Rev 12:17 that is the only group that will buffeted by hell. This little flock finds herself in the constant cross hairs of Satanic plans for her destruction. Her biggest attacks come from her own

brethren in the church who ridicule her and ostracize her for her belief in holiness and separation. She is nicknamed with the titles of *legalist* and "*holier than thou.*" However, she refuses to give one inch. Even when she's tired she still clings to truth! Since her inception at Pentecost she has fought against the degenerates of darkness.

The Dream Team; you are being called in this hour of Satan's dominion over the earth. He is God of the world that you live in. However, you have received a secret and clandestine invitation from a foreign government, a government that this world knows nothing about, you've been invited to defect from Satan's tyrannical government and to change your allegiance and to experience the Kingdom of God internally before the Kingdom of God arrives externally.

Like Jesus he seduces you with fitting in with his earthly kingdoms if you will only release your vision of victory and your hope of reigning in the Kingdom of God. You can stop the suffering today, he says, you can reduce the ridicule, he says, if only you will lean to thine own understanding rather than the Heavenly Father. Every time you submit to Gods will for you life; every time you choose the right over the wrong; every time you say *"Lord willing"* and you place your agendas at the feet of the Lord; you are giving more testimony against him at the day of his coming judgement.

You will stand before him and God as living proof that a man, a human, a son of Adam could live Gods way. In doing so, you have taken his argument away that God's laws are unfair, unlivable and unbearable. You are the living proof that God blesses those who submit to him. You are the evidence at his trial that the darkness cannot overcome every man. You are the living evidence that "*with God all things are possible.* " You are the proof that man can truly live by "*every Word that proceeded out of the mouth of God.*" You will stand there as a member of Zions government to serve as a living testimony that Gods law of love is better than mans selfish rule.

This is the very reason why he wars against you. He needs you to turn. He needs you to walk out from under submission to God and his laws. He needs to prove to God that he doesn't deserve eternal damnation because he only did what every man has done, disobey. However, in the heat of his argument, you will be there. The beloved of God, the elect, the predestined Bride will be there with robes white as snow and you will be standing with Jesus. An entire Family of God who learned obedience in this life by the things we all suffered, including Christ.

I beg of you dear reader, do not let the Sire of Sin reign in your bodies. Decide today as I have done that there is no more excuse for sin. Make no more places for the devil. Get a "*Kingdom Dream*" in your Spirit. Recognize the purpose of your salvation and begin "*Training for Reigning and Schooling for Ruling.*"

As you stand on your next Mount of Temptation, look past the kingdoms of acceptance, look past the palaces of peoples opinions, look past the facades of *fitting in* and choose God's way. Choose to believe, Choose to bow down, Choose the government of God; **Say yes** to his laws, **Say yes** to his constitution, **Say yes** to his disciplines, **Say yes** to his corrections. Embrace his dealing with you, even in the fire. See tomorrows world. See tomorrows kingdom and in doing so you will be counted worthy of the glorious,

the majestic, the eternal, the never-failing Kingdom of God.

Catch God's dream for humanity. Fall in love with what he loves, which is people! Fall in love with his hopes and his dreams and in doing so you will feel the Love of God begin to encapsulate you, it will begin to take over your language. You will begin to be moved with compassion for this world and its blinded citizens. You will drop the mantle of condemnation and you will speak life everywhere you go as you begin practicing for your position.

Who do you think God is speaking of in Revelation 22:1 when he speaks about "the River" that is flowing out from the Throne of God and the trees that are for the healing of the nations?

Rev 22:1
And he showed me a pure river of water of life clear as crystal, proceeding out of the throne of God . . . and on either side was the Tree of life . . .and the leaves of the tree was for the healing of the nations.

What is the throne of God? It's the government of God, the laws of God which produces the life of God. You and I are promised to sit in that throne or in that government. As we become one with the throne as we reside in the Throne Zone then it is you and I that will be the ones flowing forth from that government who will bring healing and restoration to all of the nations of the world. Can you not see why the "earth is groaning for the full birth of the family of God." The day of our birth is upon us. Our mother "the Church" "New Jerusalem" has been bringing us to maturity in her womb for these many

The Lord of the Sabbath

Nation shall not lift up sword against nation, neither shall they learn war anymore. But everyone shall sit under his vine and under his fig tree, and no one shall make them afraid

MICAH 4:3-4

Why does God allow such horrors on our planet? It's the proverbial, age-old question. Does God not have the power to change these horrible things? Of course he does! Why does God heal certain persons and not heal them all? Of all the questions concerning divine healing this one had always been the most difficult for me to find an answer for because I have been fortunate enough in my life to see some rather spectacular, unexplainable miracles. However, my mind I just couldn't understand why only certain people received these miracles. I am aware of many wonderful Christians who cannot seem to receive physical healing no matter how much they pray and believe. So, why doesn't God just make all of this sickness go away and heal them all?

The answer is this: He is Lord of the Sabbath! Ok, so that answer didn't help much did it? I agree but hopefully with further reading you can come to understand what this means.

A worldwide deception

Upon the failure of the first Adam, the throne of earth would continue to be held by Satan and as a result the entire earth would be held under his deception and influenced by the airwaves of his evil thoughts. This is why it was such a horror when the first Adam failed to "subdue" or "take dominion" over the earth. The first governor that God set over the earth, Lucifer was placed there to rule. However, when he was found in pride and rebellion God began his plan B. This plan included a new King a new ruler, a new government that would walk in obedience and unity with him on the earth. The first Adam had that opportunity. God would never again place anyone on earths throne whose character was unproven and whose loyalty was untested. He was willing to wait four-thousand years for that man to finally, in the fullness of time, come forth and qualify. Since Satan he is the *"prince of the power of the air"* He virtually has authority of the attitudes and the thoughts of all people.

Rev 12:9
And the great dragon was cast out, that old serpent, called the Devil, and Satan which deceived <u>the whole world.</u>

The whole world? Remember that you are included in the world. This is why we must always walk in the Spirit and make sure that we are not in deception. Absolutely, Satan has held under his influence the minds of humanity since the fall of Adam and he has done so legally with a legal claim on all the sons of Adam. This is the very reason that Satan could argue with the angel of God about the location of the body of Moses because he has a legal claim of death on every man born into his Kingdom or his government.

When Adam failed God pronounced a divine sentence of condemnation upon the earth and upon mankind and upon Satan. In Gen 3:15 we see that all of the curses were placed where they belonged. However, there is one curse that he gave that has been long overlooked. Notice that when it came time for God to curse Adam, he did not curse Adam! God cursed the earth for Adams sake or instead of Adam. Remember, Adam was God's son and God refused to curse him so he cursed the earth in his place. The curse of mans sin lives in the earth today and of course what are the wages of sin? Death! Therefore the earth has been in a constant stage of death and dying since that day. This is why Paul states that "the earth is groaning and waiting for the birth of the sons of God" because our ministry in the next age is to remove the curse from the earth and to beautify her again, to govern her and to heal all the nations of earth.

The earth bears the curse of sin. The earth is owned by God but governed by Satan. Just as a landlord owns property he allows the tenant to have limited free reign of the house. By law, if the landlord has legally leased the home then he doesn't have absolute authority to enter in and out as he pleases even though he owns the house. Of course, if the tenants are out of control then he can enter to restore order back to his property and evict the tenants. Ladies and gentleman this is exactly what God has done and soon shall do. This earth was cursed, Satan was enthroned and even Jesus told his disciples "*this is the hour of evil, this is not my hour.*" During this time, this age of darkness God has given this sentence to man.

"*Since you have desired to rule yourself, since you have rejected my government and my laws then I shall allow you to rule yourself. Six days you shall work! Six days shall be given unto you to work! Do it your way, govern yourselves, create your own laws, use your own reasoning to decide good and evil. Create your own health laws, sexual laws, marriage laws, family laws and be in control of your own destinies. I will remove my hand, I will relinquish my claim over you and allow you to save yourselves by your own righteousness. I will allow you to find the ways of peace on your own and accomplish your own dreams,*"

However, God is all knowing, he sees the end before the beginning ever starts and he saw the devastation and the destruction. He looked and saw a day like today when all the governments of man have failed. Every empire that we've ever built from the halls of the Roman senate to the seats of the British parliament have all been colossal failures. He saw the end of the six working days of man, the six-thousand years and he saw that at the end of the sixth day that man would be in total desperation and that after six-thousand years of working and six-thousand years of wars and terror and starvation and disease and death that man would have to be saved from his own devices. God saw the day when if man wasn't stopped, if the days weren't shortened that man would annihilate his own kind with weapons of mass destruction. He saw that after six thousand years of the results of Satan's deception that man would need a "*strong hand from somewhere*" to save him from himself. God knew it would take that long for mans pride to finally crumble and reach out for help from the higher hand.

This is the very reason why God reserved the seventh day and called it the Sabbath day or the Rest Day. Because, after six days of mans working and Satan's rule he would send his Christ to "shorten the days" and to save man from total destruction on the earth. This would be the day when mankind would be willing to bow down and call him Lord. This would be the day when Christ and his government of Church Age believers would bind Satan for the entirety of the Lords Day and all results of sin would be eradicated. On this day there would never be another tragedy. Evil would leave the hearts of men as God poured his Holy Spirit upon them all. Every man according to Isaiah would say "***Let us go up to Jerusalem and learn the laws of God.***"

LESSONS FROM A STUDENT

Here's an example: There was a teacher of algebra at a university campus and one day a young student raised his hand while the professor was illustrating the formula for an algebraic equation. The student with a hint of pride proceeded to tell the professor that he was in fact working the formula incorrectly and that he would be happy to show him his error. The professor looked at the student and dealt with this problem in his mind. The professor had no doubt that he was working the problem correctly. However, he faced a dilemma: His authority, his right to rule in his classroom has now been called into question. So, with all the other students watching and waiting for his response he had to make a decision.

He could have easily dismissed the student from the class for causing problems, for questioning his intelligence or he could solve the problem and shut the student up and prove him wrong or he could stand back and allow the student the opportunity to prove him wrong in front of his entire class. So, he decided upon the latter. He invites the student to the chalkboard and he basically walks away to finish some paperwork on his desk.

After about an hour, the professor looks up and notices the students all napping and the young man was still at the chalkboard working on the equation. Another hour goes by and the young man is still working. The professor though *"Perhaps I should go and help him figure it out"* but then he thought

against it. Eventually, the young man turns to the professor and admits defeat and ask for help. Gladly, the professor comes to the rescue, solves the problem and now the authority of the professor is firmly planted in the minds of his pupils.

In a garden long ago about six-thousand years ago a man named Adam raised his hand. He told God that he and his wife Eve could handle their own affairs and that they could figure out the algebra problem on their own without his help. He needed to give them some space and quit trying to dictate his laws to them and let them decided what was good and what was evil. So, God honored their request and gently backed away. He accepted the fact that they chose Satan's way of *"get"* and *"me first"* rather than God's ways of *"love"* and *"others first."*

However, God knew that eventually they would see Satan for who he truly was; a liar, a deceiver, a murderer and a tormentor. He knew that eventually they would tire of standing at the chalkboard, that they would tire of sending their sons to war, their children to the funeral parlors and their daughters to the streets of prostitution. He knew that the longer he let man work on his own the more man would fail and eventually mankind would turn to him from love and desperate need and ask him for his help. Then mankind would have six-thousand years of history to look back upon and always remember the results of sin and the results of pride. They would always have a point of reference to show them the results of living life under Satan's dominion.

Why doesn't God intervene and rid the earth of her troubles and her curse? Why does he allow prayers to sometimes go unanswered? Why does he

WHY DOESN'T GOD INTERVENE IN THE EARTHS TROUBLES?

not stop the suffering? Always understand this one thing: **God has no intentions of helping Satan!** God fully intends for man to tire of Satan's tyrannical and failed government.. God will never help man to kill his own self. God is standing and waiting for his Sabbath when he will heal all that Satan has hurt. He will restore all that Satan has ruined and when he does, mankind will love him and from six thousand years of experience they will choose God's Tree of Life. They will forsake the apple of sin for the grapes of God.

If God healed every sick body, if God stopped all natural disasters and wars; no one would ever pray the prayer "*even so come Lord Jesus.*" If man never learns his lessons of rebellion. If man never suffers the agonies and the pains of sin he will never be willing to forsake it. If God turned Satan's earth into paradise then you and I would never desire his paradise.

He is Lord of the Sabbath, the Lords Day. This will be his day, his one thousand years. At the end of that one day, that thousand years he will release Satan once more for a very specific purpose. After his one day and the rule of his sainted government over the earth; man will be given a final choice; the government of the saints of the government of Satan. There will be two points of reference for humanity to look to; they will see the results of six thousand years of Satan' government of mans work and then they will see the results of Christ's Sabbath day reign and then Satan will be released to try and deceive them once again and when he fails (and he will) and mankind freely rejects Satan and chooses God, when every knee freely bows and every tongue freely confesses Christ as their Lord then it will be time for Satan and his angels final condemnation to the lake of fire.

At this moment, the Lords day will end and God himself shall descend to the earth and renew the earth with a baptism of fire and then his plans for the universe and the increase of his government shall be revealed unto all his saints and the victory over Satan will have been eternally won!

Sadly, modern Christians are totally oblivious of the meaning of the Sabbath day and why some Christians choose to continue honoring it and celebrating it. This day is much more than a "*memorial of creation*" as if that weren't enough! This is a weekly proclamation to the people of the world and a reminder to Satan that the Sabbath rest is coming to the earth. This is a weekly celebration of the greatest coming revival that the earth has ever know. Sadly, most Christians have no idea about the Lord of the Sabbath. Great visions of victory come to those who understand and embrace the coming Sabbath of the Lord. John the revelator was caught up into the Spirit on the Lord Day. He like all the early church spent the entirety of the Lords Day, the seventh day sabbath in special convocation with the Lord. Since the Lord is Lord of the Sabbath then of course the Sabbath would be the Lords day. You see every other day of the week is mans days. Just like the other ninety percent *(beside the holy tithe)* of mans money is mans money. It is mans days to work and transact business and to follow his own agenda and to focus on the care of this life and this age; so basically man is Lord or ruler of the other six days of the week. However, the Sabbath, just like the tithe, is reserved as holy unto the Lord. Just as God is Lord of the tithe he is also Lord of the Sabbath. Sadly, this glorious truth as known and kept by the Apostolic church has been lost.

We find John the beloved in a special convocation

with the Lord on the Lord's day, the weekly Sabbath and it is on this day that he is caught up into the Spirit and sees the great visions of the future and ultimate fulfillment of the Lords Sabbath. The weekly sabbath is the type and shadow of the future Sabbath Day, the Millennium Reign so it is fitting that God chose tho give John these visions of the ultimate and final sabbath while John was in fact honoring the weekly Sabbath as was the custom of all the Apostles and of Christ himself.

In the closing of this chapter it is my prayer that we have shed some light and given you a reason to never again wonder why God allows the tragedies of earth. He only allows them so that when he corrects them all men will see the wonder and the love of our God. As long as man chooses to rule himself and break the laws of God then God is forced to allow man those six days to rule himself.

Just as a loving parent refuses to bond out a child who chooses the life of crime so does our Lord refuse to save this earth while Satan sits on her throne. However, when mankind has accepted Christ as the King of Kings and Lord of Lords then and only then will *"the lamb lay down with the Lion"*. For those of us in the Church of the Living God, our daily prayer should be *"thy will be done on the earth as it is in heaven"* and also *"even so come Lord Jesus."*

In the Word of God we are told that Jesus is only going to accept those into his government who *"**love his appearin**g."* There are millions of Christians who do not anticipate nor desire his appearing. They have fallen in love with Satans government of sin and self. They are Christians in name only. They have become initiated into the way of selfishness and "get" rather than "giving." We must pray that the love of the Sabbath Day that is coming will fill their vision and their hearts. Otherwise, I fear that many will say on that day *"Lord, Lord and yet he will declare that he never knew them."* Remember, we taught earlier that the whole world is deceived by Satan. Let me bring even greater truth to you; There is only one group of people on this earth that Satan has not the ability to deceive - The Elect of God. The Word of God says plainly that *"Satan would deceive the very elect IF POSSIBLE"* but thankfully it is not possible because the elect has seen the plan of God and they are dreaming the dream of God and are filled with the love of God and his ***soon coming kingdom!***

The
Purpose of the Church

Chapter Five

They shall not hurt nor destroy in all my holy mountain, for the earth shall be full of the knowledge of the Lord as the waters cover the sea.

ISAIAH 11:9-10

A WORLDWIDE REVIVAL

IN CHAPTER ONE OF THIS BOOK I MENTIONED THAT GOD WILL SAVE THE MAJORITY OF HIS CREATION. I promised to explain how this would happen and how that you, (*the New Testament believer)* would have a vital part to play in this miraculous happening. In this chapter I wish to explain in detail the true purpose of the New Testament church of which you and I are members of.

Across the airwaves and the pulpits of America and the world you will hear the modern day version of the gospel of Jesus Christ. However, this version is strangely different from the one preached by Christ, his Apostles and that early Apostolic church. You and I have been hearing for many years about a worldwide revival in the last days. We have heard it told that God is going to pour out his Spirit and that the earth is going to be filled with His glory. **Unfortunately, this is just not the truth!** There will never be another revival such as we have seen in the early 1900's until the Kingdom comes. The latter rain has been poured out upon this "*first harvest*" of believers.

GOD'S HARVEST LAWS

It is of utmost important that I stop here and explain to you the reason that I keep mentioning the "*first and second harvest*." Until God revealed this truth to me through various ministers, prophets and the Holy Spirit itself I must admit that I was totally clueless of Gods true plans for his Church and ultimately His kingdom. God likens his church to a field! The first humans on earth were agriculturalist or farmers, they worked a garden and brought forth food from the earth. To understand God's spiritual purposes for the earth you must understand the natural working of the earth.

In the ancient land of Isreal, today known as Palestine there is a set law of agriculture that is symbolic of God's spiritual laws of harvest. It would do you well to understand the natural laws of harvest before you can comprehend the spiritual laws of harvest. You must remember that "*as is the earthly, so is the heavenly.*" Basically, what I'm saying is that all the happening of the natural earth, her laws, her seasons, her agricultural rhythms are symbolic of higher and eternal laws; they have been given to us to teach us. For example: The element of water has been given to teach us about the cleansing and refreshing power of the Holy Spirit; Fire has been given as a symbol of God's refining power and his ability to transform you into pure gold. When we understand these natural elements we can more clearly understand spiritual elements. The writer of Romans said: "***the invisible (spiritual) things are clearly seen and understood by the natural things that have been created***" Rom 1:20

In the natural harvest laws of God and in the economy of the land of Israel, *(the only land that he claims as his own headquarters over the earth);* There is annually a small spring grain harvest and then later in the year, in the autumn of the year there is a much larger grain harvest. These harvest, the first harvest is symbolic of Gods Church, the *firstfruits.* We shall be the first fruits of Gods total harvest. However, contrary to the teachings of the church, we are not the only fruit! We are the tithe of the upcoming worldwide harvest. When God sees his *first harvest* of souls we will be the down payment and the proof that the rest of the harvest is definitely forthcoming in the "Lords Day." However, The Dream Team must be gathered first to help gather in God's dream harvest, the whole word!

James 1:18
Of his own will begat he us with the Word of truth, that we should be a kind of firstfruit of his creatures.

What did James say that you and I and all the members of Gods church are? A *firstfruit*, a *first harvest*, a *first gathering*, a tithe of the total harvest.

The ultimate and world-wide *second harvest* which is still yet to come later in God's time-line; later in

WE ARE THE FIRST-FRUITS BUT WE ARE NOT THE ONLY FRUIT!

His year, this will be the final harvest of mankind upon the earth, this will be the goal of which all the previous ages has been building up to. This is the last level of God's high-rise building that he began building in Gen. 1:1; this is the finale! This harvest is the finishing of the "*house of God*" this is what God saw from the beginning when he declared "*the whole earth shall be filled with the glory of the Lord.*" This harvest is God's dream harvest, this will be his day of vengeance upon Satan and upon sinful men. This "*second harvest*" at the end of God's year will be when he gets it all back, the entirety of his creation. This ingathering will be so large that they will cover the earth as the waters of the sea. This is what Paul plainly says concerning the *first harvest*:

Rom 11:16
For if the firstfruit be holy the lump is also holy.

In this 11th chapter of Romans, Paul is clearly teaching about "*The elect*" or "*The called-out ones*" as is noted plainly in verse 5 and verse 7. In speaking about this elect and predestined "*firstfruit*" which is none other than those who came to faith during the Church age, if indeed they become holy and sanctified; then this will guarantee the total of God future harvest. In other words, if God can find a people in this age who will choose to rebel against Satan's government and respond to his calling upon them, this will prove emphatically that in the next age when Satan is bound that indeed all of creation will come to God. You as the "*firstfruit*" are the guarantee that God's plan is going exactly as predestined to be.

So, why will those in this age have a greater reward than those who are saved in the Kingdom age? Because, those believers in that future age will never fight the same battles that we have fought. They didn't come to Christ when deception covered the land. They will not have to contend with Satan and his constant deceptions. They will have to fight no spiritual warfare, they will exist under the godly reign of the saints. They will not suffer the cruelties of life and the results of mans sin as you and I have. They will not have to believe in Christ while the world ridicules them. However, the "*firstfruit*" the ones called out in this age we will be known forever and for all eternity as those *Overcomers* who came through "*great tribulation.*" The Apostle John saw us with our robes white as snow and he said that this is the group that endured a lifetime of struggle with Satan. This group endured, many of them even unto their deaths.

This is the calling that you have dear friend! Do you realize how precious your *"calling and election"* truly is? Have you ever realized before now why you MUST overcome? When the Holy Spirit chose you in the age for salvation, you received the greatest prize that's ever been granted in the lottery of life. Paul told us to now *"walk worthy of the Kingdom call"* You have been elected if you are reading these words, to take your place among the overcomers. No longer do you have buy into the lie of the modern preacher who says that you cannot rise above sin. It is time to overcome, to come over everything that Satan is sending your way. It is high time to awaken out of sleep, to cleanse your garment, to love holiness and to separate yourself from the world. Should you do these thing and keep his commandments then you will be trusted and accepted into that government of righteousness that shall soon reign over all the earth.

May I show you an amazing scripture that plainly tells us the purpose of the church in this age? Prepare to be amazed at how this scriptures proves the ideas we are presenting in this chapter.

Acts 15:14
. . . God at the first did visit the Gentiles (notice the purpose for visiting the Gentiles, not to save them all) **to take out of them a people for his name** (nature a& character)

Acts 15:16
After this I will return and will build again the tabernacle of David that has fallen down and will build again the ruins therof and I will set it up people after living in God's perfect world and comparing it to the six-thousand years of Satan's rule, the

majority will choose to follow after Jesus. However, I also do not believe as I have been taught all my life that just a handful will live forever in heavens Disney world. There is a balance to this message and I thank God for his revelations of this balance. If God in his foreknowledge saw that he would lose the majority of his creation to the lake of fire then I beg you to explain to me why he didn't create the lake of fire for man? Why did he only create it for Satan and his angles if the majority of mankind will go to hell? If he intends to send the majority of mankind that has lived on this earth since Adam, over 155,000,000,000 then why does His Word say that he only created *"gehanna"* or the lake of fire for Satan and his angels? Just another example of two plus two equalling three. But didn't Jesus say that only a few would find the way to life? Absolutely and that proves our point; in this age only a few are being chosen to reign in that government of life. However, in the next age that will not be the case. Jesus was speaking of the age in which he was ministering in, the Church age.

When prophesying about an end time revival in our age; Sadly, these ministers have once again made the mistake of applying Kingdom age scriptures in the Church age. Jesus paints a total different picture about the end of the Church age than modern day ministers do. He asked this question concerning his second return in the Kingdom age; *"Will I find faith on the earth."* Now, this is diabolically opposed to the teachings of modern day Christianity, they propose that faith is increasing and that the church is growing and that revival is in the land. Actually quite the opposite is true. Faith is diminishing across the land, churches are closing, crowds are dwindling and sin is taking over the land with morals and values at their lowest levels in human history. Rather than man supposedly "evolving" men are in fact "devolving" culture, arts and humanity at large is disintegrating. Common manners and human dignity has become a memory of years gone by. Mankind has lost almost all social skills in the age of Facebook and social networking. Young people leave their homes in their pajamas and women dress like permanent employees of the red light district. In the midst of all of this the snake oil salesmen of religion would have you to believe that a great revival is coming. I declare emphatically that revival has ended in this age. However, I announce with great joy that your mind has never even imagined the magnitude of the revival that is coming to planet earth.

How about a revival where everyone responds to the gospel? How about a revival where every sickness is healed; a revival where all demonic influence is broken? How about a revival where we actually do bind Satan rather than just saying those words? How about a revival where true financial prosperity comes to everyone; a revival where every young persons rebellious nature is changed? How about a revival where every broken family is restored and put back together? **That revival is truly coming!** Would you like for me to tell you who the Evangelistic team will be that conducts these crusades? The visiting evangelist will be The Lord Jesus Christ and this teams of associates and ministers will be none other than the resurrected saints of his new government, *The Dream Team!*

Why isn't everyone being saved in this age, the Church age? Why does it seem that on the majority of the world the preaching of the gospel has absolutely no effect. However, on certain others *(a minority)* the gospel is completely accepted and wholeheartedly embraced. There is a reason for this!

Because, in this age, God is not trying to save the world! Yes, read that again and let it sink in - God is not trying to save the world in this age! That's not the purpose of the Church age. If so then God is failing miserably! I choose not to believe he can fail.

THE BRIDE OF CHRIST

In this day God is only saving his predestined and elected Bride. Once he comes into union with his Bride at the resurrection then he and his bride will do what a husband and wife does, they will produce many, many, many children during the Millennium *(their honeymoon)*. This Bride of Christ is not married, she is only engaged to Christ at this time; Paul calls us the *"affianced bride of Christ"* in other words we are engaged to him. Our role at this time as his *"Fiance"* is not to produce him children, it is to prepare ourselves for the wedding. Sadly the church is so busy trying to save the world and have multitudes of children *(converts)* that she is failing to keep her garments spotless, she is failing to teach her members to live the very life that Christ lived, an overcoming life. After the wedding *(the resurrection)* then together with our husband we will begin working and bringing *"many sons to glory."* The entire earth will be our field of labor and then we shall fill the earth with the knowledge of the Lord as the ***"waters cover the earth."*** The Kingdom age work cannot be accomplished by one man. Jesus was and is a man albeit a God-man. Just like the first Adam, the second Adam needs a help meet, a spiritual Eve that after proving herself to be a faithful bride she can work with him in the greatest harvest of souls in the history of the world.

Billions will be born in the millennium and the majority of them will accept Christ as their King. However, you must remember that God chose a very rudimentary way of reaching the lost which is through the instrumentality of preaching. So, even in the Kingdom age, the nations will be converted by his teachers and preachers that he sends to every nation, state, town, hamlet and village. Who do you suppose those ministers will be? Who will those kingdom teachers be? Why beloved of God, it will be all of those who he predestined in this age for salvation. It will be those who was baptized into the church in this age; those who grew in the womb of the church and they learned obedience to the laws of the kingdom in this life and they were counted worthy to inherit the Kingdom of God. These ministers will be sent throughout the world to bring healing to every diseased body and freedom to every bound person.

THE GOSPEL OF CHRIST

Jesus never made any attempt to save large crowds of people. He was not looking for the salvation of crowds he was looking for the training of the few pupils or disciples that he could trust with his *coming kingdom*. He never asked anyone to *"give him their hearts"* or to *"accept him as Lord."* Rather he predestined or called out twelve pupils, students or disciples. He taught them the only gospel that he ever preached *"The Coming Kingdom of God."* Christ had no crusades nor did the Apostles.

The modern church declares that it preaches the gospel of Christ when in fact is preaches a gospel *"about Christ"* rather than preaching the gospel that Christ preached. The only message Christ came to bring was the announcement of the *soon coming Kingdom of God.* Notice, Christ never preached one time that his kingdom was now on the earth. Actually, he had to correct everyone including his disciples who believed that his kingdom was now on the earth. (ACTS 1:6)

So, why the church? What is the true purpose of the modern church in this age? If it's not to save the world then what is her purpose? Christ came to "Call Out" which is what the word CHURCH means *"called out ones."* He came to *"call out"* a select few from Satan's government and to cause them to turn from the influences of Satan and to qualify to reign with Christ on his throne in the coming kingdom. To be transformed into the very image of their elder brother, Jesus Christ.

Rev. 3:21
To he that overcometh will I grant to sit with me in my throne.

Where are the called-out and overcoming ones to be sitting? In the government *(throne)* of Christ. We are actually going to be qualifying during this age to replace Satan on the throne or over the government of the earth. It is imperative that you understand this: The Church of this age has not been simply called unto salvation and eternal life but rather **we were called to learn obedience to the laws of God** and to develop the God kind of character in this mortal life, to earn the trust of our heavenly father.

For way too long the Church and her role has been misunderstood and therefore the church has been filled with laziness and lethargy. The Church has never been a soul saving station. The local church is not the place where sinners are to be reached (ideally) but rather it is the place where believers are to be matured and trained

If the Church is the means or the vehicle whereby God is trying to save the world then this question begs an answer. How did God save anyone before the church came into being? We know he was calling people such as the Prophets and the Patriarchs before the church ever existed. The writer of Hebrews tells us that all of the Old Testament saints were "filled with the Spirit of Christ." So, we know that God didn't need the church then to reach those people; Why? Because he used his Holy Spirit to draw them unto him. What means did God use for 4,000 years to draw souls unto him? It wasn't the church it was the Holy Spirit and I render to you that he uses the exact same method today.

THE TREE OF LIFE

Remember that God cut off access to the Tree of Life or the Holy Spirit to the entire world for 4,000 years. No one could simply come up to the Tree of Life and receive eternal life. Before they would be allowed access to the Tree of Life they would live a lifetime of proving their character and earning this Tree of Life. Sadly, the modern church teaches that the saints now have eternal life in them. However, eternal life or the crown of life or the tree of life is only promised to the overcomers and those rewards are given after this life nor during it. (Rev 2:10). So, you are asking I'm sure "If not eternal life then what do we have now?" Right now, you have a promise! I will explain this subject in the chapter entitled "Born

Again, what does it really mean."

This is exactly why Jesus said plainly that "no man can come to me except it is given to him of my Father" Because, he is the Tree of Life and no one can come to him on their own. No one can decide to come to God without him drawing you, the tree is still closed off to the world and it's only available to the "*called out ones*" in this age. Actually, God only offered his Holy Spirit in the Old Testament to a predestined few; Moses, Abraham, Noah etc. However, they did not need the church to save them; the Holy Spirit drew them to repentance and faith. In the church age nothing has changed in many regards except some minor nuances. God hasn't changed his program; he is not using the church to draw men to repentance, his Spirit continues to do that. He is using the church to mature and train the ones whom he has drawn unto himself. This is the very reason when Jesus was resurrected and at his ascension he gave gifts to his church, the Five-fold ministry, for one purpose; Not the saving of the world but for "the equipping and training of the saints." (EPH 4:11). I beg you to answer; "*training and equipping for what?*" God's church is a teaching and training church. The Holy Spirit still draws his chosen ones to repentance and faith and the Church takes those believers and prepares them for their future role in Gods Kingdom.

Now that let us turn to the scriptures for this portion of our Bible study; Matt 16:18

*. . . **I will build my Church and the gates of hell shall not prevail against it.***

This is the first mention of the word church in the New Testament. The Greek word for church is *ekklesia* and it simply means *"called-out ones"* So, basically Jesus was saying in his native language *"I came to build my group of called out ones, called out from Satan's government, called out from the systems of this world, called out from rebellion and iniquity and lawlessness"* Then Jesus went on to give a wonderful promise to those who respond to his spirits calling. He promises them victory over the grave. When he said *"**the gates of hell shall not prevail**"* He was speaking of the grave. The Greek word for *"hell"* as translated in this verse is *"Hades"* which means *"the grave."*

So to paraphrase Jesus words - here's what he actually said. *"For all of the ones who I call out of Satan's government and into my own, here's what's going to happen. When you die and they roll the stone or the gate in front of your graves; don't worry when I call you out from the graves those gates or stones won't be able to hold you back, they will not prevail against you.*

> # THE GATES OF HELL ARE SIMPLY THE DOORS OF THE GRAVE

As I have stated earlier, the true purpose of Christ *first coming* was to qualify for his throne, not to take the throne nor to sit upon the throne. The coronation day of Christ does not occur until the *second coming*, then he will take his throne. This is of extreme importance. God will never again place anyone in authority as he did Satan who has not proven that he can be under authority. This is the reason that Jesus Christ and all of his brothers (*you and I*) had to pass the test of complete obedience. To face this challenge God used the ministry of Satan. God created Lucifer and he knew full well that this archangel would rebel because God knows all things. So, God simply uses Satan's own weakness for Gods greater glory. Paul states it perfectly *"all things in heaven and earth were created by him and FOR HIM"* (this includes Satan) He uses the deceitfulness of Satan for his own good works. One of the way that he uses Satan is in the tempting or testing of his "supposed children." Anyone can say they are a child of God but very soon God will try your claim through the ministry of Satan just as he did with Job and with Christ.

MT. OF TEMPTATION THE REAL VICTORY

Everyone in Christianity gives such adulation and respect to *Mt. Calvary* and rightfully so. However, we shouldn't overlook the *Mt. of Temptation* which holds equal importance. It was on this mountain that the actual victory was won. It was on this mountain when Christ faced the same serpent that the *first Christ*, Adam, faced in the garden of Eden. The Serpent presented the exact same argument to Christ as he did to Eve, *"The twisted version of the Word of God"*. He basically told Christ that he knew of a way that Christ could become a God without complete obedience to Yahweh. Remember; he told Eve the same thing *"you can be as God to decide for your own selves what's good and what's evil"* He offered to give Christ a great position in his kingdom if Christ would do as the *first Adam* did and simply choose the tree of self-government and self-rule. All Jesus had to do to escape the cross was agree to bow down to Satan and as a result he could get the glory without the gore. However, Jesus passed a test on that mountain that the *first Christ*, Adam, failed to pass. He chose the government of God, the laws of God and ultimately the life of God. Now, here is a question for you the reader to answer; **What if Christ had chosen the kingdoms of this world?** What if he has circumvented the laws of God and chose his own way as the first Adam did? Would he have still been God? Think about it!

If Jesus Christ would have sinned and committed rebellion on that mountain, what would have happened to Gods plan? Someone says "*Christ couldn't have sinned because he was God.*" Well, if that's true then he cheated and he truly didn't experience the same temptations that you and I do and he cannot be a merciful high priest. If he couldn't sin then he wasn't truly a *son of man* and if he wasn't truly a son of man then the whole thing was a sham. Of course he could sin, just as the *first Adam* could sin. However, he did not! This is why the Father is well pleased with his son, he is perfectly obedient and he is perfectly obedient because he knows that God's laws are not grievous they are laws of love and he kept them perfectly. Because he looked back and saw how the *first Adam* or the *first Christ* failed, he saw the results of that failure and he understood that all of humanity depended upon him not to eat of that forbidden fruit.

Just as the mortal life of the God-man Christ Jesus served as a period of testing and trials that he might learn obedience so he could be trusted with God's kingdom; the very same thing applies to all of the other children of God who are now in the womb of the church waiting to be born again at the resurrection. As we walk through this life we are preparing to rule with Christ. However, that rule and that authority will never be given to those who want the easy way of selfishness. Those who refuse to acknowledge God's ways and God's laws they will believe Satan's seductive language and they will believe that they can be as God and decide for themselves how to live their own lives.

You are qualifying just as Jesus did to be given the Kingdom; to be one of his brethren, to be part of the ruling and royal family that shall soon serve with love and joy and peace over the entire earth. So, face your mountains and face the seductions of Satan with this vision clearly in view. Look past the kingdoms that offers you, the way of "*get*" and see what Christ saw. See, the results of his lies; look back on the first Adam and then look at the last Adam and decide where you wish to cast your lot. It is

WHAT IF JESUS HAD FAILED TO QUALIFY FOR HIS THRONE?

time to qualify for the throne, no matter how much the church teaches you that you are now saved and settled and it's a wrap, don't believe it for one second.

It's time to face Satan and all of his hordes of hell when they tell you that you are not who you say you are; "*If you were truly a child of God and going to rule and to reign in God's kingdom then where is your power now*" Oh how Satan sneered at our Lord when he was seemingly powerless. However, Christ saw his future ministry as *King of Kings*. Satan saw a defeated man but Christ saw "*The Lords Day*" in his mind when the very angel of darkness in front of him would be bound before his very eyes and the throne of his tormentor would be taken and turned over unto him at last. You must see the same vision, ig-

nore those who ridicule you for keeping Gods commandments. Ignore those who think it makes more
sense to go to heaven than to talk about a coming
kingdom. Simply see what Christ saw and you will
overcome and your mountain of temptation will also
become your path to total victory and acceptance
into the Kingdom of God. Christ knew that this age
was not his hour of power (LUKE 22:53) However, he
knew that day was coming. You and I must recognize
this same truth!

SERVANT LEADERS

Why is God calling the church first? Isn't that
God showing partiality for not calling everyone to
repentance? Since God is no repector of person then
how do you explain predestination? Allow me to ask
you this question and perhaps it can shed light upon
the truth. If you had devised a plan to feed the whole
world. Imagine that somehow you had acquired
the technology or the finances to make sure that no
one else ever goes hungry; would you just open the
floodgates and say "*Yall Come*"? Think about it. You
have the money and the technology to do a lot of
good for a plethora of people; you have the dream
but you are missing one vital ingredient: People, you
are missing a team to bring this food to the world.
You alone cannot manage seven (7) billion hungry
people. You have the food but not the network to
distribute it. Now, if you go throughout the world
and find one million people to help you distribute
this food, have you shown partiality to those people?
Of course not, these people have been chosen to
learn how to feed the world and they are actually going to be servants to the hungry.

God has a plan to bless the whole world. He has
the power to pour out his Spirit on "*all flesh.*" But
for reasons unknown to us he has chosen the foolish-
ness of preaching to accomplish this amazing harvest
of souls; He will need teachers and preachers and
witnesses in the next age to distribute his Holy Spirit
in every corner of the globe. He did not choose you
to be some supreme ruler while everyone else is "under" you. Absolutely not, here is the type of ruling
and reigning that Christ has in mind, this is God's
style of government; "*let him that would be chief be
servant of all*" If you want to see a beautiful picture
of Gods perfect style of government please read his
lesson to us in Luke 22: 25-30. Oh yes, you and I
are going to be chiefs, rulers and royal sons of God;
we are going to be rulers but you need to understand
what that means. We are going to bring healing and
deliverance and knowledge of God to all of humanity. **This is not a calling of privilege this is a calling
of purpose and responsibility and servant hood.**
This is why not many will be chosen for this calling
because very few can do as Christ did and "serve."
God is calling the Church first so that he can place
his dreams and his mind in us so that we can develop
a love for Gods creation and begin changing our
character and our mind in this mortal body for the
fulfillment of our future Kingdom ministry in our
spiritual bodies.

John 6:44
*No man can come to me on his own. . . my Father
must call them or invite them*

Don't you see, this is an invitation only government. There are no volunteers, it's all draftees. If you
don't believe it just ask Paul, he wasn't looking to
volunteer in God's government. However, God had
chosen Paul for this special privilege and this special

calling. Jesus told his disciples "*You didn't choose me but I chose you.*" How foolish is the rebellious and carnal mind that thinks that we somehow chose God. The Bible says that "*no man seeketh after God*" However, there are certain ones that God seeks after because he plans to change us into his image through his Word, his Spirit and his Church. Do I believe that God forces this calling on anyone? Absolutely not but I do believe that he can shine the light so bright on your Damascus road that you will eventually bow down and say "*yes, my Lord.*"

TEACH ALL NATIONS

Didn't Jesus tell his disciples to "**go into all the world and preach the gospel**"? Actually that's not quite what he said. He indeed instructed us to go into all the world and teach <u>a certain gospel for a certain purpose.</u> The only gospel he told us to teach was not a gospel of world salvation but rather "*this gospel of the coming Kingdom of God.*" Jesus said "**this gospel of the Kingdom must be preached in all the earth AS A WITNESS**" Notice carefully, the only message that Jesus cared about was the Kingdom message, the *Coming Kingdom* and this is the only message he commissioned us to preach. He did not commission us to go and "Save the world," he plans to do that in his perfect timing. However, our purpose is to simply go forth and be a witness, a shining city upon a hill; salt that flavors the earth; to announce to the inhabitants of the earth the good news of a coming better day and as we preach this message and live this life of the Kingdom as a witness against the current government of earth, then the Holy Spirit will do the choosing, the drawing and the saving as our gospel of the *coming Kingdom*

goes forth. Actually what Jesus told us to go forth and do was to go forth and simply "*live the Kingdom life*" (we teach all nations best by a living example) as a witness before the entire earth. The life of obedience to Gods laws stands as a witness to a godless world just how wonderful the *Kingdom of God* is and shall be. We are those witnesses who have experienced firsthand the joys of Kingdom living in a lawless world. How do we do that? It's very simple, Jesus gives us the instructions in Matthew 28:19. Unfortunately most people only know the first part of this verse, let's investigate:

Matt 28:19
Go therefore and <u>teach</u> all nations . . . .teach them to observe all my commandments!

Every Christian can quote this scripture. This scripture is used to raise untold millions of dollars for Christian evangelistic empires. However, this scripture says so much more than meets the eye. Now, I challenge you to read that again. Not one time did he tell us to go forth and save the world. He told us to go forth and "*preach the Kingdom*" (which is the gospel message) and to "*live the Kingdom life*" as a witness against and for the benefit of the world. How do we live the Kingdom life? How do we teach all nations? What are we supposed to be teaching all nations? Not how to just "*accept the Lord*" but rather how to "*become just like our Lord and how to live the Christ life.*" Oh how it has been overlooked but allow it to jump from the pages right now into your converted mind; ***OBSERVE ALL THINGS - KEEP MY COMMANDMENTS!*** Now in our next chapter we will discuss exactly what commandments Christ was talking about.

Commandment Keepers

Chapter Six

. . .a good understanding have all they that do his commandments
PSALMS 111:10

BASIC PRINCIPLES

ONE OF THE MOST BASIC PRINCIPLES OF UNDER-STANDING THE BIBLE IS SO OFTEN IGNORED. Here is that most important principle: **The Bible is a complete book**: You must always remember that principle when studying the Word of God. Unfortunately in today's church most New Testament believers do not adhere to the this vital key for correctly interpreting the scriptures. They study the Bible as a divided book: *The Old Testament vs. The New Testament*. Somewhere along the way we have divided Israel's holy book and caused a division that should never have been. It's almost as if we have turned the New Testament against the Old Testament. Preachers and ministers often speak as if with pride, the following words, "*We are a New Testament Church*", and by default they are in fact alienating themselves from all vestiges of the Old Testament. Failing they do to realize that the Old Testament is our teacher still! Paul says it is in fact our *schoolmaster* even at this present time, in the church age. Failing to understand the importance of the Old Testament renders useless any prodigious knowledge of New Testament understanding. When in fact, they are together the *"Two Witnesses"* that work together to bring to us the complete plan of God. It is absolutely impossible for you to rightly divide the Word of God without always searching for biblical truth in both testaments. Sadly, we, the modern church, have exercised extreme ignorance of God's eternal

GOD ONLY USES THE MAN THAT HE HAS FULLY CONQUERED

plans simply because we have failed to understand the absolute importance of the Old Testament and its relation to the New Testament. Paul told Timothy that the Old Testament was profitable for doctrine.

A MAN NAMED JACOB

Without this primary principle; *The Bible being a complete book;* then we fail to realize Gods purposes for his people. So, let's take a look into the pages of the *"other 39"*; the 39 books of the Old Testament which we have so often forgotten the importance of. In those books you will find primarily the history of God's first church, *Israel*. The word Israel simply means *"conquered or governed by God, chosen of God."* If you will remember; the man Jacob, son of Isaac, son of Abraham was a wily and deceiving character. He was a con man and a loser in the game of life with his constant disregard for others. He was living life his own way at his own speed and he was able to control his life and create his own blessings or so it seemed. He was always thinking about how to outsmart the system as we can so clearly see when he outsmarted his own father and brother. However, God had predestined this man to submit his life to Yahweh. God in his sovereignty had chosen Jacob for a purpose. That purpose could not be accomplished until God had conquered the character and the very nature of Jacob. **God can never use what he cannot conquer and he always plans to conquer what he plans to use!**

One day Jacob came face to face with his destiny, the Angel of the Lord which was the manifestation of Yahweh himself, in his theophany *(a theophany is a temporary body for a spiritual being)*. Jacob, the deceiver, the con artist, the fast talker, the quick thinker came into the presence of his God, his creator and something amazing happened. Jacob made a startling confession and when he did so it was the moment of change, the epiphany that his character so desperately needed. What was it? When he spoke these words after wrestling all night with God it was moment of majesty. He said "***I will not leave until you bless me.***" Do you know what he was really saying? "*I have been in control of my own life and with my schemes I have been able to bless myself. I didn't need any help or blessings from anyone but my own self. I was my own God and I was my own government. I lived by my laws and I decided what was good and what was evil, I created my own blessing. However, NOW I KNOW that you, the great Yahweh are in control of my life, of the heavens and of the earth. You have caused me to come face to face with my own inadequacies and now I surrender. Now, I choose to let my blessings come from my submission to you. I recognize and acknowledge that my own way of "get" and my own way of "me first" must end; now I vow to you to totally depend upon you for my blessings".*

At that very moment; when his nature changed; when his character changed; his name was changed! Why? **Because a mans name is never separated from a mans person** and in bygone days of antiquity your name was descriptive of your character and your nature. He was now qualified to be called Israel "*God has conquered*" and Israel was God's first church. Gods church is to be a fully conquered people, a fully submitted people. Only in submission to God's laws and God's ways will the true path to happiness every be discovered. As the author of this book, I have learned the lessons that I now teach to you; I learned them through experience, truly He had to conquer me!

GOD'S NATION

There were many nations in the world and God could have chosen to work with any of them. However, God made a covenant with *Abraham, Isaac and Jacob* and their descendents. Because of Abraham's obedience he chose them to establish his first natural church through the physical loins of Abraham.

God intended to be both God and King to Israel. Israel was to have no separation between church and state. Why did God choose Israel? They were not any better than all the other nations. Why did God choose this backwards and rebellious lot? Was it because he was a respecter of person or partial? Absolutely not! He wanted to use Israel to reach all of the other nations of the world. This is so plain to see in the scriptures.

> GOD PLANNED TO USE ISRAEL FOR THE SALVATION OF ALL OTHER NATIONS

God had a plan for Israel, not to save them only but to use them for the salvation of and to be a blessing to all the nations of earth. God always works his plan of salvation through a submitted *Dream Team*; through a chosen and predestined people. However with that choosing and with the calling came tremendous responsibilities and demands. Herein is where we all mess up. We all want the calling, the anointing, the choosing of the Lord. However, when that calling demands a separated life, a submission to his laws and a changing of our minds; then we decide that the price is too high. This simply means that for Israel God would give his complete focus. He told Israel "*of all the families of the earth, you only have I chosen.*"

From the moment that God chose Israel you never find him interested in any other people. If you will notice; all other nations in the scriptures are only mentioned as they relate to Israel. Did God not love the other nations? Absolutely, he loved them so much that he chose ONE NATION to become holy so that he could work through that one nation and bring heavens blessings to the earth and all the nations of earth through that dedicated and separated nation; the Church of the Old Testament. This is why Israel was called a *"kingdom of priest"* they were to serve God and man for the blessing and the joy of the whole earth; for all peoples. God's only attention and concern in all of the Bible is about one nation, Israel! Whether it's natural Israel in the Old Testament or spiritual Israel in the New Testament, Israel is his only focus. Everyone must become an Israelite to be saved *(not naturally but spiritually)* God only recognizes Israel, the children of Abraham in his eternal plans.

This was the people, the nation, the church that he had chosen to bring the knowledge of God to all of the other nations. This is why he forbid them to intermarry with these other nations because he didn't want those foreign nations to influence Israel in true worship; he is indeed a jealous God over his church. Notice how God calls Israel his *"firstborn"* or his *"firstfruit"* (Exo 4:22) It was Gods plan and intention to use his firstborn son, Israel to introduce him to all of the other nations after they had come to know God more fully. As a result all the other nations

would have desired and sought after Yahweh.

THE REASON FOR HIS LAWS

This is the very reason why God began placing so many laws upon the children of Israel. Not because he is cruel or because he wanted to control them; He wanted them to enjoy the earth and have long and prosperous lives. So, he implemented laws necessary to ensure their happiness and prosperity. As a result of their learning Gods laws of love and liberty then the natural results of living under those laws would have automatically brought peace and joy to Israel and they would have been "*A witness*" to all of the other nations of the absolute joy of living God's way. God could have pointed to the nation of Israel when he began dealing with all the other nations as the "*example nation*". He could have shown all other people a reason to reject Satan's rule in their lives. He could have pointed to the blessing, peace and prosperity of Israel as his proof that his laws and his ways are the only ways to happiness. They were to cause the other nations to desire God. They were to cause all other people to submit to Yahweh and to experience the same blessings that they would see Israel experiencing. Needless to say, Israel failed in her calling. However, there is a reason that she failed.

THE MOST MISUNDERSTOOD WORD IN THE MODERN CHURCH: -*LAW*-

The Laws of God! I am amazed at the number

of Christians that cringe when they see that phrase in print or hear it spoken. In the modern Christian church if you say anything about the Laws of God you will be expelled from their pulpits while they continue to preach on grace. Somehow they have invented a "**greasy grace**" *(grace the allows for the breaking of God's laws)* or a "**sloppy agape**" *(a perverted love, a distorted love; complete affection with no correction)* . In the modern message of the church, the grace and love of God has annulled his laws and as such they have pitted a religious war against any use of the word Law in their pulpits, books or talking points. Here is their mantra, I'm sure you have heard it. "*We are no longer living under law but we are under grace*" or "*No man can live Gods law, so Jesus did it for you, now you don't have to*".

IF THERE IS NO MORE LAW THEN THERE ARE NO MORE SINNERS

The Laws of God are eternal. These laws are not the Law of Moses. The *Ten Commandments* of God existed in the heavens before the earth was ever created. The *Ten Commandments* existed before Moses was ever born. They are Gods moral laws and nothing or no one will ever change, fulfill or annul them. Christ did not do away with them, what a disgrace to accuse the very man who kept all of Gods laws as having done away with those laws. The laws of God will exist during the Kingdom age and thereafter. All of the nations of the earth will one day be subject to these Commandments. However, God's own church despises the very mention of God's laws.

Israel was blessed with the Laws of God and these laws were for their happiness and for their joy not to be a burden. Had they only submitted and lived by those laws then they could have been used by God to save the world. Their light could have shined before the nations and they could have "*taught all nations to keep his Commandments*" They could have taught this by example and as living witnesses to the blessings contained in God way of *love and give* rather than Satan's way of *get and selfishness*. This is exactly the same command that Jesus gave his Apostles in Matt 28:19 "*teach all nations to observe my commandments.*" Yet, How many in the Christian church are actually teaching all nations to observe, recognize and to submit to those *Ten Commandments* and all the additional ordinances that Christ gave to us? Allow me to prove to you that these laws are eternal and they did not originate with Moses. Before doing so, you must understand this very important fact to understand Paul's writings about the law:

THERE ARE TWO (2) SETS OF LAWS; God's law & Moses law

God makes very clear the difference between his eternal, spiritual and moral laws vs. His earthly and temporary laws. Please not the following verse very carefully.

Duet. 5:22 - " These words the Lord did speak unto all your assembly in the mount in the midst of the fire . . . . . . and he added no more! ! !

To the eternal and morals laws that governs all of heaven and earth, the original *Ten Commandments* . . . **God added no more!** Moses is speaking here about the mountain that burned with fire when God gave them the *Ten Commandments*. He says that to those laws, those sacred requirements God added no more than those that were given upon the mountain of fire. Any other laws that were added after those ten were indeed given by Moses to the physical nation of Israel, not for salvation or righteousness but rather for "**that thy days may be long on the earth**" (DUET 6:2) in this mortal body. The laws added after God gave the eternal laws are indeed not binding upon the New Testament believer. However, the laws give by God on the mountain of fire, those were not the laws of Moses, those were the laws of God.

WHICH LAWS DID PAUL ADDRESS

When Paul is speaking against the keeping of the law he is not speaking of God laws! He is speaking of the *"added laws"* that Moses begin to add after the giving of Gods eternally binding laws, as the children of Israel began to break Gods laws. Why did Moses have to add statutes and judgements and more physical laws upon his church? Paul says plainly that these laws were added **"because of transgression."** In other words; as the children of Israel broke the *Ten Commandments*, Moses had to begin offering sacrifices for their transgressions of the spiritual laws of God. Had they never broken God's eternal laws then the keeping of those *Ten Commandments* would have indeed made them righteous. Paul says this about God's laws "**the law is holy and the law is good.**" So, how could Paul preach, as the modern church teaches, against the very laws that he is calling holy? There was never a problem with Gods law; the problem was in the people and their transgressions of his laws. So, now, to atone for their sins, their breaking or transgressing of Gods spiritual laws, Moses must now add ceremonial and sacrificial laws to pay the

blood price of sin. Pauls anger with those keepers of Moses law was in the fact that they failed to see how Christ indeed fulfilled *"Moses's ceremonial and blood sacrificial laws."* However, Christ did not annul God's eternal *Ten Commandments*.

As stated earlier and now once again for emphasis; There are two sets of laws: **There is God's eternal laws and then there is Moses's ceremonial laws and statutes** (HEB 10:1-10). Study in detail the book of *Hebrews Chapter 10:1-10* and the law that Paul is writing about will be made abundantly clear to you never again to be confused with the spiritual laws of God that shall always be binding upon his chosen nation *(church)* of Israel.

Hebrews 10:1

For the Law . . .can never with THOSE SACRIFICES which they offered year by year make you perfect.

Hebrews 10:3

But in THOSE SACRIFICES there remains remembrance of sin.

Hebrews 10:4

For it is not possible for the blood of bulls and goats should take away sin.

Hebrews 10:5

. . .but a body thou hast prepared for me

Hebrews 10:6

In burnt offerings and sacrifices thou hast no pleasure

Hebrews 10:8

. . .Sacrifice and offerings and burnt offerings and offerings for sins thou doesn't desire neither hath

pleasure in them <u>**WHICH ARE OFFERED BY THE LAW**</u>

Hebrews 10:9
He taketh away THE FIRST that he may establish THE SECOND.

Is it not plain to see in these scriptures that the ONLY LAW that was replaced was the SACRIFICIAL and CEREMONIAL laws? The laws of God, the *Ten Commandments* never mentions sacrifices or ceremonies. In fact, God says plainly in the writings of Jeremiah that he never desired sacrifices or blood offering, he never once put that in his original laws. Those were added as man continued to break Gods eternal laws. The eternal, spiritual and moral laws of God is not what was replaced, it was Moses's sacrificial laws. Yet, how the church loves to scream from the rooftop that we are *"free from the law"* like a bunch of spoiled children with their grapes of grace running through the streets without any restraints in their language, their lifestyle, their priorities, their dress, their conversation, their marriages and their actions. **Pity the man that preaches grace without law!**

If Gods law has been done away with, if Christ nailed them to the cross as one national televangelist loves to postulate then there is no more sinners on the earth today. Because, Paul said *"without law there is no transgression or sin."* I render to you this conclusion; if the laws of God are gone and Christ frees us from keeping God's laws then you can relax and have no fear; you cannot be lost because if there is no law for God to judge you by then he cannot ever, ever, ever condemn you to eternal judgement. Without a law then there is no sinners!

Notice that he speaks about the law and the sacrifices in the same context. Only this aspect of Moses law did Christ fulfill. The only reason why we do not continue to offer sacrifices is because "THAT PART" of the law has found its fulfillment. However, those ceremonial laws are not the eternal laws of God; those were the temporary laws of Moses and you will find out in Paul's writings that the only reason that Moses ceremonial laws were added was because the children of Israel had transgressed against Gods eternal laws, the *Ten Commandments*. I will prove by the scriptures that Paul never one time condemned the eternal and holy laws of God. He only condemned the ceremonial and Jewish laws of Moses. There is a huge difference between the two and if you don't get this settled in your understanding and in your theological paradigm you will never be able to rightly divide the Word of God and you will continue to live a life of iniquity *(lawlessness)* and never be accepted into God's government in the Kingdom age.

FAITH ALONE

Why does this teaching of *"faith alone"*, *"grace alone"* and *"the finished work of the cross"* make me so frenetic and vociferous in my writing? Because, it is this teaching that lent to my deceptive reasoning when allowing sin to reign in my life. It was these understanding of grace and faith that allowed me to belittle my sins and to shrug my shoulders and say *"no one is perfect"* or to say *"Christ, is the only perfect men so I will just thank him for keeping Gods laws and as far as me, it's not required"* When in my life I was faced with the sin of adultery there was nothing to really jolt me because after all if I can't keep the laws of God *(Thou shalt now commit adultery)* then Jesus will intercede for me and what's the big deal. I will commit this adultery and let Jesus intercede for me afterwards and go on with my life. Dear reader, these thoughts have brought the author tremendous sorrow in my life. God himself had to teach me the truth in a lonely prison cell. He had to show me the importance of submitting to him completely. Only when he showed me that his laws are just as binding today as they ever were did I truly come to see how lawless I had become under the message of "*grace alone.*" Grace is to the most beautiful gift of God and we could never live God's laws without him gracing us to do so. Without his Holy Spirit we could never please God in our lifestyles but with his grace we can now live the life of Christ which is a life of keeping Gods laws. Christ lives in us to keep Gods laws through us. Paul said **"it is no longer I but Christ that lives in me**." I have a question for you, If Christ is living in you what kind of life is he living in you? Surely, he is still a keeper of God's laws as he always was. Am I teaching you that works will save you? Am I teaching that you can earn God's grace by keeping his laws? Absolutely not, because you alone cannot keep Gods laws. However, the Dream Team, you and God both living and working together, can keep his laws! Keeping his laws will never save you. His saving you causes you to keep his laws. Keeping his commandments will without one doubt cause you to be "greatest in his government" or to quote Christ exactly **"Whosoever keepeth my laws shall be greatest in my kingdom"**

Dear friend, precious ministers of God, you need to make double sure that when you pound your fist onto your fundamental and evangelical pulpits and berate Gods laws and scream to your people that *"the law has been done away with"* I beg you to study and to know exactly *"which law"* has been done away with. Please, make it abundantly clear to the sheep entrusted to your care that they will be judged by their works, by their keeping the commandments of God or their lack thereof. When Jesus says depart from me "*ye worker of iniquity*" do you know what "*iniquity*" means? "*Lawlessness, without law, not keeping the law.*" God have mercy on your souls for preaching this false doctrine of "*accepting Christ in your heart*" and then die and go to heaven. **No one will inherit the government of the Kingdom of God with sin reigning in their life.** What is sin you ask? It is the TRANSGRESSION OF GOD LAWS! What are those laws? Even a child can answer that question; the *Ten Commandments* given by Yahweh in the Old Testament and then whatever additional ordinances and commands Christ gave in the New Testament such as his commands to be baptized and to observe his body and blood *(Passover, mistakenly called communion by the modern church)* and foot washing. (John 13:14-15)

This message of "greasy grace" *(grace that allows you to slip and slide all you want with no consequences)* with no obedience to Gods laws and teaching the people that God is no longer interested in us keeping his laws; beware the souls of men. The modern church teaches that we simply have faith in Christ and since he kept the law for us then we no longer have to burden ourselves with such legality. How sad! Christ didn't come to relieve you of the law of God. He came to live that law inside of you by means of the Holy Spirit to prove to the world that man could live by Gods law by the infilling of the Holy Spirit just as he received at the Jordan river. He came to live the law perfectly so that he could return at Pentecost and plant those laws into each and every member of the Dream Team, the church, the elect. God didn't send Christ to eradicate his law, he sent Christ to obey his laws and then to return to the church at Pentecost and live the laws of God through the vehicle of the church, in every member of the church; therefore muliplying the number of witnesses throughout the whole world. Exactly what are these witnesses testifying to? We are walking as living examples, witnesses, giving testimony to the fact that men do not have to be bound in lawlessness, in iniquity, in Satan's government, indeed they can be free even as we are! This is out witness! **This is ALL that Christ called us to be, witnesses.**

How plainly I can hear the words of Jesus *"If you love me keep my commandments"* I can also hear the young man asking Jesus *"Master what do I need to do to enter into eternal life"*... Please listen to the response of Christ. He didn't say *"Oh accept me and believe on me and sign the fellowship card"* No, he told this man that if you want to have eternal life "KEEP THE COMMANDMENTS." This man tried to play games with Christ and asked Christ *"which commandments"* and Christ proceeds to name several of them and this man said *"Lord, I've kept all of them"* and Jesus proved, as only he could, that this man hadn't even kept the first commandment about *"Having no other Gods before you"*. Jesus said, *"go and sell all that you have and give it to the poor"*; **Jesus knew that money was this mans God** and he had placed money before Yahweh. The young man simply walked away. Why? Because everyone wants eternal life, everyone wants to be saved but nobody wants to hear about laws, commandments, holiness or separation. No one wants to give up control of this life long enough to receive eternal life.

I want to say emphatically that if you are not a commandment keeper then you will never qualify for the throne or the government. Don't you realize that our only goal in the coming Kingdom is to teach Gods laws to the entire earth? How can we teach what we never kept ourselves? We will have no authority on the subject unless we begin living in obedience to those laws now. As we begin to experience the blessings of obedience to his laws then our lives will be a witness to the whole world, to all nations and it will cause all men to desire to know the Lord and experience the same blessing of righteousness, joy and peace in the Holy Ghost as we have already found in this mortal life.

Sadly, this is the very reason why you and I are not impacting this modern world. Our message doesn't line up with out lives. Rather than us being witnesses of a victorious life over sin and the shameful results thereof, rather we submit to and are controlled by the same sinful lifestyles, languages, actions and temperaments.

Before we go into a scriptural study of the two sets of laws allow me to prove to you that God's eternal laws existed in eternity and before creation by asking you to answer the proceeding question: **How can you commit sin?** There must first be a law for you to break or it's not considered sin, which simply means a transgression of the law. That's exactly what the word "sin" means. The New testament writer says plainly *"where there is no law there is no sin."* Transgression is described as *"breaking the law"* sin is *"lawlessness."*. When your child transgresses he or she has broken one of your rules. If you have not established your rules with your children then you cannot rightfully punish him. Can you? Your only option, if your child is unaware that he's broken a rule or law of your house, is to give him a warning, you cannot justly punish the child. **So, this is the natural proof that we must refer to in order to prove that God's laws have existed before time began.**

THE ANGELS SINNED

How did the angels sin? The Bible says *"the angels that sinned"*. Those angels could have only sinned one way; they must have known Gods laws in order to have sinned. God could never judge the angels as sinful if there wasn't already an established law in the heavenly realms. They, they angels, could only have sinned if the laws of God had been taught to them previously and if they willingly violated those laws. Without established laws then the angels would not have been in rebellion, they would have been in ignorance and given another opportunity to rule and reign. The very same commandments given to you and I were given unto these rebellious angels of transgression. Gods perfect eternal law of liberty and love existed before time began.

Notice how that 400 years before Moses came on the scene God tells Abraham **"because you have kept my laws and my statutes"** What laws? The supposed and so-called *"law of Moses"* wouldn't exist for another four hundred years. So what laws are being referred to by Yahweh himself when speaking to Abraham? The very laws that God had taught Abraham are the very laws that Moses codified and then after codifying God's laws, Moses added certain statutes intended only for the physical nation of Israel. Everything that he *"added unto "* such as the sacrifices, ceremonies and rituals has been done away with as **only those laws** were fulfilled in Christ. Everything before, the laws which have existed eternally; not the ceremonies, sacrifices and rituals but everything that existed before Moses and his additional statutes, have always and always will exist. Jesus said that *"**heaven and earth would pass away before one jot or one tittle passes away**"* from God's eternal and binding laws.

WHAT DID GOD TALK ABOUT IN THE GARDEN EACH EVENING?

What do you think God talked to Adam and Eve about in the garden every evening? Were they just shooting the bull or talking about the football scores? What were they discussing everyday? Why beloved member of the *Dream Team* they were learning his laws, his ways, his mind and his thoughts. Indeed, he must have been instructing them in the way of happiness and joy, the way of giving and obedience. Had they not known his laws then he could never have judged them. Paul says *"he that dies without the law is not judged by the law"* So, therefore we know that they must have known Gods eternal *Ten Commandments* or else God couldn't have cursed them for their rebellion.

What was Christ teaching his Apostles for three years? What did he tell them to go and do in Matt 28:19 - Go to all nations and teach them to OBEY MY COMMANDMENTS. Yet, you never hear anyone doing what Christ actually told us to do, except for a few.

DONALD TRUMP SAYS: YOUR FIRED!

Imagine this scenario if you can: Someone like *Donald Trump* chooses you, elects you to be his personal assistant in running his world-wide real estate corporation. There are many others just as qualified as you and just as appealing as you; but for some reason you found grace in his sight and he chose you. Now, imagine if you will the insanity of the following story:

On your first day at the office, Mr. Trump begins teaching you about codes of conduct, integrity and basic office standards. He gives you a handbook *(Bible)* with all that he expects out of you. He expects you to live the lifestyle that you've been entrusted with. He expects you to dress accordingly, not to use abusive or foul language in his presence of anywhere in his empire. He expects you to learn how he operates, how he thinks and basically to know what he would do in any situation and to act accordingly. However, you for some reason think he hired you because he likes you. You take no interest in his commands nor the lifestyle he expects you to live. You basically think that he has no right to tell you how to live your life and that you have the right to decide for yourself what is right and wrong for you. Actually, you've been led to believe that it doesn't matter because nowadays he can't fire you without a huge lawsuit and your job is basically secure as long as you don't blatantly turn your back on him. Well, imagine your surprise when Mr. Trump uses his favorite words on you. Your fired! But why? The answer is simple, you failed to "***walk worthy of his kingdom***". You loved being chosen but you failed in understanding the purpose of your choosing. So it is with modern Christianity; we fail to recognize that the purpose of our salvation is not heaven, it's to be a team with God, a Dream Team in fulfilling his will and his purposes on the earth both now and in the age to come.

When God sees many of his servants who accepted his grace without walking worthy of that grace; He also will say **Your fired**, depart from me you lawless one who failed to keep my standard. Their response will be "*but Lord, we believed, we confessed you, we preached to the world, we cast out devils, we healed the sick . . . . . .but we were told that your laws no longer existed..... And that's why you didn't know us!*

THE COMMANDS OF CHRIST

In the closing paragraph of the last chapter, I promised to investigate along with you in the scriptures exactly what commands Christ is referring to in Matt 28:19. Just what commands does he desire for us to teach all nations? **Are you in fact keeping all of his commands?**

It's very easy to keep them; love God and love man. Well, that's sounds easy enough doesn't it? Actually it is impossible for any human to do without the Holy Spirit. No man truly loves anyone or anything more than himself and his own. It is contrary to human nature to love or worship anything other than himself. While all men can pay lip service to their love of God and their fellow man, very few can truly show forth that love. If you ever see someone truly loving God and loving man you will see someone filled with the Holy Spirit which is the Spirit of Christ. Jesus so beautifully demonstrated for us what it means to love God and to love man. In loving God, he kept fully all of Gods commandments. In loving man, he gave himself as a sacrifice. For man he sacrificed his own desires and dreams and he adopted the dreams of his Father by loving the unlovable and by dying for the ungrateful. Why did he do it? He saw us as God sees us; deceived, pitiful and sick in our minds. Jesus became our healer by becoming a sufferer with us and overcoming all of those things that we have submitted to.

The modern church teaches us that all of God's commandments have been replaced with only two commandments "*Love the Lord thy God with all thine heart*" and also "*Love your neighbor as yourself*". After hearing that sermon we all say Amen and declare that we are free from all of those old, hard laws and we're now free if we just love Jesus and love people. How sad! The word love has been so watered down to mean no more than fluffy emotions of and paradisiacal thoughts. **However, love is not a word as much as it is an action.** Love is dangerous because love is the bringer of death to the self. When you love someone their life is your life, their cause is your cause, their dreams are your dreams; you will die for them, the ones you love. However, Jesus brings the Old Testament commandments to such a high level that in actuality the Old Testament commandments are easier to keep than the so-called new ones that Christ teaches. So, to teach Gods people that Christ did away with the Laws of God is not only misleading it is in fact a false statement. Jesus never relieves us of the responsibility of keeping God's Ten Commandments, in fact he brings even greater responsibility to us. For example, not only are we to honour our Father and mother, our relatives, our own, but now we are to LOVE as much as we love ourselves even the people we hardly know, our neighbors.

Now, think of that; Love them as much as you love you! How much do you love **you?** How much do you spend on feeding **you**, on clothing **you**, on entertaining **you**, on transporting **you?** Until you have that much love for your neighbor then you are in fact breaking Gods laws. Impossible you say? Absolutely, no man or woman can do this. However, I present this argument to the body of Christ; Only when this impossibility becomes visible and possible in your life have you truly been converted. Until the pain of humanity, the hurt of the broken can move you with compassion as it did Christ, until then you are still under the government of Satan, living the way and the selfish lifestyle of "get". What about the command of Christ to love God with all of your heart? Easy you say? Really? What does it mean to love God? It means that you will destroy yourself, your dreams, your agenda and most important your right to rule in your own life and you will whole-heartedly bow before his commands. That is what loving God means. Paul commands all believers to become "living sacrifices." Would you think about that for a moment? What is a sacrifice? Isn't is something that is dead? So wouldn't the word living and the word sacrifice in fact be a total paradox? Those two words can only fit together supernaturally never in the natural. Only when you have been supernaturally filled with the Holy Spirit can you place the words living and sacrifice in the same phrase because truly those conceived by the Spirit of God are dead to self and alive to God.

So, what commands is Christ talking about? Why of course, his eternal *Ten Commandments*. Let's explore them in detail and also lets explore the additional commands that Christ brings to us and by conjugating them together we will truly see what he means in Matt 28:19 about teaching all nations to obey his commandments. Now open the scriptures with me!

Jesus begins and ends his earthly ministry by stressing how important it is for believers to keep all of the commandments of God:

Matt 7:21
Not every one that calls me Lord shall enter into the Kingdom; but only he that doeth the commands of my Father.

Please note the words of Christ; *believing and calling on my name is not enough.* Signing the salvation card and saying that I am Lord will not grant you entrance into the government of God. Only those who OBEY his commandments will be trusted with my government. Notice the soon following verse number 23. . . he calls those who do not keep the commands of Yahweh as "*workers of iniquity.*" So, the question is "What are the laws of his father."

Matt 5:17,18
Think not that I am come to destroy the law, or the prophets, I am not come to destroy but to fulfill (bring it to its original intent)

For verily I say unto you, Till heaven and earth pass, one jot or one tittle shall in no wise pass from the law, till all be fulfilled.

Notice the words of Christ most carefully! Even in our man made laws we have what's called "*the letter of the law*" and "*the spirit of the law.*" Many times, people will try to skirt around the true intent of a law by finding a loophole around the letter of the law and thereby they make a mockery of the law. Men in their natural state are always trying to find a loophole around God's laws by pointing to places where it may not say explicitly "*thou shalt not*" and

in doing so we are in fact attempting to live by our own laws. However, Jesus came to introduce us to what the law was originally intended for: *Holiness within and without.* He came to bring the letter to it "fuller-fillment" its greater meaning, it's originally intended purpose. Then he goes on to warn us that God's laws will never, never be done away with. For example, Thou Shalt not commit adultery really only applies to married people so therefore could we commit fornication before marriage? Evidently we can since it's not spelled out in the "letter of the law." However, Christ says that contained in the letter of the law is the Spirit of the Law and as such we shouldn't desire to commit any type of sexual sins. He also came to fulfill the law by living it through all of us and as such begin filling the earth with the knowledge of God in his Dream Team or his first Fruits first as a witness.

Matt 5:19
Whosoever therefore shall break one of the least of these commandments, and shall teach men so, he shall be called least in the kingdom of heaven: but whosoever shall do and teach them, the same shall be called the greatest in the kingdom of God.

There is reason that many of us in the church did not really understand the importance of the above verse, especially in reference to "least and greatest in the Kingdom." The reason is because we thought that we were all equal, all saved and all going to heaven when we died. Therefore we had no clue what being least and greatest could possibly be referring to so we simply ignored and acted like the scripture wasn't there. I challenge you to call you spiritual advisor right now and ask him what the above verse means; you will be surprised by how taken aback he will become as he dances around the issue.

According to Jesus, only those who keep all of God's commandments are who submit to his laws in this lifetime will be trusted with great influence and authority in the next kingdom age. Those who disregard his laws here on earth will be "*least in the government*" they will not have the authority or position because of their disregard for God's laws. In the next chapter entitled "*Kingdom Authority*" your eyes will be immediately opened to the truth of the above statements from the scriptures. Now, notice most carefully the following words of our Lord;

Mark 6:9
Full well you reject the commandments of God for your own traditions. *(What are the commandments of God that he's referring to? The Ten Commandments)*

Here is what Jesus said: *No matter what teachers of truth try to show you concerning the keeping of God's laws you will always find a loophole and a way of holding on to your traditions, your religious backgrounds.* I am utterly shocked even still at how you can show people plain truth from the Word of God and they will basically shrug their shoulders and wish they had never met you; they would rather keep the connections in their local church, keep their positions and live where they are comfortable than to change their ways and submit to the commands of God. **Read the verse above and ask the Holy Spirit to reveal to you if this verse applies to you.**

Mark 7:7
In vain do you worship me, teaching for doctrines the commandments of men

This scripture quoted above has always been very difficult for me to explain or even understand. When I see people genuinely worshipping God at a church or prayer service; when I see their tears of sincerity as

they exercise themselves in demonstrative worship; as I see the rain of Gods Spirit pouring over them; I cannot imagine God rejecting that worship. I look at the Jewish people who mourn at the Temple Mount in Jerusalem with such devotion and when someone tells me that God is rejecting that worship, it's hard for my mind to grasp. When I see Pentecostals dancing before the Lord with all of their heart and when I see Baptist on their knees at the altar in worship, how can God reject that? But finally, I understand. God wants none of that, God desires no offerings of sacrifice or worship more than he wants a life of obedience to his laws and his commands. Obedience to God is in fact the only true worship.

Jesus told the sincere worshipper at the well that her worship wouldn't please God. He instructed her that God is only pleased with those who are living a life of truth and spiritual understanding. He said exactly "**he seeketh those to worship him in Spirit and Truth**" What is truth? God's word and God's laws! If you are worshipping God your way rather than complete obedience to his commandments then you actually are in fact wasting your time. God honors obedience more than sacrifice, so saith his Word. For example; On what day of the week does he require his holy convocations to be? The Sabbath; are you placing his commands above the traditions of your church? Is his prescribed way important to you, is he first in your life? What about his tithe? You can worship with every worship team on the planet and still not be pleasing to God if you are walking in disobedience to his set pattern and his laws.

Please note this powerful and chilling response that Christ gives to a young man about how he might receive eternal life. Unlike modern preachers Christ did not preach nor believe that a person is saved by believing alone or confessing Christ alone; he taught that salvation was a future promise *(shall receive the crown of life, shall eat of the tree of life)* to the overcomers, those who keep the commands of God.

Master, what must I do to inherit eternal life, Please notice the response of the Rose of Sharon; *"**Keep the Commandments.**" (MATT 19:17)* Now let us briefly look at the commands that you and I are commanded to keep in order to be considered *"greatest in the kingdom"*.

THOU SHALT HAVE NO OTHER GODS BEFORE ME

You must surrender! You must get off of my throne, you must say Yes to my will and my way. You must surrender to my authority in your life, in every way and in every area of your life. Family does not come first, careers do not come first, church and religion does not come first, I come first! The reason for this is because when you learn to obey you will find yourself on my team, together we will make a *Dream Team* and in this association you will be blessed, healed, free from sickness and you will live eternally.

THOU SHALT HAVE NO GRAVEN IMAGES

Do not allow yourself to create any false images in your mind about who I really am. Don't allow religion to design me into some evil being who longs to destroy my creation. Don't allow my glory and my love to be misrepresented as some sociopathic tyrant who must have my way or I will burn the whole world and listen to them boil in the flames of eternal fire for as long as I live. Don't imagine me as a God who doesn't care about humanity. Don't see me as controlling and dominating because of my laws. Do not re-create me with your own human ideas. See me for exactly who my Word says I am. I am love and

I am light and in me there is salvation for the entire earth.

THOU SHALT NOT TAKE THE NAME OF THE LORD THY GOD IN VAIN

Never lose your admiration, your awe, your respect and your holy reverence for me, my kingdom, my priest, my house, my son and my plans. Watch carefully how your lips release my name, my title, my holiness because from the abundance your heart will you hear your mouth speaking. Let any mention of my works be with awe and joy and gladness for as you reverence my name which is many; *Yahweh, Jehovah, El Shaadii, Jesus*, always let those names, those titles flow on the waters of reverence. As you reverence my name and all things associated with my work you are in fact surrendering, it is part of the process of allowing me to hold the throne of your heart.

REMEMBER THE SABBATH DAY AND KEEP IT HOLY

Just as my tithe is Holy and separated for me alone and as it represent the principle of *"Your firstlings unto the Lord"* as it physically demonstrates the status of my place in your life so doth my Sabbath. I've called my people to gather into a holy convocation on the seventh day of each week as a memorial of creation and as a reminder of the coming Sabbath day; the one-thousand millennium reign of Jesus Christ on earth. I planted my presence into the Sabbath day by forcing myself to rest, I created this Sabbath as my divine appointment with my children

HONOUR THY FATHER AND MOTHER

As you honour the ones on earth who gave you life you are actually honoring authority and all authority is from God. Learning to obey and honor your earthly parents teaches you that you are indeed not your own God, you are in fact under authority. In doing this you are actually honoring God. The way that you honor your parents is by living a lawful life, a hard working and honest life, a life that will make their investment into your life something that they can go to their graves being proud of. As you live a life to honor them you are in fact living a submitted life to God.

THOU SHALT NOT MURDER

As you honor life, you honor me! As you recognize that all life is given by God and that he alone is the giver of life then you cannot in any shape or form ever take what doesn't belong to you. As you honor another person by not taking their life you are in fact honoring the giver of that life. As you refuse to take life through murder of the born or the unborn you are refusing to play the role of God and as such it shows your submission to the giver of life.

THOU SHALT NOT COMMIT ADULTERY

Honor your covenant, your promises, your word must be your bond. Live for someone beside yourself. Honor your spouse and in doing so you are honoring the one who will soon marry his wife. Adultery in the eyes of God is a gross violation; it's the ultimate in selfishness and if you are involved in adultery you are thinking of your fleshly pleasures alone. This shows your inadequacies to rule in God's government. You must care for the pain that you cause others. You must care for the children whose lives you are destroying. You must care for the future generations of your family that will not have a home for family gatherings, a home of normalcy and peace and joy. As you honor your marriage you are in fact showing your respect for the holy institution and the soon coming wedding of Jesus Christ with his bride.

THOU SHALT NOT STEAL

To be trusted in God's future kingdom with possibly thousands of people in your care, you must be trustworthy. Only a person who feels that they are their own God has the mind-set to take what belongs to someone else. This must be destroyed in each of us. God commands six days of work. God values work and he loves to watch as his children work without complaint; working to be pleasing unto the Lord. In learning to work we learn the value of that work and therefore we could never steal what others have worked for. God is telling us in this commandment to value work to value people and to be counted trustworthy for his upcoming kingdom purposes.

THOU SHALT NOT BEAR FALSE WITNESS

You shall be trustworthy! Your word must be your bond. You must not lie nor disrespect the truth. Why? Because God is truth and in him there is no deception and in each of us we must attain to Gods love for truth. As we practice truth in all things; it may hurt and it may cause minor problems in the short term but as you develop love for truth you are in fact maturing and walking worthy of your calling. To please the Lord your yes must mean yes and your no must mean no. This is why we are not supposed to swear because our word alone should ring with the bells of truth.

THOU SHALT NOT COVET

As we obey this commandment we in fact begin producing the fruit of thanksgiving. As we recognize that God has given us our portion in this life then we no longer desire the treasures of our neighbor. We find happiness in what God has given us. If anyone is worshipping God while coveting with jealousy the blessings of others, they are in fact worshipping in vain. In all things give thanks, wherever you are and whatever you have recognize it as gifts from the Lord and be thankful, truly thankful.

NEW ORDINANCES BY CHRIST

The Ten Commandments were given by Yahweh in the Old Testament and they represent Gods eternal and moral laws. However, when Christ came he not only teaches us to keep the commandments of his Father but he also introduces to us some additional commandments in the form of ordinances. Now in Matt 28:19 he instructs his Apostles to teach "***Whatsoever I have commanded you***" he tells them to teach all nations to DO or OBSERVE all of the commandments. Now, he did not tell them to go and get everybody saved, he will do that in his time, he told us to go and TEACH THE COMMANDMENTS. Let us look at the few that he added to the ten so that we are careful to teach all Christians correctly in the keeping of Christ commandments.

KEEPING OF PASSOVER
(communion)

After many years of studying I have yet to find where the word communion came from as our "*breaking the body and drinking the blood*" is commonly called. The only biblical word that I can find for this sacrament or ordinance is actually the "Keeping of Passover."

John 13:1 -5
Now before the Feast of the Passover . . . Please note that Jesus himself is keeping the Passover feast

in this setting. Realizing that he is the fulfillment of this feast of Passover, that he is indeed the sacrificial lamb, he simply makes a couple of changes to the ceremony but he does not do away with the ceremony. He in fact commands us to continue keeping the Passover as he was doing. He gives us instructions on how to continue keeping the feast of Passover by now replacing the older elements of Lamb and unleavened bread with his blood and his body. For some reason the Catholic Church changed this name from Passover to Communion. However, the Apostles and Christ celebrated Passover once a year and they used the bread and the wine to represent that the Passover lamb has in fact come and fulfilled that feast of Israel.

FOOTWASHING

It is debated by many churches and Christians as to the necessity of this ordinance. I will admit that for many years I felt this was more in the category of a *"nice thing to do."* However, I have come to understand that the commands of Christ are exactly that, commands. Matt 28:19 commands for all believers to "***Observe all that I have commanded you.***" So, let us see if this ordinance is indeed one of Christ commands.

John 13:14,15
If I then, your Lord and Master, have washed your feet, ye also ought to wash one anothers feet. For I have given you an example that <u>***YOU SHOULD DO AS I HAVE DONE UNTO YOU.***</u>

May I ask you; is the above mention of foot washing a request or a command? He says, If I am your Lord and your Master then you must do as I have shown you. But why? We all ask why and at times these ordinances might seem unimportant; but in ceremony and symbols there is lessons and messages and even ways to measure our spiritual growth. You must understand that in the future government on this earth that you and I are qualifying to be members of; we will be Kings and Priest and as a result of those offices we will be serving the people. This ordinance is a test of our ability to bow down to those who cannot or will not be able to reach up to us. This is actually a kingdom test, foot washing. Gods government of rule is not a tyrannical government, it is a serving government. This is why he ordained this ordinance, you will in fact be a servant throughout all eternity and only if you find joy in servant hood here will you qualify for the kingdom.

WATER BAPTISM

Is water baptism necessary to be saved? Here's a better question. Is obeying the commands of God necessary for eternal life? Christ says that it is. So, the commandments of Christ are just as binding as Gods and if they are not obeyed you have in fact not obeyed the gospel.

Now, does water save you? No, absolutely not. Does water baptism in itself save you? No, absolutely not. However, obedience saves you and Christ commanded water baptism. "**He that believeth and is baptized shall be saved**" that is the words of Christ. I could list countless scriptures that prove the necessity of water baptism. Of course, one must not be dogmatic about these truths; should someone be unable to be baptized upon the time of their conversion through no fault of their own and should they die before that, of course they would be saved as God knows the very intent of the heart. If the thief on the cross could have had a puddle of water like the Ethiopian eunuch did, I can assure you that he

would have been baptized. Jesus himself was baptized, Paul was baptized, all the Apostles and early church was baptized and yet this church age seems to disregard that commandment as they do all the others. No wonder they will tell Christ *"Lord, Lord, we believed, we confessed, we prophesied, we prayed"* they will truly be shocked to know that they were part of that whole world that Satan deceived (REV 12:9)

John 14:21
He that hath my commandments and keepeth them, he it is that loveth me.

Those who will be told to *"depart from me"* will evidently be those who know about him but they truly didn't love him enough to *"Keep his Commandments"*

Rev 12:17
These are they . . . .which keep the Commandments of God and the testimony of Jesus Christ.

In this scriptures is a beautiful example of faith and works. The commandment keepers without faith are Pharisees. Those who have faith without the commandments are deceived.

The
Authority of the Kingdom

Chapter Seven

TRUE AUTHORITY

WOULD YOU LIKE TO RULE AS A KING IN GOD'S FUTURE GOVERNMENT? He is accepting applications from those spiritually conceived members of his called out church. His greatest gift to you will be the authority that He grants you in His government. He will trust you with the souls of all mankind in the coming age. How will he determine your position in that Kingdom? Quite simply; He's watching in this life. The eyes of the Lord *(angels of the Lord)* that are to and fro upon the earth are always watching you. They are watching your maturity into obedience and your levels of love by your keeping of God's laws. It is because of what you do in this life that you will be granted Kingdom authority. Do you remember the *"seven sons of sceva"*? (ACTS 19:11-20) This was a group of people who wanted the benefits of Christ kingdom without the laws of the kingdom. They approached a demon and tried to cast him out in the name of Jesus. They used the same words and incantations that the Apostles used but their prayer did not work. Why not? Because, unlike the Apostles they had no genuine authority granted to them through obedience. How is authority granted to you on your job? By your level of trust and your level of obedience to company policy and management. Only with the blessings of administration do you have true authority. The policeman that has the power to stop a ten thousand pound car at a traffic stop, he has no power at all over that vehicle without true authority. However, as the policeman spent his time at the academy; as he worked under all his leaders in obedience; he is granted the authority of the government. As he abides by the laws of the government and as he

in fact submits to that government then all of the power of the government is at his disposal. When he lifts his hand to the oncoming vehicle, with that true authority comes his power. You cannot sneak into Gods kingdom and expect to walk in the power of heaven. True authority over demons only comes when you have overcome demons in your life through your obedience to Gods word and obedience to his commands. Then and only then will your uplifted hands threaten a demon. Otherwise you are like an illegal alien in a foreign country. If you are illegal you get none of the benefits of the kingdom. If you are illegal then you are in fact breaking the laws of the government and therefore you cannot expect any of the benefits of that government. For those who wish to sneak into Gods kingdom illegally without the covering of grace that comes through obedience to his laws then in fact you have no true authority whatsoever. Authority is earned as obedience is practiced.

Authority typically comes in incremental advancements. Most workers do not start out with any real authority. Entry level positions carry no authority. Authority is a gift granted to those that it can be trusted with. People with evil characters, selfish natures will only abuse authority. Therefore their character must be tested, their old natures must submit to the nature of God in order to earn the true authority of the kingdom.

Jesus tells a parable about a wedding supper which represents his soon to come wedding with his church, his bride. (MATT 22:11) There was a person who tried to enter into that wedding without a wedding garment. This person believed that God's way wasn't the only way. This person felt that they could enter the kingdom without obedience to Gods laws. After all, why would a silly garment be important to God? Why does it matter if I have a certain garment? Because, God said so! It's really that simple. If you want to rule in this kingdom you must come in at the door, you must come into God's provided way, you cannot do it your way any longer. It is time for you to totally surrender to his will.

Everyone who has been called, elected and predestined in this age, the Church Age, they alone are being prepared for positions of trust that they will earn during this lifetime. God desires to share his throne with you, he desires for you to be a fully vested member of his family. He desires to place the badge of heavens holiness upon your soul; in his coming Kingdom he must have people who have been prepared in the furnace of affliction, tried in the torrents of time and pressured in the realms of resistance.

Please understand that in the Church of God there are two groups of people, two seed lines, two vines growing together, two twins living in the same house. Namely; *The Church carnal* and *The Church spiritual*. The *sold out church* and the *lethargic church*. The *wise church* and the *foolish church*. Both groups of people are indeed saved; they have placed their faith in Christ and believe in him completely. However, there is one group who has decided to *"make themselves ready"* and there is another group of people who will be *"made ready"* in the tribulation and in the coming wrath of God upon the earth. John saw a group of believers who were **"made white."** They did not make themselves white in the Church Age, they did not submit to the Word of God and they did not purify themselves by obeying the scriptures. Rather, they had to be made white, made pure by the fiery trials of God that are to come upon the sleeping church. Pray therefore that you

be watching and waiting, that you prepare your own garments so that you might be counted worthy of Kingdom authority.

When exactly did Jesus receive his full authority? When did he announce that "all authority in heaven and earth has been given unto me"? Did this occur while he was still in the furnace of affliction? Did this happen while he was in his testing period called life? Did he receive full authority one second before he has proven his absolute obedience and his absolutely faithfulness to Gods Word? In fact he did not receive full authority until after his crucifixion until after his earthly life had proven for the record that he was fully submitted and had the very heart, character and nature of God.

In the exact same manner; the other sons of God *(you and I)* who have been spiritually conceived by the Holy Spirit just as Jesus Christ was will also receive our authority at our resurrection as we stand before his judgement seat for our job interview and for his decisions as to the intent of our heart and the content of our character. At that point you and I will be granted authority over many people among the nations of the world. At this point if we have been **"faithful in a few things"** we shall then be made **"rulers over many."** Sadly it must also be acknowledged that at this very same event, the judgement of the saints, many shall stand disappointed as silence fills the judgement hall (30 minutes of silence in the heavenlies) when millions upon millions realize that they could have done so much more in preparation for the Kingdom of God.

IS THE KINGDOM OF GOD ON THE EARTH TODAY

There are three religious or theological views on the kingdom of God and it's timing.

- PREMELLENNIAL
- AMELLENNIAL
- POSTMILLENNIAL

Will the return of Christ be PREMELLENNIAL *(before the thousand year reign)* AMELLENNIAL *(there will be no literal kingdom but simply a divine rule in the hearts of men between the first and second coming)* or POSTMILLENNIAL *(the kingdom will be brought about by men spreading the gospel and then Christ will return after the world has been made better by the preaching of the gospel).* Quite sadly, the modern church having grown weary of preaching about a coming Christ and a coming Kingdom have simply changed their gospel and made is less taxing upon them by not having to explain our Lords delay and they have in fact adopted either the amellennial or postmillennial positions. It's important to note that almost every sermon that you hear today speaks of the Kingdom of God and everyone loves the subject. However, they have placed the Kingdom of God as *Augustine of Hippo* did, in the wrong age.

HIPPOS MISTAKE

Allow me to explain; *Augustine of Hippo* an early Catholic church father is in fact the creator of the

postmillennial and *amellennial* doctrines *(anytime an "a" is placed before a word it means non-existent such as "a"moral means no morals, "a"millennium means no millennium)* in all of its historical and in its current forms. He at first begin to believe that God's kingdom would not be established until after the Catholic church has preached the gospel for one-thousand years *(1,000)* and then the earth would be a utopian paradise and changed with the gospel. He then argued that Christ would come after the Catholic Church had dominated the earth and ushered Christ back to the earth. Well, after seeing the world getting worse and worse *(as Christ said it would)* rather than better and better he changed his position. Becoming disillusioned with the world becoming more and more evil he began allegorizing the scriptures about the millennium and in fact created the doctrine currently held by 90% of the church world; the doctrine of *amellennialism.* Virtually he eradicated the idea of a literal thousand year reign on earth and spiritualized it all away and stated that in fact there is no millennium but that rather the Kingdom of God is already here and in the hearts of men right now and it's actually a spiritual kingdom and not a literal, natural kingdom. *(To destroy this idea please read Chapter Two of this book entitled "The Kingdom of God")* If Augustine is indeed correct then Jesus has never and never will fulfill his role as King. Yet, as Jesus stood before Pilate he told Pilate that he was born to be a King. Although Jesus Christ fulfilled the roles of *Savior, Healer and Deliverer* he has never fulfilled the very role he was born for, *King of Kings.* That role must be fulfilled and that role will be fulfilled when as the book of Revelation teaches *"the kingdoms of this world become the kingdoms of our God"* literally! It has rightly been said that the church in America is three thousand miles wide and a quarter of an inch deep and sadly that is not an empty cliche'. This empty reasoning has allowed for *"Replacement Theol-*

ogy" "*New Covenant Theology*" "*Dominion Theology*" and various other nuances of ideas.

SO WE WAIT

For all of my dear friends whom I love in the aforementioned groups who genuinely believe that the Kingdom of God is here and that we are now taking dominion over the earth, I have one question for you; **Can't you do a better job**? Because so far it doesn't look like your batting a thousand. The earth, the world, the nations are deteriorating before our eyes while you fail to warn of a coming Kingdom; you seem to glory in a non-existent kingdom and with such preaching have deceived the church. We are now living in Satan's government, this I promise you dear reader. We are not now taking over the earth, we are right now "*Standing on the promises*" waiting in patience for the soon coming of our Lord and his glorious Kingdom. We will not give in to the pressures of this age by abandoning that message for a false gospel of a current Kingdom Now. Jesus Christ at this time is not King of the nations or the earth, it's the wrong time! As the curtain is closing on the Church age we are preparing now for the Kingdom to appear in the soon coming years as the players of the world stage, the nations are lining up perfectly with Bible prophecy: so we wait! As weary as we may become of preaching the message, still we wait. The faithful, the elect will never tire of waiting. In waiting we are possessing our souls!

Many of these well-meaning and good people will use a couple of scriptures in their arsenal to prove that the Kingdom is indeed here now. Allow me to share some of those scriptures with you and to also share their true meanings as the Word will interpret itself.

Mark 1:14
And saying; The time is fulfilled and the Kingdom of God is at hand: repent ye and believe the good news.

What is the head of a Kingdom? A King! He is in fact the physical embodiment of his kingdom. This is why he is called the "*Head of State*", in order to see the state you would have to look at him as he is the manifestation of his State. So it is with the Kingdom of God. Christ is the head of his kingdom and his earthly natural kingdom would have been set up if Israel had accepted him as their Messiah and King.

WE ARE NOT NOW TAKING OVER THE EARTH, WE ARE RIGHT NOW "STANDING ON THE PROMISES"

However, God in his foreknowledge knew that they wouldn't accept him and as such the Kingdom was never to be established on earth at Christ first coming. However, the Kingdom of God visited the earth in the King himself, Christ Jesus. As he was here and as he housed spiritual elements of the Kingdom such as righteousness, joy and peace so do these elements reside in his spiritual church. However, his governing and his earthly Kingdom will not be spiritual it will be physical although ruled by spiritually born sons of God. Only in the church age is his Kingdom realized in the Spirit and even then it's only elements or an essence of the kingdom that you and I are experiencing today, not his world ruling government. Please, please, make that clear in your thinking. We are not in the world-ruling government of Christ right now.

Without that clear understanding you will think we are in the Kingdom of God by modern preaching. We are still in the Church age and are in fact we are the Church of God not the Kingdom of God.

THE KINGDOM AT HAND

Note the phrase "*at hand*" in the above verse; skeptics try to use this verse to prove that God set up his kingdom when Christ came the first time because the scriptures says that the kingdom was "*at hand*." Please look with me at the original greek work for "*at hand*"; Greek - *Eggizo* - it is the exact same Greek word that is translated elsewhere in the scriptures as "*approaching*" rather than "*at hand*" as the translators for reasons unknown chose to use in this particular verse. If you look in Hebrews 10:25 you will find the exact same greek word -*Eggizo*- translated correctly as "*approaching*" and not "*at hand*." Now. To prove concretely that this scripture did not mean that the Kingdom had now come or was "*at hand*" as if to mean as close as your hand is *(as modern Kingdom Now preachers love to postulate),* let us allow the Word to interpret its own self.

Luke 21:31
So likewise when you see these things come to pass know ye that the kingdom of God is nigh at hand.

Now, we are presented with a real problem for those who postulate that the kingdom of God is now here in the hearts of men, ruling and reigning on the earth, especially when they try to use the verse that says the kingdom is "***at hand***" because in Luke 21:31 Jesus is talking about a day in the distant fu-

ture called the end times and he says that when you see all those forthcoming horrors taking place then you can know that the kingdom of God is -*Eggizo*- approaching or "***at hand***." Evidently by the words of Christ the Kingdom was not on the earth when he said these words.

THE KINGDOM IS WITHIN YOU?

Another favorite verse of the *Dominion, Covenant, and Replacement* Christians is found in Luke 17:21; you will hear them quote this one like it's a peppermint stick; they love it because it supposedly proves that this is a present day spiritual kingdom in the hearts of men and that we are now ruling and reigning. I have actually seen some of their tempers and it causes me to wonder exactly what they are reigning over. Let's look at their favorite scripture.

Luke 17:21
. . .the Kingdom of God is within you

Without proper exegesis *(context)* I would have to stand down and acknowledge that indeed that's what Jesus said. However, knowing the truth of the coming kingdom and knowing it's a future kingdom and with all other scriptural references pointing to its future tense, what do we do with this one? Well, of course we do good Bible study and we find the context and the original wording. Luckily for us, all modern translations have corrected this incorrect King James translation because in fact Jesus did not say those words; He said according to my study and all the corrected modern translations "***The kingdom of God is among you***" He was indeed the King of his Kingdom and the King of the kingdom was standing among them. However, let's look even deeper at whom he was speaking to when he supposedly told them that the kingdom was within them. Read the preceding verses as you always should:

Luke 17:20
And when he was demanded of <u>the Pharisees</u> when the kingdom of God should come, he answered them . . .

To whom is he speaking? The Pharisees. Am I to believe that he would tell those hypocritical Pharisees that the kingdom of God was in fact in them? Of course not. Jesus made it abundantly clear to his disciples on many occasions that he in fact had not received his kingdom as of yet and that he would not partake of the Passover with them until he partakes of it with them in his coming kingdom. Also, he told his disciples in Acts 1:6.7 when they asked him when he was going to establish his kingdom, Jesus told them "*it's not for you to know the time and the season.*" Even forty days after his resurrection he had still not established his kingdom. He gives us a very detailed answer in Luke 19 about his kingdom; whether its a present or a future kingdom. Let's study those verses.

OCCUPY TILL I COME

Now, the scriptures I'm about to present to you shows us so plainly how that you and I will receive true authority in his government. It was the forthcoming verses that helped me to completely understand the subject that I'm now writing about. Please read with me carefully;

Luke 19:11
And as they heard these things, he added and spake a parable, because he was nigh to Jerusalem, and because they thought that the kingdom of God should appear immediately.

The same mistake made by the Pharisees in the above verse is being made by almost the entirety of the Christian church in our age and most especially those who preach the *Kingdom Now* message. The disciples also falsely believed that the kingdom had come when Christ came. Read the above verse; when did they think the Kingdom of God would appear? Immediately! They believed as many do today that the purpose of Christ coming was to set up his kingdom but not so; he came to set up his Church, this is not the kingdom age, this is the church age.

Now read with me carefully the most beautiful revelation from Christ's own words about the nature of his coming government and the timing of that government.

Luke 19:12
He said therefore a certain nobleman went into a far country to receive for himself a kingdom and to return.

There is more revelation in that one verse than most of Christianity understands as a whole. Jesus is explaining about His kingdom by using a parable. He says that "*a certain nobleman*"; this represents our Lord of course, the most noble of noblemen. He continues: "*went into a far country*" this of course is indicative of his leaving the earth and going to his Father in heaven; a far country. He continues :"*to receive for himself a kingdom*" Now beloved, this proves emphatically and without further discussion needed that this nobleman did not have his kingdom before he takes this far journey. In fact go back and read the chapter entitled "*Daniels Interpretation*" and you will read where emphatically Christ did not receive His kingdom until his return to his Father. Also in Revelation Chapter five we read where he receives his kingdom after his resurrection, after the Lion of Judah prevails over death. He continues: "***and to return.***" The plans of this nobleman is to return with his government and to receive those who will reign

THE LOCAL CHURCH IS NOT AND WAS NOT BUILT TO BE A "*SOUL SAVING STATION*"...

with him in that government. So, his kingdom or his government is not brought to earth until he returns! Is it not plain to see when the kingdom is coming? Why would Jesus pray "***Thy kingdom come***" if it was indeed already here?

Luke 19:13
And he called his ten servants and delivered them ten pounds and said unto them, work until I come.

This has the most amazing revelation concealed within. Notice what happens right before he leaves. He calls ten servants. Now, the church that you and I are part of, the *Apostolic Church of God* simply means "*the called out ones*" so these that he called in the aforementioned parable is in fact "*The Church*" and notice even more carefully that he called "10" which is the number of *responsibility and leadership* in biblical numerology. It also denotes a predestined number of people, an elect, a chosen amount of people, specifically called for one purpose; to rule with this nobleman when he returns. Notice what

he tells them to do while he is gone. He doesn't tell them to "*rest in your salvation*" nor to "*rejoice in the fact that you are saved, that your part of the ten*" Absolutely not, he tells them to work; to prepare; to grow and mature into responsibility and maturity. According to the book of Ephesians this is in fact the very purpose of the church "***for the maturing of the saints.***" Notice before Jesus left the earth, just like this nobleman he also gave gifts unto the church, ***Apostles, Prophets, Evangelist, Teachers and Pastors.*** These gifts are to bring us not to salvation but to maturity. God and his Spirit brings us to salvation, just like this nobleman called the ten servants, so God has called us unto salvation. However, the job of maturing and responsibility he has left with the church *(more on this in the chapter entitled "Born Again, what do you mean")*

Sadly, I hear preachers across the world stating that the local assembly of believers or the local church is a "*soul saving station*" nothing could be further from the truth. The purpose of the local assembly of believers is not for the salvation of sinners it is as the scriptures teach; for the maturing of the believers. In our focus of saving the lost we have failed to mature the spiritually conceived sons of God and as a result they are losing their faith, they are losing their focus and they are truly destroyed for a lack of knowledge. The most ill advised Christians are those who attend a church that fails to recognize it's true calling of teaching and equipping of saints. The local assembly of believers is never represented in the New Testament as a place where sinners come to be saved but rather its the place where they come after their conversion to be trained in the scriptures and to be taught the mind and the ways of God; His laws, His statutes and His plans for their lives both their moral and immortal lives. So, the question is then asked; Where do the sinners get saved? Wherever the Holy Spirit chooses to call them; on their jobs, in their cars, in their homes, at the shopping center or any other place that you cross their path and your life serves as the witness of the gospel of Jesus Christ. Once you have been used as a minister of God to bring the message of the Kingdom of God, then and only then can they benefit from fellowship among the saints in the local congregation. It is not the commission of the local church to save the world, it is our commission to be *"witnesses and to teach all things that God has commanded."* What are we witnessing? We are showing the world in our lifestyle, our language, our words and our deeds the virtues of the coming Kingdom of God. We are showing them by our life the beauty of living Gods way, the beauty of obedience to the laws of God. We are living sacrifices walking around in a selfish and satanically controlled world and we are witnesses of the ways of God, the way of giving, the way of life and the way of obedience. This is the commission of the church, not to win the world. The Holy Spirit has the job of evangelism, he calls men to repentance and he always has a preacher with the gospel message in place to draw in the net after that soul has been drawn by God himself to godly repentance. God chose preaching to be the net that is cast out when he begins drawing someone to repentance. Our job is simply to preach the Kingdom of God and those who are being called to train now for the Kingdom will answer the call and our preaching will guide them to their destiny in God.

Luke 19:14
But his citizens hated him and sent him a message; we will not have this man to reign over us

It was not his servants that hated him, it was his citizens; the ones who make up the population of the earth that he is going to return to and rule over. People are so determined not to be ruled or governed; just look at the nations today; there is a rebellion springing up everywhere against government as people are needing someone with a heavy hand to step in and bring peace to the world. These citizens of the world sent messages daily to this King that he would not rule over them. The citizens of earth send the same message daily to our heavenly Father; their message is loud and clear; we can govern ourselves, we need no monarch, no king and no ruler; we are our own Gods. However,

GOVERNMENT IS EVERYTHING!

his servants were working and preparing to actually help him rule over these citizens who were blinded by Satan because the servants understood that one day Satan would be bound and these citizens would love their Lord when he returned. Anytime you see Christians who despise government either in the church or in the world then you have found Christians who are absolutely clueless to the fact that *"government is everything."* This is why God teaches us to obey our parents because the family structure is the first unit of government on the earth. This is why men are made the head of the home for the establishment of divine order and government. This is why women are told to wear a covering of hair on their heads in honor of government, their husbands. This is why we are told to honor our parents because in doing so we are honoring government. A husband

and wife that do not realize that their home is a miniature government will never be able to rule and reign with Christ. This is why Paul encourages not allowing the sun to go down upon the wrath among husbands and wives; you must learn to submit to one another because in doing so you are actually honoring God by honoring government. This is the first lesson of true Kingdom authority; submitting to government.

Luke 19:15

And it came to pass when he was returned having received the kingdom, then he commanded these servants to be called unto him, to whom he had given the money so that he might know how much every man had gained

I pray that the spirit of revelation is opening these truths up to you in a new way. Notice carefully that the kingdom did not come until he returned at his literal, physical second coming. But at his coming he calls his church into a resurrection to stand before him for the Judgement Seat of Christ; remember decisions or judgement begins in the family or house of God and this verse shows it perfectly. He calls these ten, this elected and predestined number; remember that ten (10) is the number of leadership and responsibility; the members of this called out and elect group are to be judged according to their works, not their confession of faith but their works. He is going to determine their level of obedience to his command that they work until he comes. Did they grow in faith, obedience and in love and the fruits of the Spirit?

Luke 19:16, 17

Then came the first servant and said Lord, thy pound has gained ten pounds
And he said unto him, Well, thou good servant because thou hast been faithful in a very little have thou authority over ten cities.

I would assume that by now your eyes are opening to this glorious truth. The first servant from the Church age is called before Christ and this church member didn't buy into the lie that there was no works involved in Gods plan of salvation. He didn't buy into the lie that he was saved to go to Heaven. He believed God's Word and went to work on his growth process of maturing, of obeying all of God's laws, of loving people and serving mankind. His pound which represents his initial spiritual conception *(mistakenly called salvation)* had grown into ten pounds or an overcoming life. Notice, please notice the reward this member of the church receives. **Authority to rule and reign on the earth over literal cities and literal peoples!** Not Heaven, not a home in the sky, not a mansion, Oh no, much, much better; he receives a trusted position in Christ government over the earth, he shall serve ten cities and convert those who were once enemies of Christ into faithful followers of Christ during the millennium. That trusted church member will have power over every demon in those ten cities, he will go among his people healing every disease and teaching and preaching the laws of God and the love of God and the life of God. He will indeed be one of those "*deliverers on Mt. Zion*" (OBADIAH 1:21) that the prophets spoke about. He will indeed be one of those 144,000 who follow the lamb whithersoever he goeth. *(Order my book, the mystery of the 144,00 for more details)* Or you can continue to believe that he will be escorted off to Heaven somewhere to sing for all eternity, the choice is yours to make.

Then Christ calls another elected church member before him and this servant has also increased in his calling and election, he has in fact made his calling and election sure but not as greatly as the first one did. However, his level of authority is given to him over five cities in verses 18 & 19. For those who don't believe there will be those with greater and lesser rewards at the judgement you need to read this teaching of Christ in detail. No wonder there will be thirty minutes of silence at the judgement as people suffer losses in their rewards, their positions and their crowns or their realms and levels of authority.

Now notice the saddest part of this story as we continue reading. You're about to read a symbolic portrayal of the majority of Christianity who have bought into the "*faith only*" and "*finished work of the cross*" lie. You are about to read about a person who believed on Christ and accepted salvation and now loses it *(Sorry to all my Calvinistic friends)*.

Luke 19:20
And another came and said Lord behold here is thy pound which I have kept in a napkin . . .

Luke 19:22
Out of thine own mouth will I judge thee thou wicked servant

Luke 19:24
And he said unto them that stood by "take from him that pound and give it unto he that had ten pounds"

Such a sad story about a person who was so-called saved. They had accepted the same call that the others in the church had received, went to the same altar and said the same prayer. However, this person just wanted to be saved and laid his salvation in the napkin of eternal security, in the napkin of greasy grace and in the napkin of eternal lies. He had no idea of his purpose for being saved the purpose of ruling and reigning in a future, earthly and literal kingdom. Don't let this be you at the judgement, God is requiring maturity and obedience if you plan to govern the galaxies with him. You must be trusted, if he told you to work until he comes, that's exactly what he's looking for when he returns, proof of your works. Faith is wonderful but without works it's dead.

Please don't be among those foolish church members who allow their oil to run out simply because they believed that this salvation was by "*faith alone*". May I quote the gospel writer once again, though so few really want to hear his words **"Faith without works is dead** (*non-existent*)" (JAMES 2:18)

Born again

the cure for Calvinism

Chapter Eight

*Behold the days are coming saith the Lord when the plowman
shall overtake the reaper and the treader of grapes him who
sows seed, the mountains shall drip with sweet wine and the
hills shall flow with it*   Amos 9:13

JOHN CALVIN

INTO THE THEOLOGY OF THE 18TH CENTURY CHURCH A NEW DOCTRINE WAS PRESENTED AND ACCEPTED BY MANY FROM A GENTLEMAN OF FAITH BY THE NAME OF JOHN CALVIN. His teaching which is commonly summed up in the following acronym T.U.L.I.P included the theological argument of eternal security or as commonly called *"once saved always saved."* Although this chapter is not intended as a treatise on all the points of Calvinism nor as a teaching of all the nuances of T.U.L.I.P for the sake of your understanding I will simply explain the meaning of T.U.L.I.P and then deal with only one of Calvin's doctrine, the doctrine of eternal security in this chapter. (*Order my book "Walking through the TULIPs for a complete understanding of his teachings).*

T - Total Depravity of Man
U - Unconditional Election
L - Limited Atonement
P - Preservation of the saints

Of course the "I" in TULIP was added simply to create the acronym. Sadly, many of the truths presented by Mr. Calvin have strong elements of truth in them but as always when taken to extreme positions and when placed in the wrong ages of God plan for eternity, the result is always extremism. Mainly for this chapter we will be looking at his position on the "P" of his TULIP teachings, the *"preservation of the saints"* or in other words, eternal security. Eternal security basically espouses the doctrine held by all Presbyterians, many Baptist and a lot of evangelical Charismatics. This is the teaching that once a person *"accepts Christ'* that they are then guaranteed eternal life no matter their future actions in this life. Basically, they can never be lost according to Mr. Calvin's postulations and theories. In fairness, Calvinism does not agree with Christians living sinful lifestyles theoretically, they espouse that should someone continue in a life of sin that they were not truly saved.

I will now explain to you how I wrestled with this theory for many years and eventually accepted it as truth before God divinely showed me the error of my way and corrected me with his Holy Word.

Before we delve into this subject allow me to explain why this is so very important in your understanding of God's plan for the ages. If you plan to walk with God as his partner in dreams, as his co-labourer in the gospel work then you must understand this vital truth presented in this chapter about the entire subject of being so-called *"born again."*

I first began my religious journey among the old-time holiness, Pentecostal or Apostolic people. As a young child preacher, beginning my ministry at the age of fifteen (15) (*I was in fact ordained on my 15th birthday)* I preached across the nation and in a few foreign countries the only message that I then knew and that was the Pentecostal message. One of the tenets or beliefs among the Pentecostals, especially the Apostolic branch of the Pentecostals was the doctrine of holiness living. Basically, we grew up with a horrible fear of dying lost and going to hell. Everything was preached against as a genuine effort to keep the influences of the world out of our hearts. We were diabolically opposed to the *"Once saved always saved"* message in those days as we took it to be a license for sinful living without any eternal consequences. In our churches you had to *"pray through"* for the smallest of sins or else you might die in those sins and go to an eternal, boiling lake of fire. As you can imagine we lived in constant fear of losing our salvation. We never knew which sinful thought or action might be the very one that robbed us of our eternal life so of course we lived very fearful lives with absolutely no security at all in our salvation. Our salvation depended upon our ability to remember to repent.

With the above painted picture in your mind you can easily see how the thoughts of Calvinism found an easy resting place in my mind when it was presented to me later in life. As I grew older in my ministry and as sin begin entering into my life and as I began to need an excuse for those sins and addictions, the entire message of eternal security began to appeal to me and find its way through the cracks of the door of carnality. Howbeit, I would never have admitted in those days that this was my reason for accepting Calvinism. I would have told you that indeed the scriptures supported Calvinism.

In fairness and to bring a balanced approach to this entire subject, Calvinism doesn't stand alone in the area of unbalanced extremism. The church of my childhood could have preached their message with more of a balanced approach as well. They truly believed that a lifetime of serving God could have been made obsolete by one sin unrepented of. While I have now come to understand their message more fully and I have in fact rejected Calvinism, I would caution the Pentecostal people to season your message with grace and you may very well find the perfect balance that your members are so in need of.

So, how could I have accepted Calvinism? Well, of course only if someone could prove it to me in the scriptures and with a well reasoned argument. Naturally, when the eternal security message came to me it actually caused me to admire the sense of rest that these folks displayed in their salvation. They didn't seem to fear losing out with God, they were just resting in the finished work of the cross. They didn't seem overly concerned with a dutiful prayer life or a daily crucifying of the flesh, they seemed to not allow condemnation over their personal sins to become a factor in their thinking; my old Pentecostal mind was actually jealous of their ability to be secure in their salvation. So, the more time I spent with them and heard their teaching and their "scriptural proof" the more and more that I became systematically convinced of the truth of Calvinism.

WHAT IF WE HAVE MISUNDERSTOOD THE ENTIRE CONCEPT OF BEING "BORN AGAIN"?

Please be reminded that both sides of this argument can present very valid and convincing proof of their doctrinal positions. While the Calvinist would present pages of scriptures to me about the so-called truth of eternal security, I could always counter them with scriptures such as *"he that endured to the end shall be saved"* or Pauls warning about himself *"becoming a castaway"* or the teaching in Hebrews about those who have *"once tasted the heavenly gift"* and turned back and their inability to ever repent. On and on the arguments would go and they always have a response to my response. However, here was the question that they always stumped me with. No matter how much I would try to argue with them, no matter how much scriptural proof I presented against the Calvinist, they always stopped me in my tracks with the following arguments of reason for which I could find no tenable answer.

AS IS THE NATURAL SO IS THE SPIRITUAL

At first they would present the principle of *the spiritual being represented by the natural* and the scriptures do teach us that "*as the earthly so is the heavenly*" (I COR 15:46). With this principle in mind they would present the following questions; *How many times can a person be born?* Then they would ask; *Can you ever not be a son of your parents?* Of course the undeniable answer to those questions presents loads of trouble to those of us who didn't believe in eternal security. It is a fact that a person can only be born one time and of course there is nothing that you can ever do that would cause you to no longer be a child of your parents.

So, we find ourselves in a dilemma; if we answer those two questions of the Calvinist in the affirmative; and we must, then they win the argument and as a truth we must all believe in eternal security. However, **what if in fact we have totally misunderstood the entire concept of the new birth?** What if in fact we have failed to understand the truth about being born again? Are you willing to find out?

According to our traditional understanding of being "*born again*" we have all upon receiving the Holy Spirit been born again, saved, redeemed and given eternal life. If that is in fact the case then we can all rest assured that we are all eternally secure. You can only be born-again one time, let that settle into your

thinking. You cannot ever be "unborn again" nor can you ever be "unsaved" if you can then you were never saved. If you have ever been given "eternal life" then if you could ever lose it, it was not eternal life, it was temporary eternal life. Can you see the absurdity of the whole argument? Unless we can find the greater truth and the deeper understanding of the new birth then we must believe in eternal security, the scriptures opposing eternal security notwithstanding.

But, what if our traditional thinking was wrong? As always the Holy Spirit leads us and guides us into all truth when we sincerely seek for answers with a pure heart and not a prejudiced and traditional mind-set. As I sought the answers from God, this one question began forming in my converted mind; *Did you actually receive eternal life and were you actually born again?* Of course I was taken aback at the question and responded as the majority of you that will read this book "*Of course I was saved, born again and of course I received eternal life when I repented of my sins.*" To think otherwise was completely outside of my theological framework and traditional mind-set. It just so happened after God begin dealing with me about this subject that I ran across a book by "happenstance" entitled "*Born Again, just what does it mean*" and in those pages, to my amazement was the very same questions and answers that I had been dealing with in my own mind.

After twelve months of constant study of this subject I have come to following conclusions that I wish to share with you: Both groups, the Calvinist and the Holiness (Armenians) each have elements of the truth but both are out of balance and have gone to the extreme. As always the truth lies right in the middle of both schools of thought. **Someone can definitely, without a doubt turn their back on** their faith and be lost! However, human frailties, forgotten sins and weakness of the flesh cannot and will not deny you the gift of eternal life. So, what's the difference? When a person quits repenting of sin, when a person no longer feels the pull of conviction, that is a person that is dangerously close to turning their backs on THE FAITH. However, as long as you feel that split system *(good and evil)* warring inside of you, that's a good sign, that means that you are still spiritually alive. You have not turned away from the truth, you still have the seed of God inside of you.

SINLESS LIVES

If indeed you have been born of God or born-again as we evangelicals use the term then in fact you could not ever sin!

I John 3:9
Whosoever is born of God doth not commit sin; for his seed remaineth in him: and he cannot sin because he is born of God.

The above scripture is where we must begin this study about being born again because this scripture gives great headaches to the body of Christ and their desire to rip this scripture from the Holy Writ. First ask yourself, are you without sin? Honestly, is your life sinless? Have you obeyed all the commands of God, all Ten? Have you loved your neighbor as much as you love yourself? Have you forgiven 70x's7 times? Have you visited the sick, the widows, the prisoners as Christ commanded? Have you observed His Sabbath, paid His tithe? Have you forsaken gossip and talebearing? Have you been faithful in your prayer

life, in putting Him first? IF YOU HAVE ANY SIN IN YOU AT ALL, ACCORDING TO THE VERSE I JUST QUOTED THE YOU HAVE NOT BEEN BORN AGAIN! Now, we are going to find out if in fact any of us has been born again yet! We are going to see if any of us have eternal life in us at this time or if it is rather a promise for the future. This chapter is going to help you so much if you will simply make yourself study these scriptures and open your spirit for the truth of God's word, no matter how different it sounds from what you've always heard. Dear friend, my ministries goal and purpose is to teach you the importance of selling out to God, to obeying God's word and to never again be deceived into thinking that you are currently born again or saved or that you now have eternal life.

According to the beloved of Jesus, John the Apostle, if you were born again or born of God, it would be

IF YOU HAVE ANY SIN IN YOU AT ALL THEN YOU HAVE NOT BEEN BORN AGAIN!

impossible for you to sin. By your own admission, you have not reached that point as of yet? Correct? So when do you believe you will reach that point of sinless perfection? According to Jesus, when you become like the angels in your resurrection, only then will you be unable to sin. **That is when you will be born again, in the resurrection, not now**! Here's the question that you and I will seek to answer in this study; Is the "*new birth*" a present or a future reality? Did Christ promise the new birth while we are still flesh? Or does he promise it to us when we have become spirits *(spiritual bodies)* in the resurrection? Have we entered into the Kingdom of God now or can that only happen in the new birth in the resurrection? Did Paul plainly teach us that *"flesh and blood cannot inherit the Kingdom of God"*? If so, are you still flesh and blood?

The Calvinist are very correct on several issues such as *Original Sin, Predestination* and *Unconditional Election* but on eternal security they have emaciated the scriptures. However, on the following point they are also correct; *as the earthly so is the spiritual,* In other words, we learn lessons of the spirit by the ways of nature. Paul tells us that even those who don't know God can see God in the works of nature. With that understanding let us actually look at the work of nature in the birthing process.

BEGOTTEN OR BORN?

Paul teaches that he had *"begotten us by the Word."* Now I want you to notice carefully the original word for begotten. This word means *conceived.* Paul tells us that he has *"conceived us"* by the preaching of the Word. **He did not birth us but rather he began the birthing process.** As is the natural, so is the what? *(The Spiritual).* So, are we now *"conceived of the Spirit"* or *"Born of the Spirit"*? If in fact we are now *born of God* or *born of the Spirit* then we have a huge scriptural problem because Paul says in *Romans 8:19* that the entire earth is waiting for a very special day; a birthing day, a giving birth of the children of God. Now, if we are already born, if we are already manifested then I ask you; what is

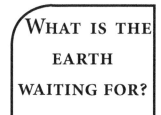

WHAT IS THE EARTH WAITING FOR?

the earth waiting for?

When the sons of God shall be born we shall be "**Deliverers on Mt. Zion**" we shall be used of God to rid this earth of the curse placed on sinful man. If we have indeed been born again as sons of God then why is the earth still groaning and begging for our birth? Because beloved, our new birth shall take place at the resurrection. **Our first birth was by water through the womb, our next birth shall take place by Spirit through the tomb.** When Jesus speaks of the *"gates of hell"* not prevailing against his church do you have any idea of what he was actually saying? Notice that he gave Peter, keys to the kingdom. Now, think about this for a moment. What does a key do? It unlocks a door, it gives entrance into another room or dimension. What was the key that Christ gives to Peter? "A Promise" that is what the key was, the only way to enter into the Kingdom of God is revealed to Peter by these words of Christ; "***the gates of hell shall not prevail against it***" What gates? And what Hell? Oh beloved, how wonderful is his Holy Word. The word Hell in this verse is not *gehanna (lake of fire)* nor is it *"Hades" (place of darkness)* it is the word *"Sheol"* which simply means *"the grave."* What was placed over the tomb or the grave of our Lord? A gate! The word *"gate"* here means *"entrance or exit."* What Jesus actually said were these words: *"The key that will allow you to enter into the Kingdom of God is your ability to pass through the entrance of your grave. When your grave cannot hold you back, when the gate, the door, the dirt of your grave doesn't prevail against you and when you pass through that gate you will then enter into the Kingdom of God".*

Until you have passed beyond the *"gate of hell"* or *"the door of your grave"* you cannot see nor inherit the Kingdom of God. So, please tell me how anyone could preach or believe that we are now in the Kingdom of God? How could anyone believe that we are now born again? When scriptures tells us that *"he that is born of God cannot sin"* and yet we all sin.

ABORTIONS AND STILL-BIRTHS

As long as a still birth in the natural is possible, so is a still birth in the spiritual possible. As long as abortion is possible in the natural so is abortion possible in the spiritual. Are we at this moment *"born again"*? If so then we can never be "un-born" but if we are in fact only *"begotten of the Spirit"* then we are in fact still waiting for our new birth! Is it possible that none of us have experienced the new birth yet? Absolutely!

Is a human born at conception? No, yet it is still a child, is it not? An unborn human is still a human and called a child. This is the very reason that we can be called children of God right now or sons of God right now and still not yet be born. We are legally and positionally children of God. However, should we fail to mature and to come to full faith and an overcoming life then we will not receive the *"crown of life."* If we already have eternal life inherit in our being then pray tell why must we receive a *"crown of life"* or eat of the *"tree of life."* Because, eternal life *"is in the Son"* and we have a promise of eternal life if we remain in the Son. Only at our resurrection will we receive eternal life inherently in our beings and then we will no longer depend upon the Son for eternal life, we shall have it inside of us. Isn't human life in the sperm? Even though you have a conception and you have the elements of life and you even have a child, still you do not have a born child and only a born child can fulfill his potential in the family and on the earth. You and I have been conceived or begotten with the Spirit of God but if you and I refuse to mature, if we refuse to stay connected to the umbilical cord of Christ which is His Church then you and I can and will be still born or aborted by Satan, the first abortion doctor, he aborted Adam and Eve from their potential spiritual birth; and thus with this understanding we can solve the eternal security and the loss of salvation mystery.

You cannot lose salvation because saved means saved. However, if I throw you a lifeline on my boat are you saved at that point? No, you are saved when you leave the water, if you hold on, if you don't let go, if you endure until the end only then are you saved. Right now, as you hold that rope you have salvation in the rope but when you touch land you will have salvation within yourself, you will be saved. At this point in your walk with God, Christ is your rope. Until the day that you become one of his brothers in the resurrection and until you have eternal life inherit within yourself, you must hold on to him because at this time your eternal life is in him and in him alone. He said *"if you abide in me and I abide in you"*

THE CHURCH, OUR MOTHER

Right now, you are an unborn child abiding in him, in his womb which is His Church and the church has one goal according to *Ephesians 4:13,* to bring you into the maturity of Christ so that you can "be just like him" and therefore experience the same new birth that he did, through the tomb!

According to Galatians 4:26, "***the Church is the mother of us all***"! The Church of Jesus Christ is his bride and her job through the *Apostles, Prophets, Pastors, Teachers and Evangelist* is to nurture you, to equip you, to mature you in the "*stature of Christ*" until you look just like him and to follow him in the new birth through the tomb.

ETERNAL LIFE, WHEN?

In all twenty-three references in the New Testament concerning eternal life they all speak *(when read carefully and in context)* of eternal life in a future tense, except for one and it's possible to even interpret that verse in a future reference. For example:

Titus 1:2
In HOPE of eternal life which God that cannot lie PROMISED before the world began

Does Paul tell us that he has eternal life or that he has HOPE of eternal life? Beloved, you and I have a promise, strong and sure that if we hold to our faith which is Christ that after we have died and slept we shall receive eternal life, in the future. I wish to say this to you; if you have eternal life in you right now then you could never die or go to a grave, it would be impossible for anything or anyone to take your life if you have eternal life right now. Unfortunately I don't have time to teach on this much needed understanding in this book but unfortunately most Christians believe the pagan lie that we all have immortal souls and that we go to heaven or hell the moment we die and thus we do have eternal life. How sad, that we as Gods church willingly remain so uninformed of Bible truth. No one goes to heaven or hell until they've had a fair

judgement. Poor Lazarus, to think that Jesus pulled him back from heaven to this life. *(Order my book: "The Hereafter" for biblical proof that the saints of God are resting, no one is in heaven or hell)* Even Jesus Christ didn't have eternal life inherit in his mortal body until "*God raised him from the dead.*" His eternal life was a gift he earned by his obedience to God in this mortal body.

Titus 3:7&8
. . .we should be made heirs according to the hope of eternal life . . . .that they which believe in God might be careful to obtain good works

Did you see that verse plainly? Hope of eternal life? Also, an admonition that the way to obtain what we now hope for is by keeping the laws of God, good works

---

PRINCE WILLIAM

What is an heir? Someone with a promise. What is Prince William right now in the royal lineage of the honorable House of Windsor, literal descendents of the House of David? He is an heir! Is he royalty? Yes. Does he have a promise of a future reign? Yes. But he is only an heir at this time, he is not a ruling monarch. He has the promise but not the "fullness" or the "reality" of the promise. However, should he attend his studies, should he keep his royal focus, should he keep his person under subjection to the House of Windsor and all of its tutelage and intricacies then the throne is a good as his, right now. However, should he turn from his understanding of his royal responsibilities then the very throne that is as good as his right now will be taken from him. So it is with the child of God who has been conceived by the Gospel into the church and they fail to mature, they fail to understand their part of the Dream Team, they fail in recognizing the responsibility of their future royal duties then their name shall also be blotted out of the Lambs book of Life.

Doesn't the scriptures calls us "*heirs of the promise*" or "inheritors of the promise?" Plainly we are called "the heirs of salvation." As of yet, we are still believing in the promises of God. As much as the modern Christian wishes to believe that we are now possessors of the land, I declare emphatically unto you that we are heirs that shall soon posses. For the next Christian that tries to sell you the bill of goods that we are now possessing the land, ask them if they have looked at the land lately? It might not be something that they are to proud to attribute to the works of God.

THE ACORN AND THE OAK

The acorn; the small, obscure and little acorn is the promise of an oak tree. All the elements of an oak tree is in that acorn. Everything that you can find in the oak tree you can find in the acorn except shade from the sun and fruit of the vine. You see, the oak tree serves a purpose for humanity. It is used to build our houses, shade our workers on a warm die, supply firewood during winter cold and for the fruit of its vine. Although the minerals of that tree, the very essence of that tree, the life of that tree is in the acorn; if that acorn does not mature then in fact the oak tree will never be born. As a child of God in the womb of his church, you have the essence of the Kingdom; you have what shall govern

his future kingdom already living in you and that is: righteousness, peace and joy in the Holy Spirit; You see, the essence of the Kingdom was given to you as down payment, as a foretaste of what the future, literal and earthly kingdom of God will be like. How many times have you been to church and hated to go back to the real world? The reason is because among the Church of God, among the people of God, the *spiritually begotten* children of God, the very essence of love and righteousness and joy and laughing and peace is shared among those growing in the womb of the church. The *Apostolic Church of God* is experiencing right now, internally, what all of the nations of the world will someday experience, we have the foretaste. However, we make our mistake in thinking that God's kingdom is on the earth just because the essence or qualities or attributes of the Kingdom are inside of his church. Just as that acorn has the essence of the tree inside of it, if that acorn fails to understand it's purpose then the tree will never be born. The acorn must be planted, nurtured and matured to ever be BORN. You and I have the Kingdom Essence but we must die completely to self and changed into the image of Christ if we are ever to be born again! The oak tree is not guaranteed, it is promised upon conditions. Salvation, eternal life and new birth is not guaranteed to even the Apostle Paul; no wonder he didn't count himself as to have already apprehended but he was determined to press forward until he was born again!

Romans 2:7
To them who by patient continuance in well doing seek for glory and honour and immortality, eternal life.

The questions begs an answer; what in the world can this scripture mean if we already have immortality or eternal life? Paul knew better than this modern gospel, he knew better than this false gospel. He said in Gods holy writ that the only way you and I will ever receive our throne of royalty, our eternal life and our new birth is if we continue in patience and well doing. What is well doing? Keeping Gods commandments!

The child's potential

The unborn child has no life in itself. If he loses contact with the umbilical chord then all hopes of his future life dies; he is totally dependent upon the life of his mother. The child has no independent or inherent life until he breathes the breath of life, his first cry. This is why God hates abortion because the potential of the child is never realized until the child is born. The potential of the unborn children of God is aborted when they lose their faith in Christ and when they quit maturing in obedience to the laws of God. What if *Dr. Martin Luther King Jr* had been aborted? What if *Henry Ford* or *George Washington* had been aborted? Their potential would have died with them. This is why Satan fights against the unborn children of God who are struggling in the womb of the Church to just hold their faith. This is why he wants you right now. As long as you are unborn then you won't be one of those that will be there when he is bound by Christ, you will not take part in putting him under your feet, as Paul said the sons of God would one day do. But as you overcome him, as you hold on to a bleeding cross and an empty tomb, as long as you know your potential as royalty in the coming Kingdom of God, as long as you realize that you are part of God's *Dream Team* for the earth then you will never be aborted or still

born. You will keep maturing until the old you begins looking just like Christ. The only way that you can meet your elder brother at the resurrection of the Family of God is if you look just like him. Paul said that at the resurrection *"we know not what we shall be but we shall be just like him."*

The family of God

When will be just like him? At the resurrection, our bodies will be changed just like his, we will be a Son of God just like him, we will have his authority and his power over the nations and we will rule over the earth! This is the reason to stay in the race, this is the reason to never give up... Not because of hell and not because of heaven but because of your God given potential to reign with Christ, to bring healing to the nations, to convert the souls of billions and to literally save the world!

> **At this moment our eternal life is in Christ... one day it shall be inherit in us!**

At this moment our eternal life is still in Christ *(I John 5:11)* but then at the resurrection when *"this same Spirit that was in Christ shall abide in you, it shall also make alive your mortal body and you shall be changed"* then and only then will you be eternal, then you will have earned the crown of life, the tree of life and the Lord of life. The entire earth is waiting for your birthday because when you are born then the entire family of God in heaven and earth will move to this planet and set up headquarters in New Jerusalem and Christ will destroy all of his enemies that fight against him at his coming and will show the whole world his power and then every knee will bow and every tongue will confess that he indeed is Lord, everyone on the earth will know him as *Lord of Lord and King of Kings* and then he will pour out his Spirit upon all flesh, the little children, boys and girls will rejoice in music and dancing (*I'll prove in the chapter Joel's prophecy that prophesying in this verse means exuberant singing and dancing*) Your teenagers will have divine revelations, your old men will be plump and healthy, all of this will happen in the Lords Day, the eternal Sabbath. (*JOEL 2:28*)

According to *Romans 1:4*, Jesus was proven to be the *Son of Man* by the water birth through the womb but he was proven to be the *Son of God* by the resurrection. You and I will be no different, we can all call ourselves children of God right now but the proof, the declaration will come if "*the gates if hell*" cannot hold us back. While we are indeed unborn and legal children of God today, we shall soon be born and fully adopted sons of God in our resurrection. Interestingly enough this is a subject you rarely hear preached anymore, *the resurrection* and yet it is the entire purpose of the church and our birthing process.

When did Jesus announce that all authority in heaven and earth was now given unto him? After his resurrection, after he earned the right to make that declaration. The power over death was his last enemy and death shall be our last enemy and like Christ when we are resurrected, we shall have the same authority and power over the nations.

Rev 2:26

He that overcometh and keepeth my works until the end, to him shall I give power over the nations.

When will this authority and power be given? When you have matured enough to be born in the resurrection, when you have earned God's trust as a member of his *Dream Team.*

A lot of the misunderstanding comes from the lacking translation work done by the King James translators. Allow me to explain: The original word for "*begotten*" is the same word that several times, for reasons unknown, the translators used the word "*born*" instead of "begotten" in certain verses and sadly this is very confusing because they themselves had to rely on their own understanding to know when to use the word "*begotten*" and the word "*born.*" **Remember well this reminder:** The King James Version nor any other version of the Bible it inspired by God. Only the original text (*the Masoretic Text*) in their original language and text are inspired writings. Always do a word study on words and find their original meaning and context. In this case, "*born" and "begotten*" are used interchangeably from the exact same greek word.

NOW LETS STUDY EVEN DEEPER:

Romans 8:11-25

Vs 14

For as many as are led by the Spirit of God they are the Sons of God.

Please note that the above verse does not say that as many as "*accepted Christ*" or that "*believed in God*" were sons of God. It says that only those who are being led by the Spirit of God or the Word of God into full maturity or into full truth, only they are the Sons of God. Now, someone might read that and say "*See, we are the sons of God right now, born again right now*" However, you might want to hold off on that declaration because the future verses will set this whole verse in context for you, let's continue.

Vs15
For you have not received again the Spirit of bondage but the Spirit of adoption whereby we cry Abba Father.

What have you received right now? The Spirit of Adoption, not the full adoption. You are not a fully adopted son right now, you have the SPIRIT OF ADOPTION or the SPIRIT OF SONSHIP. Just as the acorn has the essence of the oak tree inside of it and the potential to become an oak tree if it meets the conditions, so is the conceived Child of God. What is the condition to grow according to this verse? Crying Abba Father! Leaning on, obeying and trusting fully in your father. If you are truly a conceived Child of God, you are leaning on and trusting in your heavenly Father for everything you need and in doing so, you are being led by the Spirit of God and as such your throne is as good as yours, if you remain in the "*Crying Abba Father*" position!

Vs16
The Spirit of God bears witness with our Spirit that we are now the children of God

If you have been conceived of God Spirit then you will know it and he will know it because of your continual crying of Abba Father, help me Father, let me please you Father, teach me your ways oh God, teach me your laws oh God, I only want to please you. This is the proof, the witness that you are a conceived Child of God and on your way to your full birth.

Vs17
And if children then heirs; heirs of God, and joint-heirs with Christ, if so be that we suffer with him, that we also may be glorified together.

If we do what? If we suffer with him! Only then will we receive the promise that we've been promised; to be glorified with Christ! To rule with Christ, to sit on Christ throne! Right now, we are heirs not receivers of the promise. Like the Old Testaments saints mentioned in Hebrews 11, we will ***all die in the faith not having received the promises but seeing them afar off***. We are heirs right now! Nothing more, but oh my that's so much more than the world is. They are heirs of eternal death and we are heirs of a glorious kingdom and eternal life.

Vs 18
For I reckon that the sufferings of this present time are not worthy to be compared with the glory which shall be revealed in us

The sufferings, oh my how the message of the gospel has changed. How the message of the 1st century *Apostolic Church of God* has changed. In those days a message was preached of "*the Kingdom of God*" and of the reward promised to those who "*patiently endured with well doing*" and upon doing so they would receive eternal life.

Today's message is this: *Accept Christ, believe that he was the Son of God and you will walk into an abundant life here on earth and you will be blessed beyond all your neighbors; you never have to worry about being* *lost again, your reservations are secured, and don't worry about pleasing God, no one can do that, Jesus did it and that's enough; and then you will die and go to an eternal paradise in the sky.*

Paul says that there is only ONE WAY that this promise of eternal life, this glory will be revealed in you; through suffering. This is why scriptures tell us that Jesus had to "**learn obedience by the things he suffered**." Before you're allowed to reign in an eternal kingdom; many, many test will be sent to you to prove your character, to prove your fidelity and your love for the ways of God. You will be given that crown after he has said "Well Done" that means that you did some things well, you obeyed his Word, you hid his Word, you loved his laws; you were faithful and now you can be made a ruler over many people, nations, cities and lands. Have you ever seriously wondered what that *"ruler over many"* verses meant? Think about it, if your in heaven with all saved people and everyone gets the same reward, who are you going to be ruling?

Vs19
For the earnest expectation of the creature WAITETH for the birth (manifestations) of the Sons of God.

If we have already been born then what is the creation waiting for? Oh, there's coming a day when the earth will blossom like a rose at our birth when the "**Deliverers shall stand on Mt. Zion**" to deliver this earth along with Christ from her curse. All her deserts will blossom with roses, there will be streams in the deserts, all of her waters will be healed, all of her animals will be fed from the land rather than off of one another, all of her children will never be sick again, all of her elderly will be made healthy

and whole...... But that cannot happen until "**thy kindom comes**" and until you find your place in that kingdom.

Vs21
Because the creature itself also shall be delivered from the bondage of decay into the glorious liberty of the children of God.

Just in case you thought I was going overboard in describing your role in the coming kingdom, allow verse 21 to sink in to your converted mind. Why is the earth waiting for your new birth? Because the earth is decaying, it is in corruption and you will deliver this earth from that decay!!!!!! When will you do that? When you are set free from this house of clay and given your glorious liberty and when the tomb opens up for the world to see on public display the glorious birth of the spirit born sons of God!

Vs 22
For we know that the whole earth groaneth and travaileth in pain together until now

Paul said, even right now, the earth is still waiting and groaning. Well, how could that be if Paul was a born again child of God at that time? Dear reader, if you were born again at this moment, you would be just like the wind. Just like Jesus was after his resurrection, he walked through walls, he appeared and disappeared, he changed his physical form many times in his new spiritual body. He could manifest in flesh if needed so that he could eat with his disciples. This is what your new body will be like and when that happens the creation will no longer groan because all of the brothers of Jesus Christ will seize this world, cast out Satan and bring the laws of God to the nations.

V23

Not only they but ourselves also, which have the firstfruits of the Spirit, even we ourselves groan within ourselves waiting for the adoption to wit the redemption of our bodies.

Did you see it? Did you see that even the conceived children of God are groaning with the rest of this cursed earth because we know that "something isn't right" we are decaying right along with the earth. We are just as bound as the creation is . . .we are waiting . . . .we are waiting. But, what are we waiting for you ask? Oh read the verse again, WE ARE WAITING TO BE BORN! We are waiting for the ADOPTION which will happen when? *AT THE REDEMPTION OF OUR BODIES!* Beloved, you are not a fully adopted son of God right now, you are conceived, the image of Christ is FORMING in you as a child in the womb is forming. However, the day of full birth, the day of full adoption is coming and Paul tells you right here when that day is AT THE REDEMPTION OF THE BODY, at the resurrection you will be born again! The first time through the watery womb, the second time through the darkened tomb!

V24

For we are saved by Hope . . .then do we with patience wait for it

Wait a minute! We are saved by what? Hope! Hope of what? A future resurrection, a future kingdom, a future government of God. We hold on to that hope and patiently waiting for it,,,, we are BEING SAVED. The patience is forming us into his image. Dear friend, you are not saved right now, you have Hope! You are patiently waiting and in that waiting

you are *"saving yourself from this evil generation."*

V29

For whom he did foreknow he did predestinate to be conformed unto the image of the Son of God.

Now for the truth of predestination! You are predestined not for hell or heaven but rather to rule with Christ and you if you have been called in the church age you are called or predestined to be changed into the image of Christ and counted worthy to rule with him. Yes, there are those who he has not called, their turn will come. At this moment, he is calling you, your turn is here, you are predestined to hear this call and to be conceived by his Holy Spirit and to be matured in to the exact image of your elder brother, the Lord Jesus Christ.

NICODEMUS

Now let us consider the words that Jesus spoke to Nicodemus that for so many years I have completely misunderstood until these times. If you will remember this is the conversation between Jesus and a man who wanted to enter into the Kingdom of God when it comes to the earth. Jesus proceeded to tell him about the new birth and how he must be born again before he can enter into the kingdom of God. Before I can deal with this conversation allow me to digress and touch upon an important principle that's necessary in order to under this conversation between the man named Nicodemus and the Christ.

What is God? He is a Spirit!
What is his composition, what is his matter, his make up or his chemistry? Absolutely Spirit! Is God flesh and blood? Eternal bodies do not need blood nor oxygenated air, the life that flesh and

blood bodies receive now comes from the blood and the air, the new body will have life inherit within itself with no need of blood nor air. This spirit body will depend on nothing for its life flow. While it most certainly will be ablt to enjoy food and it may enjoy sunlight but it will not need any of it as we do just to live. This glorified spirit body will be like the angels according to Jesus teaching and he tells us that the angels cannot die. **So, God is not flesh and blood, correct**? However, is being a Spirit being what makes God who he is? Spirit is WHAT GOD IS but it's not WHO HE IS. Actually being Spirit doesn't make God any more God than being a spirit being makes Satan what he is; indeed both God and

is light or invisible but his character, no one shares his character in the whole of creation but Christ and the faithful angels. Now, who is the only one from earth that has his character? Jesus Christ - His what? His SON! Now, read this carefully! **God will never trust anyone in his government who does not have his characte**r. Satan had God's composition but not his character.

God can create a lot of things but there is one thing that even he cannot create instantly in you and that's character. That is the very purpose for your earthly journey: before you are given an eternal, never dying body you will first develop a Godly

GOD WILL NEVER TRUST ANYONE IN HIS GOVERNMENT THAT DOES NOT HAVE HIS CHARACTER

Satan, they are both Spirit! Even the angels are spirit beings. So, being Spirit doesn't make God who he is only what he is. Demons are spirits because they are none composed of flesh and blood. All spiritual beings have the same composition or make-up as God has. So, what makes God, God? Not his composition but rather his character.! His composition is the same as all the heavenly family but the only flesh and blood being that ever attained to his character and his composition is Jesus, his son. Besides Christ, only the faithful angels have his character and that is the character of Agape Love! Love, that you cannot begin to fathom *(the next chapter will describe this love of God)*. God is light and God is love. Light is invisible like an X-Ray light, it cannot be seen. This is why light was created before the sun was created in Genesis Chapter 1, think about that one. The reason is simple; God is light, his invisible matter, his Spirit

character that can be trusted inside of that eternal body. Until the love of God permeates you, until you feel his agape love for humanity you cannot and must not be given an eternal body. If you have hate in your heart here on earth, that hate must never find an eternal body to live in, it must be conquered and overcome and transformed into the love of God. How dare the modern preacher tell you that you are going to be given a God body *(spiritual body)* without developing God's character! God reproduced his character in Christ before reproducing his composition in Christ. In other words the second Adam had to pass the character test, the agape love test and the very character of God had to be found in him before Christ would be given ***all power in heaven and earth*** just as you shall be given all power upon your change and upon your full birth as a joint-heir with Christ. All of the conceived "*brothers of Christ*' must also ***"learn obedience by the things we suffer"*** we must also allow men to hate us without ever fighting back, we must allow *"the mind of Christ"* or the "Character of God" to be formed in us while we're still in the womb yet unborn before we can ever be born into the Family of God as spiritual beings with eternal bodies. If you want an eternal body you must get an eternal mind-set.

Remember this well! The human sperm carries life but it doesn't carry maturity! The mother brings the life to maturity. The Holy Spirit brings you the essence of life, the new nature but the church must bring you to maturity and Christ is in his church, Christ operates in his church. Pity the man who think he will rule with Christ in a coming Kingdom and he cannot go to a local church and submit to local authority nor get along with his brethren. How will you judge the world if you cannot even love those in the household of faith?

GODS REPRODUCTION LAWS

Please read in it's entirety
Gen 1:20-25

Notice that all of the animals are created *"after their own kind."* Like always begets Like, apples always produce apples. Baptist always produce Baptist, Pentecostals always produce Pentecostals and so forth. There is a law of reproduction in place that demands that *"like begets like"* or anything that you produce will be just like you. All creation is placed under God's reproduction laws, all is demanded in these verses to produce "after it's own kind." Now would God establish this law and not keep it himself? Wouldn't his sons, his offspring have to follow the same pattern, wouldn't they have to be of his same composition and character? Just as a dog doesn't have cats, a spiritual being doesn't have flesh and blood children. That is not *"like begetting like."* Spiritual beings must reproduce spiritual beings and natural flesh and blood beings produce the same. God's purpose for your earthly journey is this! After he has called you and predestined you to be begotten of his Spirit and conceived by his preached Word, after you have learned obedience in suffering and after you have learned to love his laws and his way and when you have been found worthy as an overcomer then you are to FINALLY BE BORN AGAIN after GODS KIND, born of the SPIRIT and of THE WORD! GEN 1:26. He made us in his IMAGE in our mothers watery womb but he will make us after his LIKENESS through the tomb! This life journey is for us to be changed, transformed first in character and then in composition, formed into his likeness! Sons who have been tried in the fire and found faithful. Now we can be born of the Spirit!

God is not a man and therefore his sons will not be men, his sons will be in the family of God which is a spiritual family, spiritual bodies that can cross the galaxies at the very speed of thought. He is not looking for flesh and blood sons because all flesh is the enemy of God and cannot please God. As long as you struggle with flesh you are struggling with the very enemy of your father in heaven. God's only plan for flesh is to destroy it and burn it up and let it die.

So the question now is, When will we be like our elder brother?

I John 3:1-2

Behold what manner of love the Father has bestowed upon us that we should be called the sons of God . . .

. . .beloved now are we the sons of God and it doth not yet appear what we shall be but we know that when he shall appear we shall be like him for we shall see him as he is.

Notice that Paul says that we should be so thankful that God in his sovereign grace and mercy is willing to even refer to us or call us sons in these flesh and blood bodies. However, even as conceived children still in flesh and blood he calls us sons. However, we know that when we are born again in the resurrection that we shall be changed and at that moment we will be just like Jesus in a glorified and resurrected body and the scriptures tell us that Jesus won't be ashamed to call us brothers. Think about that, if Jesus has to rule with you for all eternity and at this moment it was your time for judgement, would be ashamed to call you brother?

Just as my son was my son in his mothers womb he was yet unborn, unmanifested and unrevealed, legally and positionally he was my son; so in the same manner God now calls us sons even in the womb of His Church. However, it wasn't until my son took the breath of life that he could ever be of any use for the family sake. So it is with the conceived sons of God.

So finally here we find Nicodemus and Christ talking about the Kingdom of God. Jesus told him that until the resurrection or until he had the key to the kingdom which is the resurrection key, until he had that new birth that like all flesh, he could not receive the Kingdom of God. Of course, like so many today Nicodemus didn't understand the sayings of Jesus. Christ proceeded to explain to him;

Whatever is born of man is a man, he's natural, he's flesh and blood, he's sinful. Whatever is born again or born of God is an offspring or son of God, he's a Spirit just like God and he cannot sin. As long as your in the flesh and blood body then you cannot inherit the kingdom of God because the key to that kingdom is a resurrection and at this point in time Nicodemus you those gates of hell will prevail against you, the gates of the grave will hold you back from that first resurrection and because of that cannot enter into the kingdom of God.

So, Nicodemus looks at Christ perplexed and still not understanding, so Jesus continues;

Nicodemus when a person is born of the Spirit or Born again they will be just like the wind, you cant see them, you cant hear them but they are always there. They come and go as they wish undetected or like the wind that can manifest physically. Just like the wind can manifest in the blowing leaves or the bending trees so can the Sons of God manifest if they so desire.

Nicodemus still wants to enter the Kingdom of God and Christ preaches to him the whole gospel. He tells him about the Love of God and how that he, Christ, was sent to save the world. However, he said that the world wouldn't receive him. He proceeded to tell him that everyone who forsakes their lawless ways and their evil deeds could indeed be born again in the resurrection. Jesus said "**he that loveth truth Nicodemus, will come to the light that his works may be on display.**" (ST JOHN 3:3-21)

Yet, the modern church says that works has nothing to do with salvation! My oh My how different their gospel is that the one Jesus just preached to Nicodemus

In closing; No, you cannot lose your salvation but you can lose all that you have; your Hope of salvation!

The Journey

Chapter Nine

Thus the Lord my God will come, and all the saints with
You . . .And the Lord shall be King over all the earth
ZECHARIAH 14:9

LABOURING TO REST

IF WE ARE NOT YET BORN AGAIN AND WE ARE WAITING FOR THE RESURRECTION TO FULFILL OUR INTENDED SPIRITUAL PURPOSES IN THE EARTH, THEN WHAT ARE WE TO DO IN THIS AGE THAT WE NOW LIVE IN? Actually, this portion of the Journey is possibly more important than the destination. **We must prepare now to enter into the Lords Day**, the Sabbath rest that will soon visit this planet called Earth. Paul makes the most interesting statement about this coming rest day; He tells us in Hebrews 4:11, "*let us therefore labour to enter into his rest.*" Was Paul playing with words in this verse of scripture? After all, how do you labour to rest? Is that not the ultimate dichotomy? Labouring and resting wouldn't normally be in the same flow of thought. However, our beloved Apostle had revelation that sometime surpasses his reading audience.

Have you ever prepared for a vacation? The vacation is intended to bring you rest and relaxation, yet the weeks leading up to the resting vacation can be quite laborious. You are spending time to make sure that nothing ruins your rest, your vacation. You are checking with travel agents, making last minute arrangements for a pet sitter, for a house sitter, you are labouring to rest. The word labour in this context and in it's original meaning refers to a "*hastening*" or "*paying attention to*". Indeed when each Friday rolls around I find myself taking care of last minute details; fasting and handling of necessary chores so as not to have my Sabbath rest interrupted on Saturday. I find myself on Friday actually working to ensure that I will be able to actually enter into that weekly rest. Fixing the car, repairing the roof, preparing the Saturday meals is all done the days before the Sabbath.

As you and I prepare ourselves to enter into God's Messianic kingdom in the coming Lord's Day we also must begin in this lifetime preparing and making sure that we will in fact enter into that rest. Our job in this life is to heed Pauls warning and not fall into "*unbelief*" while waiting. This is why Satan tries to "**wear down the saints.**" You are being watched, assessed and evaluated by how you are holding to the faith of the Son of God. While you are here, the mind of Christ is supposed to be forming in your mind. The Holy Spirit is preparing you to govern with Christ by changing your attitudes, your personality, your thoughts and your actions. In fact, he has called us as a nation; the Church of God is a nation of people, of precious people that God adores. We are his chosen people and he desires to write his laws into our heart while were on this mortal Journey.

AGAPE LOVE EXPLAINED

In the last chapter I began speaking to you about the agape love of God. You will begin to notice as the Holy Spirit begins transforming you that you cannot help but love what God loves and that would be people of His world, His creation. Do you ever get frustrated trying to bring people to Christ? Do you ever find yourself looking down at people who just can't get their lives together? Do you feel angry when you see how wicked our world is getting? When your relatives just cannot kick the addictions of shame, do you lose your desire to help them? Do the politics of Washington cause you to become apathetic? You must not allow these feelings to become part of your mind-set. Do you find yourself looking at the gay community and just wishing they would all somehow evaporate back into yesterday closets? Do you look at the murderer and wish they would just go ahead and pull the plug on him? Do you wish that everyone who keeps rejecting God would just get the rewards that they have coming to them? Lose that attitude, perish the thoughts, there is no room on the Journey for those ungodly attitudes.

Here is what will help you in the future; you must always remember that since the Garden of Eden the entire population has been cut off from the Holy Spirit except for a predestined few in each age. No man has ever gone searching for God, you didn't and I didn't. Had he not come looking for you or me we would be one of those people who continually push religion aside. The whole world is deceived (Rev 12:9) according to the Bible and only a few are chosen by God in this church age (John 6:44)

If you will live your life the right way, if you will grab this understanding of the Coming Kingdom and cherish the hope of the resurrection and recognize your royal calling then people will see the essence of the kingdom inside of you and you will be a light on a hill. You will fulfill the role of royalty visiting the earth and everyone will desire to know about your hope, the royal house that you ascend from and the bloodline that you have so gloriously been translated into by your faith in Christ and his cross and his empty tomb and his coming Kingdom.

The Apostle Peter says that if you will harbor this hope of the new birth, he says that those who are elected and predestined to be chosen in this age, those that the Holy Spirit is calling to take this Jour-

ney, they will in fact find you and they will in fact ask about the hope inside of you.

I Peter 3:15
Be ready always to give an answer to every man that asketh you a reason of the hope that is in you with fear and meekness.

_____

THE MISERY OF MANKIND

Although you and I have been called out of this worlds systems, her customs, holidays, her mind-set and her religions; we must still live here among her poor, lost, deceived and bound people that do not have this glorious hope. They have all the fun they can with all the drugs and drink that they can find because they harbor no blessed hope; they are of all men most miserable. That misery tries desperately to display and charade itself in false happiness; that misery will smile for a camera, scream for a football team and laugh at a drunken friend who has become inebriated and blinded by their own shame; but that miserable person when the false happiness is revealed to be a sham, when the sexual affair didn't satisfy, when the effects of the drug have waned they cry in the darkness.

We must begin to be filled with God's character for hopeless humanity and the nations of the world that are dying and don't know it. God actually commands us to love this world! I write a lot about keeping the Ten commandments and yet six of those commandments are summed up with this one; *Love your neighbor (the world) as much as you love yourself.* When is the last time you wept for hurting humanity, for a broken people for a cursed earth, for a weeping world?

When God begin working in my life this year, when I began keeping his laws in my personal life, I noticed a most unusual thing happening to me, especially in my prayer life. I began to have an overflowing concern for other people. In my prayer time I became less self oriented in my prayers and found a flow of names coming to my mind as I prayed for complete strangers that I hardly remembered. While praying for these people and while feeling a true compassion for the world and the broken lives of so many people, new tears found their way to my eyes.

THE DESTINATION WILL BRING A CHANGED BODY. . . THE JOURNEY MUST BRING A CHANGED MIND

God spoke to my spirit in his gentle tone and told me that indeed I was becoming like him, he loves people.

I found myself genuinely praying for my enemies, not the old generic prayer I once prayed for all my enemies but rather naming their names and being moved with compassion for them. You see prayer for others is not really about changing their lives it's actually a cleansing of your own life and its making room for greater measures of the Holy Spirit of God as he forms you into the image of the loving Christ.

So many people fail to realize that the only change that will take place in the resurrection will be in the body, not in the mind. The purpose of The Journey is the preparation and transformation of the mind of man to become the mind of Christ. *Therefore let*

this mind be in you that was in Christ. Until you are first changed in your Spirit or mind then you can never be changed in your body. Although I may wish to give you the body of a dog; without the mind of a dog, the combination would never work. A dogs body must be accompanied by a dogs mind.

Although God may desire to give you a changed and glorified body it can only be accomplished with a changed and glorified mind. The destination is a changed body, the Journey is a changed mind. The destination is a glorified body, *the Journey* is a glorified mind. Until you have been changed in your thoughts about humanity and about Gods ways then you will never qualify for the government of the glorified. Until you can love people you can never govern people, until you can be moved with compassion you can never be moved into the throne.

ISRAEL'S TRUE PURPOSE

When God called Israel, he called them to be a kingdom of Priest. They were to stretch forth one hand to God on behalf of the people and one hand to man on behalf of God. They were the intersections between hope and hopelessness, they were the crossroads between curses and blessings. When God told Abraham about his calling and his future purposes he tells him *"I will make of thee a great nation and you shall be a blessing"* (GEN 12:2) In other words Abraham, I'm not blessing you to bless you, I'm blessing through you! You are to become the very blessing that I am giving you. By your blessing you shall be a blessing. He then continues telling Abraham *"in thee shall all the families of the earth be blessed."* (GEN 12:3) You must understand that God didn't choose Abraham out of favoritism; God chose

Abraham for an amazing responsibility, to bless the nations of the world through his seed. God chose Israel as an example nation, a peculiar people, a chosen nation for one purpose; that the whole world might seek after God through their example. When God calls Israel his "*firstborn*" son or his "*firstfruit*" is that not saying by default, does that not indicate in a silent yet thundering sermon that in fact there will be a "*second born*" son? Who will that "*second born*" son be? **The nations of the world or the Gentiles!** Notice what God says about Israel, a type of his church in the earth today;

Jer 2:3
Israel was holiness unto the Lord and the firstfruit of his increase

The firstfruit of his increase! What can that possibly mean? The increase shall be the final and greater harvest of souls that shall come to him during his Millennium reign. He wanted Israel holy as he wants his present day church holy, not because they were more special than everyone else but because through their holiness they would have won the nations to God by their example and by living in his blessings.

Duet 4:5
Behold I have taught you statutes and laws . . .that you should keep them in the land that you possess...keep therefore and do them . . .in the sight of the nations which shall hear of these laws and say surely this great nation is a wise and understanding people. For what nation is there so great? Who hath God so close to them? What nation is so righteous and has such wonderful laws!

Can't you plainly see the role of Israel? Not to be the only ones saved or holy or chosen! No, they were to be the example nation or the wittness nation so that in God's timing all the other nations would desire him.

This is the very purpose of the church in the earth today! If we as the *Apostolic Church of God* rise to the occasion, accept the call, obey his laws and believe in his Christ then we shall be holy and if the "***firstfruit be holy then the whole lump will be holy***" (ROM 11:16)

THE HIGH PRIEST AND HIS PRIEST

Within the priesthood there should be a burning desire to bless God and to bless people. The priesthood is for the salvation of the world; you and I are literally the salvation of the nations. Had it not been for you and I and the Journey of life that were on and our untold potential then God's justice would have demanded the destruction of mankind already. However, because of us working with Christ in the ministry of priest, His mercy reaches to man through His spiritually begotten sons of God. Simply think about it, the very fact that Christ is called the High Priest should be quite telling; it should indicate to you that if he is the High Priest, there must be other priest for him to have the precedence over. Those other priest, that company of priest, that priestly nation that is called to love the world and to serve God is indeed the present day *Apostolic Church of God* in the earth. Some of our members are breathing and some are resting in their graves but corporately we make up the clandestine army of the Lord, we make up the silent soldiers of eternity as we wait for our turn, our hour and our Lords Day.

WHO IS YOUR NEIGHBOR

So, who is our neighbor that we are commanded to love as much as we love ourselves? When Jesus tells his Apostles to *"go into all the world and teach men to observe all that I have commanded"* then this means that he has commanded you and I to love our neighbors AS MUCH AS WE LOVE OURSELVES. We must be honest, we must confess; Have we in fact observed all that he has commanded? No wonder that many will say unto him at the judgement *"Lord, Lord we believed"* and he will say unto them *"I never knew you."* We are commanded to love this world with an unnatural and humanly impossible love. Our neighbor; Is it Mrs. Jones across the lane who always brings us cookies for Christmas? Or is it Mr. Johnson who watches the house for us while were on vacation? Actually, the scripture reveals to us who our neighbor is.

Luke 10:29
. . .and he said unto Jesus, who is my neighbor?

Christ answers this young lawyer as only Israel's teacher could; with the story of the good Samaritan. He tells him about a stranger who was robbed and left for dead. A priest passed by and pretended not to see him *(how many of God's modern priest, you and I, have done the same thing)* A Levite passed by and did the same thing. These two men were very religious, they lived good, clean, godly, drug free, addiction free and alcohol free lives. Their finances were in order, their homes were idyllic and they simply wished that the lesser people in the world could just get it together and find God the way they had. We are the very elect, the chosen people, they thought!

On the Journey to our destiny in God, as members of God's *Dream Team* we must acquire the agape love of God in our character as we *"labour to enter into the day of Rest."* How can we love the nations in Gods future government if we cannot love the neighbors in our world. Finally, there came a Samaritan, the Jews would have considered him a dog but he helped the poor man. Then Jesus ask the most profound question;

Luke 10:36,37
Which now of these three, thinkest thou, was neighbor unto him that fell among thieves . . . . Go and do thou likewise!

Who does Jesus say that our neighbors are in this parable? Everyone! The whole world, all of Gods creation is your neighbors, your responsibility and they have been placed into your care and your ministry, you are being watched! If you walk in their midst on any particular day, if they are graced by God enough to cross your path then they become your responsibility. Are you now responsible for saving them? For evangelizing them for converting them? Absolutely not; you are indeed resposible for being a witness to them of the glorious liberty of the gospel. Your life, your attitude, your personality, your kindness, your joy, your peace is to draw their eye and in doing so also draw their hearts so that they might ask you for "the reason of the hope the lieth within you." At that moment when THEY HAVE ASKED you are to be ready to give an answer. Of course we are assured that we must not take any thought of what to say at those times because the Holy Spirit if we are filled with the Holy Spirit will speak through us to the lost person. The angels of heaven record every cup of water that you give to your neighbor. As you reach to heaven also reach to man as you prepare for your eternal destinies as servant rulers in God's government.

AN IMPOSSIBLE COMMAND

In one of the two great commands of Christ, he acknowledges that all men love themselves. We look out for us and our children and we hope that everyone else can make it the best way possible. As long as our four and no more are provided for then we are satisfied. There is nothing wrong with that kind of love for you and yours, it is indeed a natural love. You should love yourself enough to take care of yourself and not be a burden on society; you should love your children. If you do those things, loving yourself and yours, you have done what every man is humanly capable of doing, that is natural love and Gods Spirit is not required for that, we ascertain that kind of love from the human Spirit. *Anton Lavey* the founder of the *Church of Satan* in San Francisco, Ca was able to love himself, his wives and his children and his church, nothing supernatural is required. But Jesus commands something very unnatural; that we have the same concern and compassion for every one of Gods creation.

Matt 7:12
All things whatsoever you want that men should do to you, do yourself unto them, for this is the law and the prophets.

I'm amazed at how a local church is willing to help someone if that person is willing to straighten up and join their church and line up with their standards of living. However, this is natural love; anyone can love the person who is obeying them and doing as they are told. Only God and the priest of God can love those who walk in rebellion *"While we were yet sinners, Christ died for us"* can we love people who are yet in rebellion? The love of God inside of you is what a hurting world so desperately needs. The judgement of people must be left into the hands of the Lord as we are told to "judge nothing before the time." Until our Lord establishes his kingdom you and I as his Dream Team are supposed to be a witness to the whole world of the amazing life that now lives in us. We are not called to save the world, we are called to be a witness, a live lived, a story told in human form. That witness will attract men to the Church and that alone is the only effective means of evangelism. Jesus said that church folks will *"compass land and sea trying to convert people and when the person is converted, it's a flase conversion and they've become more of a child of hell than the religious person is"*.

On the Journey be careful that your voice and your conversation doesn't reveal your disgust with the world conditions. Always express the hope that is within you. When you hear bad news, when they pass the gay marriage act, when abortion is plaguing the land, let your conversation always point towards the better day that is soon coming when the earth shall be healed of he plagues. If you are not careful, your disgust will grow into impatience, bitterness and hatred. Right now, you are going through a change, you are partnering with the great Yahweh of heaven in his dreams for mankind, you are catching the vision and it must come through you to the rest of the world. Speak only as he speaks, be moved with compassion for mankind, never hate and never bitterness *"for such were some of you"*

Titus 3:1-2
Tell them to be subject to principalities and powers, to obey judges, to be ready to every good work, to speak evil of no man, to be no brawlers, but gentle, shewing all meekness unto all men.

If we are going to be real with ourselves; we must ask ourself are we obeying not only the Ten Commandments but even these great commands given to us by Christ? The verse above would be worth you reading again, slowly and with careful regard. How are you doing in obeying that command? Not so good? It's OK, start now! Make up your mind that Gods creation is your ministry, they are given into you hands to care for and to love and to be a witness to. You can never win the lost until you have touched the lost. You cannot preach to a people that you have not reached unto. There is a reason that Christ was moved with compassion for the sick, the hungry and the poor, he loved them! Do you love them? Do you run from the needy? Do you visit the sick? Do you visit the prisoner? Do you feed the hungry? Do you go out of your way to love the unlovable, the people who will probably never get it together? If not, I would dare say that you need for God's Spirit to increase within you, stretch yourself and be filled with God's love today.

I Timothy 2:1-2
Give prayers, intercession and thanks for ALL MEN, including those in authority over us in this age, for this is the good and acceptable in the sight of God our savior; who will have ALL MEN to be saved and to come unto the knowledge of the truth.

All men, give thanks for all men! Even evil men, even broken men, even addicted men, fall in love with mankind because God loves them. Do you give thanks for all men? Do you pray for All men? Do you love all men? If not, change today, make up your mind that as a partner in the dreams of God that you will begin seeing all men as he sees them, as his creation!

The
Overcomers

Chapter Ten

> . . .He that overcometh . . .will I give power to rule over
> the nations.
>
> *Rev 2:26*

THE OVERCOMERS

SEVEN (7) IS A DIVINE NUMBER IN BIBLICAL NUMEROL-OGY AND IT DENOTES COMPLETION AND PERFECTION. This is exactly the number of times that the word *Overcomer* is mentioned by Christ to the seven (7) churches in the book of Revelation; specifically chapters two (2) and three (3). A certain group of Christians is specifically mentioned in these chapters; this group is very special to our Lord and in fact throughout the entire book of Revelation they are the only people that He is focused on. We know from other scriptures in the same book that there are countless other Christians who stand "**before the throne**" and who simply walk in the "**light of the city**" but there is a very specific, very esteemed group of believers that is spoken to in this writing and they are lovingly called "*The Overcomers*" they in fact are "The City, the New Jerusalem, the Bride of Christ" and they in fact are not before the throne but rather "*on the throne.*"

This group of people are promised exceedingly great rewards for their lifetime of overcoming Satan, their flesh, their temptations and their own selfish desires. They are referred to also as "*those who keep the Commandments and the testimony of Jesus Christ.*" They are in fact the group of Christians who have not only kept the laws of God but they have fully recognized and embraced the love of God which is the testimony of Jesus Christ. These Christians are not simply saved, they are overcomers. These people are not simply believers, they are doers. This elect group, this prized possession of our Lord; these jewels of Jehovah are indeed the few and the proud. Only to this group is the future government of God promised. Only to these people will the throne or the authority of God's kingdom be offered to. Your choice today as you read this book is to remain a Christian in name only or to become an Overcomer. You can continue to fellowship with and live among the *Church Carnal* or you can cast your lot with the despised few whom this world is not worthy of. You can choose to sell out for Jesus completely, you can decide that this glorious and soon coming Kingdom of God is worth overcoming for. You can decide today that all the addictions, all of the sins, all of the pleasures of life cannot be compared with your potential to minister to the nations in the Cabinet of Christ government in the soon coming Kingdom.

Why would you give up a role or a position in the greatest government the world has ever seen? Why would you give up a chance to bring peace to the nations, healing to the masses and salvation to the world? This is what your being called for, this is what your true destiny is; but if you do not understand these things then you will always accept a life of defeat. However, those who accept a life of defeat by Satan's kingdom will never qualify as an Overcomer! Let us look at some of the promises given to this elect and chosen group of people for whom the whole book of Revelation is primarily written,

THE PROMISES

THE FIRST PROMISE

Rev 2:7

. . .he that overcometh will I allow to eat of the tree of life which is in the midst of the paradise of God.

If you do not overcome the sins of the world, if you do not fight a good fight and overcome your flesh then you will not be part of the first resurrection. You will endure the tribulation and during that time you will be tried in the fire and "*made white*" (DANIEL 12:9, REV 7:14) you will go through that horrible time of purification in Gods wrath upon the earth and you will be broken to the point of gladly bowing your knees to the Lordship of Christ. The aforementioned scriptural references show us that the wise will submit during this time of testing while the wicked will have to be destroyed because they will refuse his rightful claim to earths throne. Sadly, the only language that men understand is the language of power and men will force Christ to demonstrate his august and elephantine power against the armies of men. Before he can bring peace to our planet He will first speak with the language that men know and respect, the language of power (REV 19:21) With one breath he will cause men to tremble at his presence as their very skin disintegrates in his presence at his coming. Before he can rule them with care, love and concern he must first rule them with a rod of iron (REV 19:15). There is a purpose for this display of strength; his enemies must be destroyed for innocent men to see once and for all that he truly is the Son of God. The very moment that men recognize his strength they will beg him to save them from their own destruction and from evil world rulers who will at that time be wreaking havoc among the nations and then theywill gladly bow their knees before him; at this point every knee shall bow and every tongue shall confess (ROMANS 14:11) that Jesus Christ is indeed the King of all Kings, the Prelate of all Prelates and the God of all gods.

However, there is a group of people who will be part of that first resurrection; they will not have to be broken during this time but rather they shall be sealed and protected during these years of God's wrath (REV 7:2-4). They shall live as immortals during the millennium reign on this earth and never die again. The Overcomers will be just like Christ; they will be allowed to receive into their own bodies the gift of eternal life. Until they eat of the tree of life which is simply a symbol of the Holy Spirit and Jesus Christ, the Word of God; until now they have depended totally upon the eternal life that is in Christ and could only be saved by remaining In

BEFORE HE CAN RULE THE NATIONS WITH CARE, LOVE AND CONCERN HE MUST FIRST RULE THEM WITH A ROD OF IRON

Christ. However, at the moment of their new birth, when they are born from the tomb rather than the womb in the first resurrection they themselves will have the exact same eternal life that Christ; this eternal life shall be theirs in reality and not just by promise. These firstborn or firstharvest sons will at the soon coming moment be full fledged brothers of Jesus Christ at their full adoption which takes place only at "*the redemption of the body*" (ROMANS 8:23) they shall be equally be filled with the same authority and power, the same bodies, the same minds and sitting on the exact same throne. Just as the eldest son always hold pre-eminence in the family structure so Jesus will always have pre-eminence in the family of sons but only in respect to his esteemed position as the first-born and as a result just like the law of the firstborn on earth he shall be granted a double portion in the kingdom but this in no way diminishes the role of all his brethren who shall share in his glory, power and dominion. Again, this group of people have "**made themselves ready**" they have kept their garments unspotted from the world, they have lived a life of continual sanctification and separation from the world. They have allowed the Word of God to judge them, correct them and wash them. As a result these people will be divinely protected during the tribulation and shall not suffer the wrath of God. They are promised Eternal life without the torment that so many Christians will endure. By the millions unlearned and deceived Christians believe in some sort of a secret pre-tribulation rapture before these events transpire on the earth. How very sad that the majority of Christendom has been lulled to sleep as the foolish virgins were with such non-biblical nonsense. There is only a second physical, bodily coming mentioned in God's Word there is not one mention of three comings; for anyone to believe in a secret, pre-tribulation rapture they must admit that they in fact vy default believe in three (3) literal and physical comings of the man Christ Jesus and not two (2) *(obtaining my book "The Rapture" will explain this teaching in much greater detail)*.

These Overcomers are promised to eat of the tree of life which is Christ Jesus in the paradise of God which is the Kingdom of God his re-created Eden here on earth.

THE OLD-ORDER CHURCHES

Allow me to address a very personal issue at this point. I was raised and born into a very classical Pentecostal, Apostolic or Holiness family. In our old-order Holiness church we held to a very strict interpretation of the scriptures. If the Bible even hinted at something being a sin then we evaded it at all cost. These people: my family, my colleagues and my friends are often made fun of by their brothers in Christ for their strict adherence to the scriptures. Rightly so, they accuse those of us in the old order church *(I do not personally adhere to all the old order teachings but the teachings that can be proven in scripture I will always hold until my death)* of being legalist, hypocritical, out of date and out of touch with reality. For example; in our old-order churches we believed that clothing represented our inner character, we preached against makeup, jewelry, mixed bathing, facial hair, shorts, women wearing pants, men wearing long hair and women wearing short hair and the list continues. For many years I have sought for a balance to this subject because in fact there is scriptural support for many of these standards that our old-order churches adopted and on the other hand a truthful person must admit that many of our standards have no basis in relevant scriptures. There is a fine line here that must be walked because truthfully we were wrong in as many areas as we were right in. For example; rather than living what we felt was required we actually judged everyone else's salvation by our own understanding of the scriptures. We preached and believed that people would die lost and go to hell for all eternity for not living up to these standards that we held to.

To all the readers who think it strange that people would actually hold to these old orders please be reminded that these standards were set by people who loved God with all of their hearts and simply desired to be obedient to *every jot and every tittle* of his law and his commands. With sincerity of heart the old Shepherds of Gods flock saw the dangers for Gods people in many of the questionable things that the world participated in and they preached against those things accordingly. However, in doing so, the Spirit of the Pharisee crept in among us and out of ignorance we judged our fellow man by the requirements that God had placed on us. Just like Israel of old we failed to realize that God had not called the Gentiles or other Christian groups to live by the same laws as he had called Israel or his chosen church to live by. Over the years, I sought and struggled to know what to preach about these standards. Here were my choices; forget them all and follow the rest of the church world into complete disregard for any set standard and just believe as they do that Jesus kept the law and we need not try. They erroneously teach that we just simply believe on him and that's a wrap. However, the more I personally desired to forget the old order standards and embrace the ideas of the liberated Christians who were rejoicing in their freedom from obeying God's laws the more glaring the scriptures became about certain issues and how that God desires total separation from the world.

No one can deny that in all of God's Word a woman always had long hair and Paul commanded that she have long hair. What do I do with that scripture? Ignore it and explain it away as the liberals do? They tell us that this teaching was only for that specific period of time in history and yet in the Old Testament all women in Israel had long hair and then years later in Revelation, John sees the animals in his vision as *"having the hair of women"* which denotes that long hair on a woman was not even worthy of discussion as it was the norm among the people of God. All churches in the genesis of this century taught that their women should have longer hair than men and they all began to change and sopt the customs of the world about the time of the womens liberation movement. So, I had no choice but

to ask God for the answer to this dilemma. On the other hand I also saw how wrong we were in making these standards matters of salvation because quite simply I know many, many Christians who do not live by our old order standards who have impeccable proof in their fruit that they are indeed converted children of God. But how could this be? Why do they not have to live by the same standards or laws that we did as Apostolics It didn't seem fair and in fact seemed paradoxical and filled with inconsistency.

Only when I came to see the truth of rewards in Gods kingdom did it all begin to make sense to my logical mind. There are those who have sold out completely even to the point of being ridiculous and those people shall receive a great reward for their sacrifices because truly their sacrifices are indeed sacrifices of obedience. If truly in their heart and not just out of tradition; if they believe that they are obeying the scriptures to the absolute fullest intent of its meaning then they shall be called great in the government or kingdom of God. Jesus explains to us beautifully that those who keep *"every jot and tittle of his Word"* they shall be *"greatest"* in his government or his kingdom (MATT 5:19). However, he explains as well that there will be those in his future world that did not keep every law nor every command and they shall in fact be saved but they shall not rule or reign in his government because they were not fully obedient. Rather than selling out completely they chose to obey some of the Word and ignore the rest. Many Christians do not willingly ignore the commands of scripture they are in fact ignorant and unlearned of these commands. They have ignorantly and without knowledge of truth sat under leaders who have told them that they didn't have to worry about pleasing God because Jesus pleased God and that 's all that matter. These well meaning and sincere Christians who truly believe in Christ and have accepted his gospel have swallowed this lie completely as a fish swallows a hook, ignorantly. Therefore, they simply have not the knowledge that many have been blessed with. Many do not know to pay their tithe, many do not know to keep the Sabbath, many do not know to take the Passover *(mistakenly called Communion)* many do not know to wash the saints feet as Christ commanded, many do not know to assemble themselves with other believers, many do not know to work for rewards in Gods kingdom, many do not know to separate themselves from the customs, holidays and traditions of this evil world. Therefore, to those Christians they will be rewarded accordingly.

AS YOU MATURE IN GOD YOU WILL LOVE WHAT HE LOVES AND HATE WHAT HE HATES

Jesus says that those Christians will receive fewer stripes of punishment at the judgement than those of us who know his Word and know his truth and have received his calling into all truth (LUKE 12:48) However, the Overcomers who have read the Holy Book and they see and are fully persuaded (ROM 14:5) in their minds the need for a separated life; they shall receive great rewards, positions and authority in Gods future government.

The longer I serve Christ the more he teaches me. The new employee cannot be expected to carry the same responsibility of understanding the mind of the employer as the one who has been working for many years. In the same manner as you grow in God you will begin to love what he loves and hate what he hates. You will desire to please him fully in your language, in your dress, in your character, in your conversations in your prayer life and in every area of your being. I make a personal plea to those among the old-order churches that I dearly love; Thank God for the revelation of truth that you have but leave the salvation of Christians who may not see your path in the hands of a loving and just God. At the same time; Woe unto you if having known the ways of God and having known what the scriptures teach on certain lifestyles and certain things that are displeasing to the Lord should you turn from them and turn back to the world or even to the deceived church world, you will receive many more stripes in the tribulation than the Christian who truly didn't know the laws of God. Never again judge another Christian, be fully persuaded in your own mind about what Gods Word requires of you and live that life gladly as unto the Lord. Never one time regret being obedient to what you believe the scriptures commands. Like Paul teaches us "***let no man judge you in keeping the Sabbath. . .but only the body of Christ***" in other words, do not allow the worlds criticism of your peculiar lifestyle matter to you; only listen to the teachings of Gods true church and his body of believers.

Personally, I am ridiculed quite often by well meaning Christians, even the very strict Pentecostals, Holiness and Apostolic people since I decided that God requires us to honor and keep the Sabbath. While I do not expect anyone to understand or even agree with my keeping the Sabbath, I must be fully persuaded in my own mind that God is pleased by my keeping this day holy unto the Lord. I alone must be faithful to what he has taught me and I make a huge mistake when I judge any Christian that God has not dealt with on this subject. Again,

I repeat for emphasis the words of our Lord; "*he that keepeth the Words that I have commanded you shall be called greatest in my kingdom*" I plead with those that God is calling into a more dedicated life of service to understand fully that you will be ridiculed and called fanatic even by the Church for living a separated life. They will call you Pharisaical and legalistic but I beg you to look beyond the verbal ramblings of men and see the eternal rewards of Christ. He said that when he returns he would bring rewards with him to give unto every man "*according to the works done in his body*" (II Cor 5:10)

The question then arises "*Is it necessary for salvation to keep the old standards of the Church*" my answer to you would be, absolutely not. However, your deliberate disobedience of the clear teachings and commands of God (not man made standards) will cost you your soul because to disobey his law with full knowledge of his law is sin. Salvation is free, it's a gift and requires no works on your part. However, the Kingdom of God or his government is not free and only those who "*take it by force*" will be granted a place in the Kingdom of God.

Matthew 11:12

And from the days of John the Baptist until now the kingdom of Heaven suffereth violence and the violent take it by force.

This scripture is very telling when properly understood. What did Jesus mean when he said that the Kingdom of Heaven is taken by violence? Ah, the beauty of it. This word *violent* in it's original Greek vernacular is spelled "*biastes*" and simply means "*Strong*". The only ones who will be given rulership in the Kingdom of Heaven on earth, will be those who have "*matured into the full stature of Christ*" and as a result they have become strong and they with that acquired spiritual strength have overcome the flesh and taken by force their positions in the government of God that is soon to come. Since the days of John the Baptist when he effectively opened up the Christological age *(the age of Christ ministry, 3 years)* at that moment in time the call began to go forth for Overcomers to arise and "*seek ye first the Kingdom of God.*" Until that point the entire world for four thousand (4,000) years had walked in deception with the Holy Spirit being unavailable to anyone except to a very elect few such as the Prophets. However, when Christ ministry began he came for one purpose to began calling out his church that they might begin "*training for reigning and schooling for ruling*". He began calling out the weak that they might begin their development into spiritual strength. Sadly, the word *violent* in this particular verse is a horrible translation of the original word which means **strength**. Christ is right now through the ministry of His Spirit, the Holy Spirit seeking the strong; the ones who will qualify for the kingdom, the ones who will Overcome, the ones who will triumphantly take their place or as the original Greek word "*biazo*" more accurately means "*crowd oneself into*" the Kingdom of God as a trusted, faithful and obedient follower of Christ and his every Word. If you have heard the higher call, if you have heard the screaming of Heaven eagle, if you have heard the Prophets message, if you have seen the brighter light of the coming Kingdom of God and shared in his dreams for this earth, if he has elected you to holiness and to rulership then you will never again have one problem with obeying every word even to the point of being ridiculous. *(Thanks Uncle Sam for that line)* If you will allow me the literary license to now render the words of the above mentioned verse in its actual and original meaning from its Greek foundation.

And since the ministry of John the Baptist until the present time the government of God allows itself to be seized and gained by the strong, only the strong will obtain their place in the government of God, they will force themselves into it by strength.

THE SECOND PROMISE
Rev 2:11
. . he that overcometh shall not be hurt of the second death.

While millions of Christians around the world will be given the opportunity to wash their robes white in the blood of martyrdom and while countless ones will truly repent during the millennium *(no matter what the non-biblical Left Behind series teaches)* there is no guarantee that you will be able to endure such horrors during God's wrath upon the earth and as a result you may or may not stay faithful until the end as the scriptures challenge us to do. So, the only sure way to avoid tasting the second and final death, the is to become an Overcomer in this life and to wash your own robe with obedience to His Word so that you might be sealed for protection during those days of woe. Only if you are in that group of people who keep his Commandments and obey his Word completely will you be guaranteed to never taste the second death. Just as God protected his Church in the Old Testament, Israel. Just as he sent a Great Tribulation to Egypt with his wrath, his obedient Church was sealed and protected from his wrath. They were not raptured but they were protected. However, anyone among the Israelites who didn't have the seal or the token they suffered the wrath of God even though they were so-called saved, even though there were true members of the Church they had to endure the stripes of disobedience.

THE THIRD PROMISE
Rev 2:17
. . .he that overcometh will I allow to eat of the hidden manna and will give him a white stone and in the stone a new name written which no man knoweth save he that receiveth it.

These are the words of a man in love! This is marriage talk and these Overcomers collectively make up that mystical and universal lady called the Bride of Christ. Incorporated into the creases of her dress and resting in the golden locks of her hair are countless millions through the ages who have climbed the bitter peaks of sacrifice for our Lord Jesus Christ. This group lay resting in their graves awaiting that moment when the above promise will be made a reality. You see, that hidden manna is the supernatural provisions that will be provided to the bride in our day of trouble upon the earth. The hidden manna will sustain us when the rest of the world has lost their minds. Then he promises us at our wedding day, the judgement seat, a new ring with a stone in it that will be crystal clear. The word white in this verse is actually a poor translation and it should be "*brilliant*" or "*clear*". This is going to be the wedding ring of authority placed upon the Bride. This ring as in all kingdoms denote authority. In earthly kingdoms of old, the Kings ring held the full authority of the King. If you received a letter with the seal of his ring then that letter was carried with the full weight of his majesty's empire and demanded your absolute obedience. If you were the Queen then you had access to the power of the ring upon your humble request and you had access to all the benefits of that stone. In this verse the Overcomers are promised the exact same ring or authority that Christ wears. Our rank in the future government will be known by this ring. Unlike the "***nations of the saved***" (Rev 21:24) who are simply walking in the light of the city, we, the obedient Bride of Christ, the Overcomers, we are that city. We will be living in that city. Our rank, our positions in his government will be denoted by that symbolic ring that John sees in this spiritual vision.

The marriage institution

Also, notice he promises us a new name. A name is indicative of your nature and your character. Your new name will be the proof that while here on earth your character, your nature and your mind was indeed changed into His mind. Your new name is a symbolic representation that you decided to take leave of your own identity and your own name and submit to His name and his responsibilities and His work. This is the very reason that on earth we see in a type when a woman allows her name to be removed and a new name to be given to her, this is a silent sermon to the world of a coming day when the Bride of Christ will accept her new name, new identity in the Kingdom of God. This is why in our day the institution of marriage is under such attack because every time a wedding is performed between a man and woman, a groom and bride it is another silent sermon of Christ and His Church and their soon coming wedding day. This is why we must honor this institution because it is bigger than a man and a woman; it is a living, breathing message that must never die. It is a constant reminder in the psyche of society of the ultimate wedding that all

of our weddings are mere symbols of. In the same manner the institution of the Sabbath day is a silent sermon of Gods coming eternal Sabbath and his firmly planted position as our Creator.

The only way you will ever earn the ring is to change your old selfish character and nature. Your nature earns your authority in His kingdom. Your new name will be followed by Elohim as that is the name of Gods plurality and as members of his literal family we will all be part of Elohim as legitimate heirs to the God Kingdom or Kingdom of God.

The Great House

We have other scriptures that prove to us plainly the differentiation or the ranks of saved Christians in the coming Kingdom of God.

II Timothy 2:20
But in a great house there are not only vessels of gold and of silver; but also of wood and of earth and some to honour and some to dishonor.

As you read the above verse and the ones immediately preceding and pro ceding it you will begin to have a wonderful revelation of the varying roles that we shall all fill in God's government on earth. We are told that in the House or the family of God, the actual God family; In the Great House that God has different dishes in his cabinets for his different purposes. There are some Christians who have not attained unto a position of honour and trust therefore they can never be used in entertaining royal guest in the kings house. Rather they choose to be dishes of disgrace; dishes nonetheless but unable to fulfill his higher purposes. There are dishes in His house that he is so proud of; He displays them in cases of gold and on tables of pearl. There are those in His Church, the Great and glorious House that will never earn a place in the golden china cabinet. They are satisfied with the dog food being placed on them and serving the lower purposes of God's church. However, the vessels of honor; they shine, they are obedient and they shall serve purposes beyond even their own imaginations for all eternity. All things in the vast universe will be placed under their feet or their authority.

Will the other dishes be destroyed? No, they will be used but they will never know the majesty of the golden city, they will never live in the court of the King but rather they shall live among the nations. Does that satisfy you? Just being saved isn't enough! Where is your passion? You answer to those questions will prove if you are truly "*seeking first the Kingdom.*" If you are not seeking first the Kingdom then you are in fact seeking first your Kingdom and you will never know the joys awaiting the Bride of Jesus Christ. Have you allowed the preacher to convince you that your purpose in being saved is just to escape to a place called Heaven and thankfully avoid Hell? If so, you have been robbed, you are sadly uninformed of your true potential and understandably you are living a defeated life. You have no true purpose if you do not have a Kingdom purpose. You are living in circles because you are clueless as to your destination. You are not serving God and you are not called out of this world to go to Heaven, you are called to rule this earth and to reign

YOU ARE LIVING IN CIRCLES BECAUSE YOU ARE CLUELESS AS TO YOUR DESTINATION.

with Christ for all eternity. You are being trained by His church for your future job responsibilities as members of the Royal House of Yahweh (Jehovah).

THE SONS OF ZADOK

All scriptural teaching must find roots in both the Old and New Testament to pass the test of the "*double witness.*" No matter what you have been taught the Old Testament is just as inspired by God and it's still good for doctrine and our understanding of the true plans of God. Concealed in those sacred and breathing pages you will find another example of the ranks of Gods people. The story of the Sons of Zadok are filled with revelation for the Sons of God. Before we can appreciate the ministry of the sons of Zadok we must know who Zadok was. Basically, one word describes this particular High Priest of Israel, *Faithful.* He stood with truth, he stood with David, he stood for God's laws when all of Israel turned their back and backslid, even all the other priest of the tribe of Levi. He remained faithful to his King and his God when the whole nation turned against them both. He was loved of God because he kept every Word and every tittle of Gods law and was serious about his calling as High Priest. His sons were evidently taught the same character traits as they were also pleasing to the Lord. At this point there is now two priestly orders in Israel, the Levites and the sons of Zadok. Now, who were the Levites? They were the chosen or called out people who served God in the temple. This was the type and shadow of today's church since we are all priest unto God now; we are perfectly typed by the Levites in the Old Testament. Something amazing is revealed in these verses where there is a clear distinction made between the Levites and the sons of Zadok. Now, understand clearly that the sons of Zadok were actually Levites themselves. They were legitimate descendents of the tribe of Levi but somehow their family as led by their Father had sold out to God more completely than the other Levites. Their particular family had been found pleasing unto the Lord because of their faithfulness to the Word of God and the keeping of his laws. As a result in the following verses you will see God actually making a separation in rank among his church of the Old Testament. He is doing the very same thing in his New Testament church. While all members of this church are indeed priest unto God, their is going to be a group of sons who carry the anointing of Zadok, they are completely sold out, they are fully committed they have decided to join *The Dream Team* and share in the dreams of God. Please read carefully the following verses as the light of God shines upon the words to reveal the magnificent hidden truths.

Ezekiel 44:10-15

10 - And the Levites that are gone away from me when Israel went astray . . .they shall even bear their iniquities

11 - Yet, they shall be ministers in my sanctuary, having charge at the gates of the house and ministering to the house, they shall slay the burnt offering and the sacrifice for the people and they shall stand before them to minister unto them.

12 - Because they ministered unto them before their idols and caused the House of Israel to fall into in-

iquity; therefore have I lifted up my hand against them and they shall bear their iniquity.

13 - And they shall not come near unto me. . .nor come near to my holy things in the most holy place . . but they shall bear their shame of the abominations which they have committed.

14 - I will make them keepers of the vessels of mine house . . .

15 - But those priest of the Levites, the Sons of Zadok that kept the charge of my sanctuary when the children of Israel went astray from me, they shall come near to me to minister unto me and they shall stand before me to offer unto me the fat and the blood saith the Lord God.

16 - They shall enter into my sanctuary and they shall come near to my table to minister unto me and they shall keep my charge.

Notice carefully as you read again the words written above as spoken by almighty Yahweh. The Levites had followed the rest of the nation in their compromise of the Word of God. They had drifted from "*holiness unto the Lord.*" They had mixed the gospel of their day with the traditions of the pagans and the world. As a result they could not be used by God in the original purpose that he created them for. Because of their disobedience they were now relegated to "*just being saved.*" While they were allowed to keep their salvation and their calling they were forever banned from the holy things, the inner sanctuary, the place of intimacy with God. They were allowed to be in the body of Christ but not in the Bride of Christ. The body of Christ is made up of all believers but the Bride of Christ is made up of overcoming believers. The Bride comes from the body, she is that choice part of the body, she is a chosen part just as the sons of Zadok were.

So, now I must deal with the argument that is so variably made and the question so often asked when these truths of rank and order are presented. Does God have favorites, are we not all his children, does he choose some and reject others at random? Allow me to ask you this question. If you own a business and you have ten children and the time of your passing is soon to come and your only desire is that the family business remain strong, what would you do? Of your ten children would you not love them all if you happen to choose the three of them who is most responsible to lead your work or your business? Of those ten (10) children perhaps only three (3)

WE ARE ALL CREATED EQUAL BUT WE ARE NOT ALL REWARDED EQUAL.

actually seem to diligently care about your dreams, your work, your business. While the other children were carousing and doing their own thing for their entire lives, the three (3) you have chosen made all the right choices. They went to college, they worked with you in the wee hours of the night, they watched you sweat and bleed to provide for the family; of the ten (10) children, who will qualify in your will as leaders of the family? Answer honestly, are you showing favor or wisdom? Are you being unfair to the other seven (7) or are you rather looking out for the other seven (7) by placing them in the responsible care of their more responsible brethren? Jesus Christ plainly says in his teachings that those who have *"been faithful over a few things will be made rules over many"*. What does that scripture mean, do you

have any idea? Did Jesus not tell his chosen Apostles that they would *"sit on thrones ruling the twelve tribes of Israel"*?(MATT 19:28) Is that unfair? What did the Apostles have that you and I don't have? Why do they get to rule over us? Because Government is everything to God and there will be a hierarchy in his government no matter what your prior teachings have taught you. We are all created equal but we are not all judged equal. I offer this pleading challenge, do not allow the watered down gospel message of this lukewarm church age to rob you of living an Overcoming life and taking by sheer strength your earned position in the government of God.

Here is another example of how the scriptures can say whatever we desire if taken out of their intended context. One of the readers of my manuscript before it went to publishing brought to my attention the parable of Christ when he spoke of all laborers in his kingdom receiving the same reward, even those who come in at the last hour. However, this parable has absolutely nothing to do with God's kingdom rewards; this is a parable directed to and only about the status of the Israelites and the Gentiles. At that time, the Israelites were Gods only people, they were first. However, the Gentiles or other nations were last in God's plan for salvation. This parable is explaining that very soon those who were last will be paid the same payment as those who were first, eternal life.

Take special note of Gods feelings towards these faithful and obedient sons of Zadok. They were invited into the privileged place. Herein is more proof that while God is not a respecter of person He is a respecter of works and faithfulness and obedience and if you happen to be in that category you will be favored by God just as the sons of Zadok. With that favor you will not just be a "guest" at the wedding but you will in fact be participating in that soon coming wedding that takes place at the beginning of the millennium reign. Only those who try to enter the Kingdom of God without the garment of holiness will be cast out of the Kingdom, all others will be part of that wedding ceremony. These sons of Zadok are types and shadows of the same overcomers that John writes about in his apocalyptic book of Revelation. What exactly did these sons of Zadok overcome? The answer is plainly shown in this chapter, they Overcome the apathetic spirit of laziness and compromise. While the rest of the church lived as close to the world as they could, these sons lived as close to the altar as they could. While the church of Israel was saying that Gods laws no longer mattered and while they made fun of these sons of Zadok for being "*too heavenly minded*" God was watching their works and he was well pleased.

In this church age of Laodicea you and I are living amongst the very same conditions as the sons of Zadok did. They lived among religious Levites who loved the idea of God but despised the actual laws of God. They were willing to worship their God in music and dancing but not in obedience and lifestyles. We live in a church world that has fallen asleep, disregarded the laws of God and convoluted the Word of God. Yet, God loves those people who are blinded by deception and walking under the Spirit of slumber. They will bear their iniquities just as the Levites did. During the tribulation that is soon to come upon our planet these saints will be broken unto the point of repentance and then they will be allowed to stand before the throne while the Overcomers will be sitting upon the throne of Christ.

The Fourth Promise
Rev 2:26
He that overcometh and keepeth my works until the end to him will I give power over the nations.

How many times have you read the above verse? Before the reading of this book did you have any idea what it meant? Think about it, if we are all flying away to heaven then how are we going to rule over the nations? The answer is so plain, Heaven is not the believers destination; a re-created earth that will be just like Eden and in fact will be heavenly, that is the true destiny of the believer. Who shall be rewarded this reward of having authority over the nations? Only those who Overcome Satan and sin in this life and those who continue to do so until the end of their lives. How do we Overcome? Again the answer is revealed in this very verse! We Overcome when he keep His works. I almost couldn't believe the meaning of this word when I began my research. The original Greek word for "***work***" in this particular verse is "***ergon***" which simply means employment or business or occupation. The way that we overcome is by faithfully working in His business in His employment. When His work becomes more important than your work, when his dreams become your dreams, when his plans become your plans; only then can you overcome Satan. For everyone who works for him, for everyone who puts their "*time in*" for everyone who suffers for him and endures to the very end; they shall be given authority over the nations of the earth. As Jesus promised "***the meek shall inherit the earth.***" As I have dealt with this subject in prior chapters entitled "*The Kingdom of God*" and shall do so again in a forthcoming chapter entitled "*The World Tomorrow*" I will not belabor the point here; However, the following scripture will be a great place for your mind to begin comprehending what our ministry will actually be among the nations of the earth in the very near future.

ISAIAH 2:3
And many people shall go and say, Come ye, and let us go up to the mountain (government) of the Lord, to the house of the God of Jacob; and he will teach us of his ways and we will walk in his paths: for out of Zion (his government) shall go forth the law (the Ten commandments) and the word of the Lord from Jerusalem (His Church, His Bride, His Overcomers)

REV 21:24
And the nations of them which are saved shall walk in the light of the city (they don't live in the city but there are others who will live in the city)

THE FIFTH PROMISE
Rev 3:5
He that overcometh, the same shall be clothed in white raiment; and I will not blot out his name out of the book of life but will confess his name before my Father and before his angels.

Another glorious promise is given unto these Overcomers, this special Dream Team who have proven themselves worthy of the Kingdom of God. They are promised to be clothed in white raiment. In other words they will be counted as righteous and dressed for their rank. In all Kingdoms and governments different vestures and garments are worn to denote ones position and authority. Should you see a man wearing a black robe then you can be assured he sits in a seat of judgement with the full authority of the court

of the land. Should you see a man with a badge, a uniform and a weapon then you can be assured that he is a man of the law. In ancient Rome, purple robes were worn only by the Senate and they were known by their purple vestures. The Overcomers will be dressed for their rank as those who washed their robes in the blood of the Lamb and lived overcoming and victorious lives. In all instances of scripture when angels of the Lord are seen, they are always wearing white vestments denoting their pureness, their holiness and their order of rank. One day you and I shall be dressed according to our rank in Gods coming Kingdom.

God has promised that all of the Overcomers will never have their name blotted out of the book of life. Contrary to the extreme teaching of eternal security there will be some who do not endure to the end and as a result they will not receive the crown of eternal life and they shall have their names removed from the book of the living and they shall die an eternal death.

THE SIXTH PROMISE
Rev 3:12
He that overcometh will I make a pillar in the temple of my God; and he shall go no more out: and I will write upon him the name of my God and the name of the city of my God which is New Jerusalem, which cometh down out of heaven from my God and I will write upon him my new name

Reading these wonderful and glorious promises causes me to wonder why all Christians wouldn't want to strive for this position in the government of God. Think about it; you shall be a pillar in the temple of God. Who is the temple of God? The Church of the living God, the Apostolic Church of God is the modern temple of God. A temple not made with hands, a temple of living stones, of breathing stones which are the people who make up his glorious church. However, it is worth noting that every Great House is held up and supported by the pillars. Every building is made prodigious and beautiful with those massive columns that are displayed for their strength and their position of greatness. Not every member of the body of Christ will be granted this position as the great pillars in the house of God or the God family, the family of God. Only those who have stood under the crushing pressure of an earthly life and refused to crumble, refused to bow the satire call of the flesh will be allowed to shine as a pillar in Gods building. However, when you have stood under the pressure of Gods correction, when you have stood against the temptations of Satan and the call of the wild then you have proven yourself to be a pillar, a strength beyond human understanding. As you grow strong in the Spirit by prayer and fasting you will begin taking your place in His government and you will serve his Body as rulers and as kings in the Kingdom of God. Notice carefully that Christ promises to write the name of God upon the Overcomers. Remember that a name is simply a symbol of your character. If you are an Overcomer it will only be because your character has changed as Jacobs did into the character of God and when that happens you will then be granted the very name of God or the character of God for all eternity. You will never go out anymore from the city of God, you will in fact carry the name of the city or the authority of the city within you. You in fact will be that new city, for the New Jerusalem as explained in forthcoming chapters is nothing less than all of the members of the Bride of Jesus Christ, the government of God who has been born again in resurrected bodies into their new robes, their new names and their new min-

istries. He promises to write upon us His new name which is His character. The reason he can give us His name is because we have developed His character and obeyed the words of Paul by "*letting the mind of Christ be in you.*"

THE SEVENTH PROMISE
Rev 3:21
He that overcometh will I grant to sit with me in my throne, even as I also overcame, and am sat down with my Father in His throne.

Assuredly, this must be the greatest of all the promises made to the Overcomers. While many will stand before throne and around the throne, there will be a group who shall be sitting in the throne. Please remember that these are mere symbols in revelation and a throne is not necesarrily literal in this book but rather indicative of a realm of authority. Just as the Queen of England constantly reigns on the throne of England she does not in fact sit on a literal throne coninuously but her authority the eminates from the throne is where she sits, in her authority. As Overcomers will be positioned in the same realm of power and authority that Jesus Christ now sits in and shares with His Father. How shall we gain this glorious position? Exactly how he earned it, by overcoming. He says in the above verse that we must overcome even as He overcame. What did He overcome? Satan, temptations, the flesh and the carnal mind. He overcame on the Mount of Temptation when he faced the selfishness nature of Satan that wanted him to disregard the laws of God and the will of God for His own human desires. On that great mountain where we all must one day trod, Jesus Christ overcame his own will and submitted to the Word of God. At that moment he proved emphatically that the ways of God were greater than his own desires and as a result He overcame his greatest enemy, the selfish human nature. He yielded that day to the government of God in His own life and he showed us the way to the Overcomers throne.

BE FILLED WITH THE SPIRIT

After studying these very specific promises to the Overcomer we must now ask the question; how do we achieve this seemingly impossible goal? Facing the reality of daily life can quickly rob us of these heavenly goals in our life. The daily grind of employment and raising our families can dim the light of spiritual aspiration so quickly. Many of you while reading this life changing book will feel the stimulation of the Spirit of God as your spirit man is aroused and liberated and as new life flows into your being. However, shortly after laying down these pages, the view of the heavenly Kingdom of God wil slide into the penumbra of daily livingl it will be shadowed and dimmed by your view of the unkept house or the unpaid bills or the unhealthy marriage and your focus will quickly change from the eternal to the temporal. This does not have to be the case, but there is a secret to living the Overcomers life. You must be filled with the Holy Spirit. Mistakenly we once believed that this meant a one time filling or baptism of the Holy Spirit of God. While we all could remember when we "received the Holy Ghost" we couldn't tell when was the last time we had been "filled" with the Spirit. The secret to the life of the Overcomer is not the initial baptism of the Holy Spirit but rather the continual filling of the Spirit of God in our daily lives. Before you can live the Overcomers life and before you can be filled with the Spirit of God on a continual basis you must first realize that you are the clay and the He is the potter. You must recognize fully that God is your Sovereign, He is your Creator and He is your King. You must come to the point of brokenness and humility when you willingly bow completely to His Lordship in your life. Only when you surrender your throne will you gain His throne. Only when you surrender your dreams will you dream His dreams. Only when you realize your worthlessness will you realize His worthiness. All of this requires a broken and a contrite spirit. All of this requires an awakening of total dependence on God for the very breath you breathe. However, this surrender to God is humanly impossible without the constant infilling of the Holy Spirit.

The early church and their Apostles were constantly being filled with the Spirit. One trip to the altar will never work. Your life must become a life of prayer and fasting. Praying every morning and every evening, praying over every meal, praying over every decision, praying over every sickness and every concern. There is a reason that we pray and it is not to move God but rather it is to move us. We must be moved from our own will into His will. We must be moved from selfishness to selflessness. We must be moved from our way of thinking into His way of thinking. Prayer is the vehicle that moves us, not God. Only in prayer are we recognizing our inability to control our own lives. Only in prayer are we completely submitted subjects of Heavens king. When we truly recognize our weakness and His greatness, only then can we truly pray. If you have a problem praying its simply because you have a problem recognizing your own need for God. You still unknowingly perhaps do not recognize how pitiful you truly are to be in control of your own life.

Have you ever heard the old saints of the church say "Lord willing" about everything they talk about? That used to really get on my nerves as a young man because my grandmother said "Lord willing" about the smallest detail of her life. However, the reason that young people do not say "Lord willing" is because they have not come to understand their desperate need for the guiding hand of God in their life. The ability to say "Lord willing" and mean it from your heart comes from the man who had been broken by the storms of life and has come to recognize his own inadequacies, he has come to realize that God's will is all that truly matters. We must learn to say these words and that ability only comes from a life of prayer and submission.

THE TRUE PURPOSE OF PRAYER

We may often wonder; "Why does God want us to pray"?. Is prayer a magic solution like the spells that a witch might cast in her desire to make things go her way? Do we pray to change our circumstances or rather to change our character? Do you pray when you need a miracle only? Then you are praying as the witches pray; you are attempting to control God with your incantations called prayer. A witch's spell is not much different. She will cast her spells to control nature or to control life events while giving no thoughts to the will of God. Many times we pray in the same manner, thinking we can just change things with our prayers; no matter the harm to anyone else. Do you really expect God to answer some of our selfish prayers? Prayer isn't about you it is about God. Prayer isn't your vehicle to change God it is your

vehicle to change you. Rather than changing events try changing you; this change can only occur as you stand before the misty mirror of reality in the palatial pavilions of prayer. It's in the clothes of mourning and submission that we recognize our own futility and his own magisterial might. His love for us is sometimes only found in our disdain for ourselves. When you see how worthless you truly are, how sinful you truly are, only then can you see how amazing His grace really is.

LEARN TO ASK

Jesus said "*if you abide in me and I abide in you, you shall ask . . .*" Here is an amazing revelation: Many people think that God must surely grow tired of all of our asking and our petitions that we present to him on a daily, hourly and momentary basis. However, quite the opposite is true! Do you remember what it felt like when your children depended on your completely for everything? Do you remember when they needed you for a mere twenty dollars for a date? If they had to ask you for anything they would spend several hours before mending any broken fences between you and them. They drew closer to you as they prepared to ask for that money. There was something very sweet about their dependency on you because their dependency on you required them to focus on you and to repent to you for any wrongdoing and to show you extra love and compassion. However, as life moves them away into adulthood and they no longer ask you for anything then the relationship changes and there comes a disconnect on a certain level. Where your advice was once like ancient wisdom to them, now it's considered out of date and unimportant. God is the same way, He loves when we ask, when we pray, when we lean on him for everything. As we pray, as we ask then this proves emphatically that we are abiding in Him and He is abiding in us. Even when we pray over our meal and ask His blessings, we are admitting that we depend on Him for the very food we eat and there is special sweetness between you and your Father when you ask Him for the daily needs of your life. As long as you are dependent upon Him it will be proven in your asking. Ask God for everything. Ask Him to wake you each morning and prove that you understand that you have not the ability to wake yourself. This time of asking produces a sweet relationship between you and your Heavenly Father. If you truly abide in Him then you will ask. As we ask we are admitting that we have no provisions except what He provides. We yield unto Him when we ask Him for all things. Pray when you first wake up each day, before you sleep, all during the day, over every meal and learn that only when you pray do you honestly believe in His authority over your life.

WHEN DID THE APOSTLES RECEIVE THE HOLY SPIRIT

The Apostles were not originally filled with the Holy Spirit on the Day of Pentecost as we have so often and so long believed. Actually, what happened was, they were filled again with the Spirit of God on the Day of Pentecost. Jesus did not tell them to Jerusalem and tarry for the baptism of the Holy Ghost, he told them to go and wait for the "promise of the Father" and what was the promise? The promise was made by the Father in the Old Testament that he would "***Speak to this people in stammering lips and other languages***" the purpose being that he might call forth a church from among the nations of the world. Jesus was taking to His disciples about their new job of teaching all nations to observe His commandments. When they naturally recognized their inability to speak the languages of the worlds nations, he responds and tells them that this miracle of breaking the language barrier will happen very soon and they they should go to Jerusalem to wait for this promise to be fulfilled. *(My book entitled "Any Evidence" explains the happenings of the Day of Pentecost more fully).* Originally the Apostles received the Holy Ghost on a very special day after the resurrection of Christ. He appeared unto them in His glorified body and breathed upon them and commanded them at that moment to receive the Holy Spirit.

John 20:22
And when he had said this, he breathed on them and saith unto them, Receive ye the Holy Ghost.

He commanded and they did! Here is Jesus, declared without one doubt to be the Son of God by his new birth from the tomb, he breathes on them in his glorified body and commands them to receive the Holy Ghost, do you think they obeyed? Of course they did, at that moment they received the glorious baptism. So, what happened at Pentecost, doesn't the Bible say that they were "***all filled***" with the Spirit in the upper room? Indeed it does and indeed they did but that was not their first filling it was their continual filling just as you should be continuously filled with the Spirit. What happened on the Day of Pentecost is the exact thing that happened some weeks later in the following verse.

Acts 4:31
And when they had prayed the place was shaken where they were assembled together; and they were ALL FILLED with the Holy Ghost, and they spake the word of God with boldness.

Who is the ALL being referred to here? The same Apostles that was filled with the Holy Ghost in the presence of Jesus some months before. Now, we find them just like on the Day of Pentecost, being filled yet again with the infilling of the Holy Ghost, adding to their measure of the Spirit. Can we now argue that they received the Holy Ghost for the first time in Acts 4:31, of course not just as they didn't originally receive it in Acts chapter two. Notice that they had the exact same evidence of this re-filling as they had on the Day of Pentecost, not speaking in unknown tongues but rather they boldly declared the Word of God. This is what the onlookers at Pentecost saw that caused them to consider these men drunk because these timid fisherman spoke with a new boldness, their entire personalities changed as a drunk man changes when inebriated. Exactly the same miracle is witnessed in a church service when the Holy Ghost is poured out afresh on the congregation, ther is a renewed boldness to do the work of God, to live holy, to pray for the sick. Days later that boldness begins to wane and the Church finds itself in need for another filling of this power from on high. In passing I will mention yet another misconception about the day of Pentecost that is more fully dealt with in my previous book entitled *"Any Evidence."* There is not one scriptural proof that there were 120 people in the upper room on the Day of Pentecost. Actually, the only declarative proof that we have is the infilling of the Apostles. When you read chapter one of the book of Acts you will find 120 believers that have gathered to meet the Apostles after their return from meeting with the resurrected Christ. Upon their return to Jerusalem these 120 believers are gathered. However, the outpouring of the *"Promise of the Father"* did not occur until ten (10) days later in Acts Chapter two. If you can fairly deduce that indeed one hundred and twenty parents and business people all stayed congested in an upstairs apartment for ten (10) days without leaving then perhaps you can surmise that they were all there ten days later. However, please note that the scriptures speak only of the Apostles when Peter stood up. We are told that Peter stood up with the eleven (11) not the one-hundred and twenty (120). No mention is made of any one else being there, only the Apostles. Also, for the next five chapters only the Apostles are working in the work of the Lord, only the Apostles are performing miracles until Stephen comes on the scene in chapter six. If one-hundred and twenty were filled on the Day of Pentecost shouldn't there have been more than just the Apostles working in the power of the Holy Ghost? It is my personal understanding that the Apostles were the firstfruit of the church, they alone had the commission to reach all nations and they fulfilled that commission at Pentecost as they alone spoke in the foreign languages of the world. Once again, there is no absolute evidence that there were one-hundred and twenty people who participated in this world missionary outreach at Pentecost.

The Apostles were also filled with the Spirit yet again a few chapters later in the book of Acts. The early church was filled with the Spirit every time they gathered together. There must be a constant refilling or filling up of the Spirit of God. How foolish it would be for me to fill my vehicle with fuel and anticipate its ability to travel for the next ten (10) days without a refilling. When we received our initial infilling of the Spirit we made the mistake in believing that we have received all of God's Spirit into our lives. Paul instructs us to "be ye filled with the Spirit."

There are different measures of the Spirit of God. Jesus Christ had the Spirit of God without any measure and there is a very good reason for this. He had a full measure because His vessel was free from sin and therefore all that dwelled inside of Him was the fullness of the Spirit of God. However, it must be noted that He didn't have any more of the Holy Spirit than you or I can have. Many people find those words offensive because after all wasn't Jesus Christ the very Son of God? Arn't you? He was no more a Son of God than you are. The scriptures say that he is our elder brother not our different brother. As He walked this earth, He did not walk it as God he walked it as man and as a result he was just as you and I are. If indeed He walked this earth as a God man as so many wrongly claim then He in fact did not fulfill his role as Son of Man because He couldn't be tempted of evil if He walked the earth as God since the scriptures tell us that God cannot be tempted with sin. The man Christ Jesus, the pre-ressurected man was absolutely no more God than you and I are. Think about it, what if Jesus would not have won the battle on the Mt. of Temptation? What if in the garden where He prayed, imagine if He had refused to drink the cup of His fathers will, would He have still been God? These questions beg your answer and not your judgement. If your answer is, He had no choice but to obey then you have made him nothing like us and therefore He truly is not our High Priest because He truly did not endure the exact same temptations as we do. The reason that Jesus had the Holy Spirit without measure is because when he received the baptism of the Holy Ghost in the river of Jordan he walked an obedient and sinless life; he kept the laws of God perfectly and as a result there was no restriction to the flow of the Spirit of God in His life. The reason he performed the miracles that He did is not because He was God or else He could have never told you and I that we would do the same miracles. He performed those miracles because there was no blocking or no boundaries in His personal life that would grieve the Holy Spirit and the Spirit of God had free reign in His life because of His obedience to His Father in Heaven. Paul teaches us that Jesus was declared to the Son of Man by his birth through the womb and he was declared to be the Son of God through the tomb. (ROMANS 1:4). For not even one second am I teaching that Jesus wasn't God but rather I am bringing the balance that He was God in his pre-birth and post-ressurection but during His earthly life he laid down those garments and picked up the robe of a man and walked exactly as a man with absolutely no divine intervention. He did not cheat on His test in life. He did not have access to anything that you do not have access to. He simply learned as a child the importance of His obedience to His Father and as a result he walked in the absolute fullness of the Spirit as you and I are encouraged to do. How can we be filled with the Spirit? Obedience, Obedience, Obedience to every jot and tittle of His Word. If you want an increased measure of the Spirit of God then you must increase in your capacity of submission and obedience. God is not looking for worshippers, the angels worship him; He is looking for obedience. I watch as the millions gather in powerful worship services and bow, kneel, lay prostrate, run, shout, dance, cry, weep, mourn, laugh and the list continues and all of this is referred to as worship. However, the Father only seeks one type of worshipper, those who worship Him by living a Spirit filled life of truth which is obedience to His Word, completely. He accepts no worship nor sacrifice outside of obedience to His Word.

Is there any part of Gods commands that you are breaking? I'm referring to all Ten, I'm referring to the two greatest of ones of the Ten, the one that encapsulates all of the others; Loving God with all of your heart, soul and mind and loving everyone on earth just as much as you love yourself. Do you qualify for a full measure of the Spirit? Check yourself by the commandments and see if you are breaking any of them, if so, Stop. Today, make the decision that your life will be a life of worship, a life of obedience to every Word even to the point of being ridiculous in the eyes of men. Have you judged anyone? Have you hated someone? Have you lied, Have you cheated, Have you lived in sexual infidelity? Have you desired the things that you don't have? Have you visited the prisoner? Have you checked on the fatherless and the widows? Have you kept the Passover *(falsely called Communion by the Catholic Church)* Have you washed the saints feet? Have you been baptized by full immersion in water in the lovely name of our Lord? Have you obeyed every word? Have you kept yourself separated from the world? If not then no wonder you and I don't have a full measure of the Spirit because we are to filled without ourselves to be filled with Him. I quote the words of the dear Kathryn Kuhlman when she said so often "Not some of self and some of thee but none of self and all of thee." This is the very reason why some Christians have greater measures of the Spirit then others, they have learned from a lifetime of living for Jesus that we must fully sacrifice ourselves and become walking dead men if we ever plan to be members of this Dream team.

Jesus Christ remained *"filled with the Spirit"* on a daily basis. I remember well when I decided to sell out completely for our Lord Jesus Christ. I was alone in a small prison cell where I endured the chastening stripes of our Lord for my sins and my disobedience. While there I would listen all night to the screams of people who were literally losing their minds; I saw things that I shall never utter especially on the written page but it was enough to teach me that God was ready for my full commitment. When I fully decided against sin and against disobedience God began working so many miracles in my life. The moment I decided that I would never hold one penny of God's tithe again, I would never dishonor His sabbath, I would never tell another lie, I would never be involved in any type of sexual immorality, I would never cheat or steal or be dishonest; at that moment the prison doors literally opened for me and a ten (10) year sentence was miraculously done away with and to this day no one knows how. I had to make up in my mind to fully and completely obey God and obey His laws and His commandments. From that day to this, I have noticed and continual increasing measure of the Spirit of God. As the measure is increasing so are the revelations, the prayer journeys, the glory and the joy of the Lord in my life. To increase the flow the sin has to go. Perhaps your sins are not at blatant as mine were. Perhaps your sins are hidden in your attitude and your lack of love and concern for Gods people, perhaps your sins are hidden in your selfishness and your religious pride; wherever it is, rid yourself of it all. Purge yourself and God will not have to purge you; Judge yourself by His Word and He will not have to judge you; prepare yourself and He will not have to prepare you! Leave no room for sin in your life, run from it, grab ahold of God's altar and never leave it if that's what,s required. Sin is your enemy, it will destroy and your family and your future. Sin will unman a man, Sin will infect the soul, Sin will leave you wondering what happened, sin will leave you blinded and as a fool. Until sin becomes your enemy then God can never become your friend. What is sin? The word sin simply means "Missing the Mark'. What mark? The goal or the mark is the laws of God, the command of God. When Jesus says *Depart from me you workers of iniquity"* He is saying *"Depart from you lawless ones"* The word iniquity simply means "lawlessness."

Having written to you about being an Overcomer, I have attempted to show you the goal which is the throne and I've attempted to show you the path to that throne, the less traveled path of obedience. However, there is another dimension on this path that I believe has been too often overlooked and this mystery is actually found in the Sermon on the Mount as delivered by Jesus Christ himself when he said these age enduring words, "The meek shall inherit the earth"

For nearly forty years I have heard this verse quoted, I have preached from this verse and was completely surprised when I realized that I have absolutely no idea of its true meaning and its true intent. While speaking to a friend one day over the phone she mentioned to me that perhaps the word meek had been misapplied or misinterpreted. She pointed out to me that our understanding of meek seems to include thoughts of quietness and gentleness and having no opinions, basically having a lambs nature. Indeed this was my understanding of meek. However, as was pointed out to me, Moses was the meekest man that ever lived and yet Moses did not fit the description of meek as he stood before Pharaoh and as he led his people with such authority and talked non stop delivering the law and deliver-

ing his judgements and statutes. So, what does **meek** mean? Actually I was surprised to learn that the word **meek** simply means **poor.** Poor? So, was Jesus saying that only the poor will inherit the earth and qualify to rule in His government? That's what He was saying to the natural ear but to the spiritually discerning ear he was bringing the word poor to it's spiritual intent. He clarifies this in His later teaching when he refers to the "Poor in Spirit, they shall see God." The meek are those who are poor in Spirit not in the things of the world, not in wealth, but poor in Spirit. What does a poor man do? He begs, He depends on the help of others, he is powerless over his own life, he calls out for help, he recognizes that he is nothing without help from the rich. In the same manner until you become poor in spirit and until you see yourself as the poor man sees himself, in need of a God, in need of a saviour, in need of a hand out from His Majesty then you can never qualify for the Kingdom of God. As long as you believe the your success and your dreams have been fulfilled by your own doing then you dear reader are not poor in Spirit and you are not meek. Moses was the meekest man because Moses knew that he needed God.

I used to not understand why the elders wouldn't dare eat a meal without praying. Now I know! They knew who provided that meal, they knew that without a Heavenly Fathers blessings that there would have been no physical health and strength for them to arise and provide their daily needs. I now stop and pray about everything because I have become poor in Spirit, I have come to realize that I dont need to drive without asking for His protection, I don't need to start my day without asking for his guidance. Truly we must become poor and dependent upon God for our every breath. Only when we realize out poverty and where our help comes from can we ever inherit the throne. As long as you believe that your education and your scams and your conniving and your employment and your family name have brought success in your life then you are not meek, you are rich in this worlds goods but you are not rich in spiritual measures. Today, repent for your lack of meekness. Pray over everybody and everything, say "Lord willing" after every statement, not out of cliche' but of a sincere heart. Learn what the elders knew after a lifetime of serving Jesus that "only what's done for God will last. Today is the day for you to be filled with the Spirit, over and over, day after day. When we gather with other believers, we leave refreshed, why? Because together we have all been filled with the Spirit yet again. After a prayer session you feel so refreshed because once again you have been "filled with the Spirit" you have increased your measure, do this on a daily basis and watch your Spiritual authority began to grow. Watch your prayers for the sick become more profound, watch the miracles began to creep up all around you as your measure increases.

The Coming Rest

Chapter Eleven

The wicked shall cease from troubling . . .
the weary shall be at rest

Job 3:17

THE SAINTS SHALL REST

AFTER THE JOURNEY; THIS EXPERIENCE CALLED LIFE WHERE YOU AND I ARE DEVELOPING OUR GODLY CHARACTERS THAT WE MIGHT ASCERTAIN OUR GODLY BODIES *(SPIRIT BODIES)* IN THE RESURRECTION, WE SHALL REST. The earth shall rest and the sinners shall rest even Satan will rest for a whole day, a thousand years. Before I begin teaching you about the coming rest for this earth; you must first be in total understanding of God's time clock and how it works. God has a plan as I dealt with in the chapter entitled "*The Blueprints*." His plan is longsuffering and seems like it is taking forever to accomplish. Do you know what it's like for an adult to take a vacation with a child? How many times do you hear "*are we there ye*t?" The reason the child ask so many times is because he is clueless of the measurement of miles and time and destination and purpose. To him, you should have arrived the moment you left. However, in our adult minds we have an understanding of the times, the miles and the distance. We understand that everything is measured in time. As adults we grow frustrated that our children can't comprehend the very things that we are just as guilty of not comprehending when it comes to God and his timing. We ask so often *"Is he here yet"* when thinking of his second coming. However, if you will learn the following scriptures that I will show you and plant them firmly in your mind and in your Spirit you will never ask that question again because you will have an understanding of the times and you will enjoy *the Journey* until the rest arrives.

7,000 YEARS

Although I touched on this subject of God's seven day plan in a previous chapter, I did not delve into the minutiae or the details of that plan with scriptural evidence. I want to take this chapter and show you in the scriptures exactly where we are in God's timing. On this Journey we may not know the day or the hour but the Apostle Paul says that we do not have to be taken unaware, to us he will not come as a *"thief in the night."*

Does God have an actual time plan? What is the duration on that plan? Jehovah, the great Yahweh of eternity is a God of specificity, just as his sun comes up at the same time every day; just as his planets pass through the zodiacal highway each season at the exact same times; just as old man winter blows his burst of shivers and death without fail; just as robins sing the same song in the exact same seasons; just as his created beings must all stay in a womb for nine months, so he is just as specific with his time plan for man; both the house of Israel and the other nations *(gentiles)*.

Think about this; why did God create a seven day week? In all of the history of civilizations and with all of mans different attempts at time keeping, why has the seven day week always remained? Why did God even create the week? Is there a purpose, a constant unspoken message being given to creation in this constantly returning seven day week? The truth is that **God established a time keeping <u>pattern</u>** with the creation of the seven day week. His plan for humanity is revealed in this very specific length of time, seven days. Always remember that in the numerology of scriptures the number seven belongs exclusively to the perfection and completion of Gods work. This is the very reason that the number six is the number of man and this is the very reason that the number of the anti-Christ is six, six, six (666) because no matter how many sixes are attributed to the anti-Christ, he will never be a seven! Seven belongs to the work of God and there is a truly amazing reason why! God works in patterns, symbols, numbers and parables; he always has and always will. For those who take the time to study those patterns, symbols, numbers and parables they will begin journeying into the very thoughts of God and in doing so will begin to peek into the secrets of his eternal plan and will become wise in the ways of God, firmly taking their places among God's *Dream Team*. This is why the saints will not be caught off guard at the second coming because we are "watchers of the Word" we understand this seven day pattern and it is my prayer; after reading my book that you will understand this plan as well.

Have you ever read all of the genealogies of the scriptures, all the verses that mention *"he begat a son, a his son begat a son"* and hurried through those genealogies to get past them and find the less mundane scriptures? Truthfully, there is a reason that these genealogies are so important and must not be skipped over. In the genealogies of scripture is the secrets to Gods plan. Each genealogy was meticulously kept and recorded for our understanding of the times, thank God for these genealogies as you shall soon see as we progress in this Bible study. The perfection of this keeping of time is for a purpose. I want to change the style of this chapter and present a serious of questions to you and in those questions it is my hope that they will focus your thoughts and increase your desire to find a biblical answer and cause you to be studious of the scriptures.

BIBLE STUDY QUESTIONS

What type of attitude did Peter say that many people would exhibit in these last days?

The answer is found in II Peter 3:3-4; He said that in the last days that *"men would be scoffers and mockers"* of the entire concept of the literal and physical second coming of Christ and his earthly kingdom. He said that you would know it was the last days when people became tired of preaching a second coming and began changing the gospel as so many have and began preaching as the preterist do (*preterism is the belief that Christ returned already in 70 A.D. at the destruction of Jerusalem under the the rule of Titus Caesar*) and as the *Kingdom Now* teachers do that the kingdom has already come and we are now living with a *"returned Christ"* inside of us and the Kingdom is in our heart. While elements of that message is true, they have absolutely become scoffers of those of us who still preach about *"pie in the sky"* as they mockingly refer to it in their so-called sermons. The very spirit of this age is displayed on Christian television all day long. Those who believe the message of a literal second coming are being scoffed at even by the Church and her leaders. Those of us who believe in a literal coming kingdom are being treated as Peter prophesied we would be, with contempt. May this writing encourage you to keep looking for the literal second coming of our Lord Jesus Christ. I will show you in this chapter his patterns and his ways and his method of keeping time. If you will learn that pattern then you can know the very season of his coming and you will not be as the five foolish virgins were who wasn't aware of the times of his coming. Remember that I taught you in a previous chapter one of the great principles of Bible study is often referred to as the principle of *"here a little and there a little, precept upon precept and line upon line"* that is biblical jargon that basically means that the understanding of Gods plan is not found in just once scripture but rather scattered through his Holy Book are bits and pieces that he reveals to those who are hungry for understanding. One of the very important pieces is hidden away almost unnoticed by so many Christians in the book of Second Peter.

How long does a day last in the time plan of God?

The answer is found in *II Peter 3:8-9*; Please note that earlier in this same chapter (*always find the context*) Peter is teaching about the second coming and those who will be scoffing about Christ delay. In this same chapter he gives one of those golden nuggets of understanding concerning the seven day plan of God. He says in the above referenced verses these words; "**Beloved be not ignorant**" God does not want you ignorant of his time keeping method, of his patterns, symbols and numbers. He wants you informed, not mystified and wondering about his coming and in this verse he is going to reveal to you his best kept secret that even Satan himself understand while the whole of Christianity remains ignorant of this truth, willfully so. Here is the golden key to the door of prophecy: Verse 8b "**One day with the Lord is one thousand years and one thousand years is a day"** If your converted mind can ever grasp this key then you will never again be ignorant of his plans. When one thousand years have passed, that is one day with God. So keep this in mind when study-

ing the seven day week and all will become clear as crystal before your reading eyes. Most Bible scholars stop at verse 8 and fail to read verse 9 wherein even more revelation is revealed to the lover of truth. Not only does Peter reveal the secret of God's method of time keeping but in verse 9 he reveals exactly why God has chosen such a lengthy period of time. He answers the above mentioned scoffers as only an inspired writer could. Notice carefully verse 9; please read the exact verse in your Bible while I will paraphrase what he is basically saying;

Verse 9 " *The reason why Christ is taking what seems like forever to return is this; God has one desire and it is the salvation of every soul on this planet who has ever lived. To cause that dream to come pass he created a time line, a plan that would allow man thousands of years to try living by his own governments and his own ways. Realizing the stubbornness of man, God knew that only after man arrived at the point of total downfall and destruction would he ever be willing to submit to Gods rule, so God in his long-suffering has allowed man that length of time, knowing that if he was patient and waited that one day all men would come to see his glory and repent of their sins"*

Sadly, we read through scriptures too quickly without thinking of their greater meaning. In verse 9 Peter reveals the reason why God is waiting so long. Never in the history of our world ladies and gentleman has man had the ability that he now has. Think about it, has there ever been a time in history where every human being could have been annihilated in one day? Only in our day can a man such as our President totally annihilate life on this planet with the launching of nuclear, biological and atomic warheads. THINK ABOUT THAT. We have never as a species been to this point. There is coming a war very soon when indeed our total extinction will be about to happen when men everywhere will beg for a solution and that solution will come when God shortens the days for the very elects sake because if he didn't *"no flesh would remain alive."* Can you not see? Can your converted mind not comprehend dear reader what Peter is saying? He's saying *"Don't scoff at our Lords delay"* he tells us that God's delay is Gods desire that all men would use this delay and repent. This is the will of God; the plan of God and the secret that you and I now hold in the treasures of our mind. Peter then continues in verse 10 to explain that to the world the Lords Day will come as a thief in the night but to those of us who are looking for and working towards that day, we shall not be caught unaware! To recapitulate: How many years are encapsulated in just ONE of God's days? One-Thousand years!

Is the reign of Christ on the earth to last for one-thousand years?

The answer is found in Revelations 20:1-6, please take time to read the verses, never take my word or any ones words regarding these truths, be *"fully persuaded in your own mind"*. In these verses you will find the following truths regarding the coming Kingdom, it's reign on the earth and it's time line or sequence of events. First, Satan is bound in verse two (2) for how long? For one day or one thousand years, this gives us the exact length of time when the earth shall be at rest from Satan's evil sway. The nations will be at rest for this one day because Satan's evil will no longer be broadcast into human spirits throughout the entire earth for one-thousand years. This is why men will *"turn their swords into plowshares or farming equipment"* because Satan, the original murderer will be gone from the earth; his

hold, his deception will be lifted from the earth for one whole day; the Sabbath Day, the Lords Day, the Day of Rest. For one thousand years, we will no longer struggle with the temptations of sin; everyone born during that millennium will not have to endure the inherit and spiritual struggle between good and evil that you and I have had to endure, Satan will be gone! There is a rest coming to your planet for this last and final day in God's seven day week. This is why this day is called the Lords Day because all the previous six days in the week of time has been mans or Satan's days, it has been our days to rule the earth, Satan's days to rule through us and by his rule we will bring ourselves to the point of total destruction as we nearly did at the tower of babel so many years ago. Verse 3 tells us exactly why he will be bound, *"**that he should decieve the nations no more.**"* God isn't going to bind Satan on this Sabbath day to show his strength; no he's doing it to save the world. Think about it dear reader, without deception wouldn't everyone desire the same life that you and I have in Christ? Who wouldn't desire a life of living Gods wonderful moral laws? Evidently nearly the entire populace of humanity does not desire the God life, the way of give, the way of love, the way of mercy. What's the explanation for that? They are deceived. When you and I see someone strung out on drugs, ruining their lives, we wonder why they choose that life. We sit perplexed at how a man would leave his beautiful wife and children and his lovely home for another woman who isn't even as beautiful as his wife; how can this happen we shake our heads and ask . . Deception! Can you imagine a world without deception? What will that world be like? Their eyes will open, the scales will fall off and all men, everywhere will seek after God and his ways, every knee will gladly and willingly bow, every tongues will confess that Jesus Christ is indeed our wonderful Lord.

This is the very purpose for the coming Sabbath day, the coming Lords Day, the coming rest that Paul speaks of in Hebrews chapters 3 &4.

Now notice verse 5 in Revelations 20: Again, the thousand years is mentioned to remind us of the specificity of God's days and his plan of keeping time. Those who do not rise with the saints in the first resurrection will sleep another thousand years or another day. *(I will not, as tempted as I am, attempt to explain in this chapter or this book the details of these resurrections as I have already written that book entitled "The heresies of the Hereafter" I would strongly encourage you to get that book, the truths contained therein will be beneficial to your understanding of these events that are soon to transpire.)*

Again in verse six (6) the one-thousand years is mentioned yet again as the duration of time of the Lords Day, the Sabbath Day; remember that Jesus is Lord of the what? The Sabbath. A Lord is a ruler, Christ has not ruled or been Lord over the last six days, man has. However, he will be Lord over the Sabbath. This is why our keeping of the weekly Sabbath is so vital in our understanding of the coming Sabbath. Satan so desires to remove the constant thinking of his destruction from our mind, he has stolen the weekly Sabbath from the world but he shall never touch the coming Sabbath as he shall be bound during that time. (Order my book, "*The Sabbath, so what*") if you truly desire to understand this most beautiful truth. Again in verse seven (7), the thousand years (7,000) is mentioned again and here is when Satan will be loosed from this prison *(this will be explained in detail in the future chapter entitled The Feast of Israel)* Why is he being loosed? The truth explained in the forthcoming chapters will astound you as you begin to see how perfect God's Seven-Day

plan really is.

Does Isaiah compare the time of Messiahs rule to a Millennial "rest"

The answer is found in Isaiah 14:3,7 also in Hebrews 4:1-11. Study these scriptures for yourself! In Isaiah's writing in verse three (3) what word stands out to you? Is the word rest not the subject of the verse? Is it not a coming rest? Sadly, many modern preachers try to say that this rest came with Christ. However, Isaiah is not speaking about the first coming of Christ, he is speaking of the second coming when the EARTH shall rest. To prove this, one only has to find the context in verse one (1) of the same chapter and here we find a regathering of all of Israel unto their own land, this shall happen in the Millennium as it's already began happening since 1948. Please, recognize these truths when modern Christianity tries to tell you that the rest mentioned here and in Hebrews is the rest of Christ, it is not! It is a literal, earthly,millennium rest that is promised by Isaiah, not a spiritual rest. To continue proving this to yourself, read verse seven (7) of Isaiah Chapter 14; *"The whole earth is at rest"* dear reader, look around you, is the whole earth at rest now? Or is the whole earth groaning and waiting for this coming rest which shall be brought to her by the sons of God who are resurrected at the beginning of this one thousand year mellennial rest? During the coming Lords Day, Isaiah says that the whole earth will break forth into singing. Joel prophesies of the Day of the Lord, the Sabbath Day, that when it comes, the sons and daughters, the little children shall dance, sing and speak with inspiration, the teenagers will have divine revelation, the elderly will be healthy and plump and happy *(this is the original wording of Joel 2:28 before the King James Translators translated them)* and he says that on that day that "**all flesh will receive the Spirit of God**" and the laws of God would be written upon every heart in the whole world. I shall never understand why Christianity can preach about a place called heaven that scripture never mentions and yet ignore the hundreds of scriptures pertaining to the coming Sabbath Day, only one word comes to mind; Deception. God says in Revelations 12:9 that the entire world is walking under deception, could that mean you? Let that question challenge you, don't let it anger you. Drop your religious pride and truly ask yourself the question, are these verses in this Bible? Why haven't I ever noticed them before?

Now, if the word "*rest*" as written in this chapter of Isaiah is the same word for "*Sabbath*" and if the Sabbath Day is literally the seventh day then when Isaiah sees and prophesies of a "Seventh Day" coming, can that not only mean that there must have been "six days" previously? Again, Isaiah is confirming our understanding of the "*days of prophecy*." Think about it deeply; if Isaiah is speaking here of a coming rest, sabbath or a seventh day then there must be six days preceding the seventh day. Indeed you and I are living in one of those preceding days before the seventh just as our ancestors and antecedents lived in even more previous days of this timetable than you and I are.

Let us now venture into the explanation of *Hebrews chapters 3 & 4*. For so many, who do not understand the coming Sabbath Day of rest as prophesied by all the major and minor prophets and Christ himself, they mistakenly misinterpret *chapters 3 & 4 of Hebrews*, they spiritualize away the true meaning of these chapters. I once did the same thing when I would argue against those who believed in the Sab-

bath. I always said that *"Christ became our Sabbath"* and I always went to these chapters in Hebrews to prove it. However, at that time, I had no idea that there was indeed coming a literal Sabbath day to the entire earth. So let's read carefully and learn the full meaning of Pauls writings which have been so emaciated. First, our goal is to find the context of his writing. Before doing so, let me tell you the arguments I once made and others today make. They teach as I once did that Christ is our rest. When we accept Christ then he does away with God's laws, he fulfills those laws and although we are still bound by nine of the Ten Commandments, we are somehow loosed from the fourth one, Remembering the Sabbath. But, is this what Paul taught in Hebrews 3 & 4, the truth may surprise you. To find the context we must read further back into Pauls writing; let's find the context by venturing back to Hebrews.

NOTE: I DELIBERATELY WILL NOT POST THE ORIGINAL SCRIPTURES HERE AS IT IS MY ATTEMPT TO FORCE UPON YOU THE ACTUAL STUDY OF THESE SCRIPTURES. IN YOUR EFFORT TO PROVE ME WRONG OR TO EARNESTLY KNOW THE TRUTH, MY NOT POSTING THE SCRIPTURES WILL PROMPT YOU TO READ THEM FOR YOURSELVES, HOPEFULLY.

Hebrews 2:17-18 (please read these verses, I will paraphrase)

In the above verses, you read about the role of Christ as High Priest. You read about the subject of sin and the reconciliation thereof. You also read how Christ himself came to earth and struggled with the temptations of Satan and sin. The struggle with Satan is the war that all inhabitants of the earth find themselves in, this is what causes our lack of rest. Jesus had no rest from this struggle until a certain point, his resurrection. If you will take a moment and go a few chapters over to *Hebrews 4:10,14-16,* you will find revealed in those verses when Jesus actually entered into his rest, when he "***passed into the heavens or the spiritual dimension***" at his resurrection is where Jesus entered into his rest from the struggles of sin, temptations and Satan himself.

Did we not study in previous chapters about a coming time at our new birth when all of those who will be born of God will no longer endure this struggle of sin? That truth is found in I John 3:9. When we are born again in the resurrection as Jesus was, the struggle with sin will be over, we will be at rest. If you cannot truly say to me that you no longer struggle with sin, if you cannot declare that impure thoughts don't fill your mind, if you cannot say that you are without any trace of sin then you must admit that this mentioned rest must be relegated to a future time and not a present time. While we have a down payment of the Spirit and we have a hope that brings us a measure of rest, we have not entered into the fulfillment of the promised rest. Christ himself did not enter into his rest until he "***passed into the heavens***" or in other words "*passed into the spiritual*" the spiritual body.

Now that we understand the context of Pauls writing we can now understand his teachings on the rest mentioned in Hebrews 3 & 4. For those who wish to declare as I once did that we entered into our rest when we were saved, my only response would be as my children respond to me, with one word, really? Actually, the believers have more of a struggle than the sinners do. In this life, the struggle is greater for us then the unconverted. Upon our conversion a greater battle began then before we were converted; the struggle intensified as we fight to crucify the flesh. Perhaps you are at rest but the

majority of Christians are at war. The only place that we have rest as Christians is in the "*hope of rest*" that is waiting for us at our new birth, our spiritual birth in the resurrection, just as Christ experienced at his as explained by Paul, so beautifully. Now, Paul issues a warning to those who are fighting with sin, fighting the good fight of faith *(I've never seen someone in battle resting)* He gives them a warning in these two chapters of Hebrews, we will take it verse by verse, only to silence the critic.

NOTE; AGAIN, I WILL PARAPHRASE THE VERSES FOR UNDERSTANDING, YOU SHOULD READ THE VERSES IN YOUR BIBLE ALONG WITH ME.

HEBREWS 3:1 -5 - This entire treatise is about one subject; **Our High Priest and his ability to help us with what? Our sin struggle**! He is faithful to be a high priest over his house, the House of God just as Moses was faithful to intercede over his house, the house of Israel. He is faithful to help us in our temptations as Hebrews 2:18 so perfectly explains. Jesus is the Holy Spirit and his Spirit that he sent to us upon our conversion is what helps us in this struggle with sin, helps us to become overcomers of those sins, he is faithful to fulfill that role in our lives.

Hebrews 3:6 - This verse reveals to us the House or the Family of God and our purpose on the earth. As the Family of God on the earth we are to allow this faithful high priest to help us to hold on to our faith. Jesus said while he was on the earth that when he returned he would "***hardly find faith on the earth.***" He is faithful to those who cling to him to keep our faith alive. He empowers us to obey Gods laws and to walk in obedience to the Heavenly Father. This is his present job, his role in heaven right now and he does his job well. How long must we hold on to him? Until the end. Now, if we have eternal life right now as preached by the modern church, why must we hold to him until the end? Because beloved, until the end eternal life is in the Son; at the end eternal life will be given to us all, separately and individually as born again sons of God, members of God's own family! Oh the wonder of it!

Hebrews 3:7 - 12 - Now, here comes the warning! Remember the previous verses or you will lose the context. What is Paul instructing previously? HOLD ON to your faith and in doing so you will be able to fight the good fight, you will be able to overcome sin in this life until your rest comes. This is a warning about the possibility of NOT ENTERING INTO THE REST. Now beloved, I have a simple question from a simple man; How can you not enter into what you have already entered into? If indeed we have already entered into the Sabbath Day of the Lord, the rest of God then HOW can Paul warn us about the possibility of not entering into it if we are already there?

Hebrews 3:13 - Don't allow what? Sin! Again, Paul makes it clear what this entire coming rest is about, the end of our battle with sin when Satan will be bound in the coming Sabbath. Don't allow sin to rob you of this coming rest. But what is sin? Sin is the transgression of God laws and what causes us to transgress or break Gods commandments? An evil heart of unbelief. What is Satan trying to steal from us in this battle of life? Our belief and our faith in the laws of God, the things of God. Only if he can take your belief will you ever transgress against the laws of God. When you stop believing, *(take it from a man who has been there)* when you stop believing in the plan of God, the ways of God and the things of God you will begin transgressing against God.

Hebrews 3:14-16 - When will we be made partakers of Christ? Wow, how the truth is different from the modern day gospel that says we are already partakers of Christ, we are already saved, we are already in the Kingdom! Paul says that this partaking of Christ is a future event that will happen at our resurrection in the coming Sabbath Day, the Lords Day. He says that we will only enter into that partaking, that rest from sins struggles IF we hold to our faith, our obedience all the way to the end just as we did at the beginning of our faith. May I point out here that every scripture so far in our study is all pointing forward. Now, Paul was living under the New Covenant as we are; he was writing to "saved" people as we are and yet he is not speaking in the present tense but in the future tense. Where did the modern church get her license to change this rest to the present when Paul is so plainly pointing to the future?

Hebrews 3:17 - Who did not enter into the rest? Those who sinned! Those who broke Gods laws, those who walked in disobedience, they did not enter into the coming rest. What is the warning here for you? Be careful that you don't do the same thing. Until you reach the end, the promised rest, don't do as Israel did, don't lose the faith, don't settle for Egypt, don't do things your way; HOLD ON your rest is coming!

Hebrews 3:18 -19 - Only the obedient in this life will be allowed entrance into the Kingdom of God, the believers promised place of rest.

As we enter into the next chapter, are you beginning to see the context in Chapters 2 & 3? Keep the context in mind as you delve into the next chapter or else you will lose it's true meaning. Let's continue:

Hebrews 4:1 - Note this point very carefully! This is a PROMISE not a POSSESSION, there is a vast difference between a promise and a possession. The rest of the believers is a promise, always remember that. This is not yet received by anyone on this earth today. If this promise is already received then pray tell how in the world could you "*come short of it*" as Paul warns against? If you are already there and all of this is already been given to you then you could never "*come short of it.*" Could you? Am I missing something here? If you have given me a house and a title to that house and a key to that house, could you possibly warn me after the fact "*Now, do everything right because if you don't you may not get that house*" But, I already have the house so how could I not get it? Do you see the absurdity of believing that we have already entered into our rest and yet warning us to be careful unless we should NOT enter into our rest?

Hebrews 4:2 - What caused Israel to not enter into her promise? They had Moses law but they had no faith in the giver of that law. Today, you may well keep the strict letter of the law but if your faith is not in Christ for your salvation then you also will not enter into that rest. Let me clarify my point. As many of you have figured out by now in this book, I believe in keeping the commands of God. However, if you look to any of those commands, any of those laws for your salvation then you are a legalist. While I do many things in observances and keep many rituals such as Baptism, Passover *(falsely called communion)*, the Feast of the Lord, the Sabbath, Foot washing, Tithing and many other observances, my faith is in none of them. My faith is in Christ alone and in the finished work of his coming kingdom. Only when his Kingdom work is finished will

his work be finished and he will give all things to the Father, his work was not finished at Calvary, his suffering was finished there. We do not keep God's laws for salvation, we keep them because of salvation. A child doesn't cry to be born, he cries because he's born. We don't do anything for salvation we do everything because of salvation. Just as you don't tell a sheep to grow wool, you don't tell a spiritually conceived child of God to obey Gods laws, it's natural.

Hebrews 4:3 - Only those who are walking in obedience to God, those who truly believe, only they are entering into their rest, only they are making the entrance, only they will make the resurrection and find the key to the kingdom, the resurrection. This group of believers have a down payment of this rest, they have experienced the righteousness, joy and peace of the kingdom of God beforehand; before the rest of the world will experience it. We have the essence of the kingdom right now. However, until our resurrection we will not receive that full promise; only a taste, only an earnest, only a shadow of it. But if we continue to believe we do enter. This life is the "entering in" We are entering for as long as this life takes. The converted life is the beginning of the entering, we do enter!

Hebrews 4:4 - God rested on the Sabbath as a type of his coming eternal rest. However, God's rest was interrupted by sin and he has been working since then to prepare the kingdom for his dear son, Jesus Christ . However, he will have eternal rest when all of his creation is safe and at home with him at long last free from Satan's dominion, then we shall all rest with him for eternity.

Hebrews 4:5 - Paul says, "*Now, talking about the present day, if they shall enter in*" In other words just as those in earlier days had a promise of a future entering in so do we in this day have a promise of entering in, in the future. However, if we are true believers we will begin entering into that rest right now. We start making our entrance upon our conversion and the entrance will be complete at the resurrection.

Hebrews 4:6-8 - Amazing; Paul plainly says here that "the promise" remains for SOME! There will be some, an elected, chosen, predestined group of overcomers that will indeed enter into that rest at the first resurrection and they shall enjoy immortal life during the reign of Christ. But listen to the warning; Who will enter? Only the obedient. Obedient to what? The laws of God. The overcomers will be those who entered into their rest by obedience to all of God commands and their obedience will be based upon their faith in the Lord Jesus Christ as they allow him to live his life in and through them; a life of obedience. Notice in verse 8 that "**another day**" of rest is spoken of by Jesus *(Joshua is a mistranslation by the KJV)* Jesus speaks of a coming "day" not "days" of rest. Remember, the subject at hands, the 7 day plan of God. Only one of those days is the Sabbath day or the Day of rest and it will be given in the 7,000th year of mans existence, not before. You and I are not living in the "DAY" mentioned by the prophets, we are in the 6th day. The day of promised rest is the 7th day.

Hebrews 4:9 - Now we arrive at the cherished scripture of those who oppose the keeping of God's Sabbath day. For herein they suppose the Sabbath has been done away with and fulfilled in Christ and yet Christ kept the Sabbath himself. What does this verse mean "*There remaineth therefore a rest for the people of God.*" It sounds like Paul is saying that the

people of God have found that rest promised in the scriptures and therefore we can all forget about the Sabbath because it has been fulfilled. However, upon careful study, such is not the case.

The Greek word translated "*rest*" in every other verse in Hebrews 3 & 4 is *katapausis*. But, the word translated "*rest*" in this one and only verse in these two chapters is "*sabbatismos*" So, had this verse been translated as it should have been it would have read entirely different, it would have read "*There is yet to come for the people of God, a Sabbath day.*" The Anchor Bible Dictionary will prove this point for you if my writing leaves any doubt. The Anchor Bible Dictionary also states the following: "*the author of Hebrews proves through the joining of quotations from Gen 2:2 and Psalms 95:7 that the promised Sabbath rest still anticipates a complete realization for the people of God in the end time which had been inaugurated with the first appearance of Christ*"

The word "*sabbatismos*" as used in this verse is very unique from all of the other "rest" mentioned in these verses. All biblical dictionaries and resources of antiquity prove the clear meaning of the word "*sabbatismos*"; Sabbath Rest! That is the meaning of *sabbatismos*. This same word appears in the ancient *Plutarch* and in those writings of antiquity it explicitly means "*Sabbath observance or celebrations*". With our understanding of the word "rest" enlightened we can plainly see that Paul is actually saying that for the "people of God" there is a coming day of rest still promised if we hold on to our faith in Christ and our obedience to his laws. Could anything be any plainer? How have we abused this chapter for so many years of Christianity

Hebrews 4:10 - Who is the "He" being made mention of in this verse? "**He that is entered into his rest**" has mistakenly been taught as meaning the New Testament believers. However, this is not the case at all. "**He**" **that has entered into his rest is Jesus Christ**. As always the scripture will interpret itself and leave no further doubt as to the "He" of this verse. Remember who this entire chapter is about? In verse one (1) of this chapter who is being discussed? Jesus Christ, our High Priest and it is he that has ended his work in this age and indeed has entered into his rest with God. To further prove that the pronoun "He" in this verse is Christ, simply look at verse 14 *"Seeing then that we have a great high Priest that has passed into the heavens (spiritual realm), Jesus the Son of God."* From verse one of this chapter all the way to the end of the same, everything is about Christ and his promise of a coming, eternal rest to the believers. At this moment Christ is the only man of earth who has indeed been resurrected and entered into the promised rest from sins struggle. Now, he helps us with this struggle until our time of "glorious liberty" shall also come to us; indeed there remaineth a Sabbath for the people of God.

Hebrews 4:11 - This scripture is the most convincing of all in my mind that you and I have actually not entered into the promised rest. How do you labour to rest? I dealt with this question in detail in the previous chapter so I shall not belabor the point in this chapter. However, there's a good reason why we must "labour to rest." If you haven't read the previous chapter of this book it will be made abundantly clear therein.

Hebrews 4:12-13 - In these verses Paul instructs us as to how we can labour to enter into that rest. He teaches us that our labouring is basically a "prepara-

tion" or a "*preparing as a bride adorned for her husband*" and how is this preparing being done? With the Word of God, the Laws of God and the manifested dreams of God. His Word is actually judging his children right now as we prepare digesting the Word of God into our minds and being transformed by the same. We are *labouring to rest* by feeding on the Word and allowing the mind of Christ to fill our minds and his Spirit to help us overcome this struggle with sin.

Hebrews 4:14-15 - Again, I have already presented the meaning of these verses previously in this treatise. They show concretely that it is Jesus that has entered into his rest when he entered into his spiritual body at his resurrection and has in fact ended his struggle with temptation and sins of the flesh. His temptations are mentioned in this verse and most importantly his overcoming of those temptations. This gives you and I the assurance that if "*his mind*" is in our minds then we too can do the same thing, we can overcome! We can be obedient to God's laws just as he was because it is *"no longer I but Christ that lives in me."*

Hebrews 4:16 - This sums up the entire meaning of these two chapters. Notice Pauls words about "***the time of need.***" This means your time of struggle with sin, in those times he will help you in that struggle until your promised rest from those struggles indeed come to you just as it finally came to him. His grace will help you not to "***come short***" of the promise of rest and of entering into the Lords Sabbath Day that shall soon grace planet earth. He is now in his rest simply waiting for the Father to place all things under his feet! Until then, he is free from the struggles of the flesh and dear reader you too soon shall be when Satan is bound and his temptations will leave the earth and all the earth will sing and rejoice in that rest. It is my prayer that you now understand the true meaning of these chapters and that you will never be convinced that Christ came to set you free from keeping God's laws. He set you free from the penalty of the death should you ever break those laws. He came to pay the penalty for those who have indeed broken the laws of God. The penalty was removed, not the law! With that clearly understood now let us continue studying God's 7-Day plan and our questions of study.

BIBLE STUDY QUESTIONS

How much time has elapsed since mans creation

Unfortunately, many Christians and creationist still proclaim that the earth is only 6,000 years old. Science and God's Word proves the fallacy of this argument. I dealt with the scriptural study of this subject in the chapter entitled "*The Blueprints*" it would be worth your reading if you haven't done so. The earth is millions of years old. However, the re-creation, the renewing of the earth happened nearly 7,000 years ago. Remember at the beginning of this chapter I mentioned the importance of the genealogies of scriptures, we will now see just why those genealogies are so crucial in biblical understanding.

Does Genesis 5:3-29 and Genesis 7:11 show that exactly 1656 years transpired the creation of Adam and the flood of Noah?

YES IT DOES! So, if one-thousand *(1,000)* years equals one day with God, Noah's flood happened at about one and half days into Gods total time plan. (

Shane Vaughn

Note carefully: Genesis 5:3 shows that Adam was 130 years old when Seth was born. Now, add up the ages of each forthcoming child from Seth at the birth of his sons, plus the age of Noah at the time of the flood and you will find exactly 1656 years)

Does Genesis 11:10-32 show that exactly 427 years passed between the Flood and the death of Terah.

YES IT DOES! This is the exact same time that Abraham leaves Haran according to Acts 7:4.

Was Abraham 75 years old when he left Haran?

YES HE WAS! The answer is found in Genesis 12:4. Now notice the details of Gods perfect Word and in his keeping of time for future generations. Genesis 17:1-10 will prove to you that exactly 24 years passed since Abraham left Haran. 24 years after his leaving he is given the Covenant of circumcision. To see Abraham's age at the time of this Covenant simply compare Genesis 12:4 with Genesis 17:1.

How many years have now passed from the Covenant of circumcision with Abraham to the Covenant of Sanai with the children of Abraham?

The answer is found in Galatians 3:16-17. This period of time is called The Exodus period. Exactly 430 years passed between Abraham's Covenant and Gods Covenant with the children of Israel at Mt. Sanai.

ARE YOU FOLLOWING THESE YEARS?

How many years passed from the giving of Covenant at Mt. Sanai to the 4th year of King Solomons reign when the temple building began?

The answer is found in I Kings 6:1; all scholars place the building of the temple at 966B.C.

Now to see gods perfection in keeping time simply add together all the numbers:
1656 + 427+ 24+ 430+ 480+ 966 = 3984

This date shows us that Adams creation happened about 3984 years before the building of Solomon's temple. While according to scholars and keepers of time there is probably a fifty (50) to sixty (60) year discrepancy in the changing from the Gregorian and Roman calenders we can still get very close to the timing of Jesus Christ on the earth as a baby. Basically when Jesus came to the earth, mankind was closing out the 4th day and entering the 5th and 6th days of Gods timetable. This is the very reason these centuries since his birth can be called "*the last days*." Literally it is the last two days in God's plan before the 7th day finally comes. In actuality, our year 2000 is ahead of biblical time by about 30 years because of the miscalculation of the genealogy of kings, and their reigns. However, you can be assured that the end of the sixth (6th) day is upon us.

The church age didn't actually begin until 31 A.D. on the Day of Pentecost. Therefore the end of the church age would fall very close to that exact date some two-thousand years or two days later.

Take a moment and notice a statement from Christ that is so often overlooked as he spoke in those spiritual tones for spiritual ears.

Luke 13:32
. . .I do cures today and tomorrow and on the third day I shall be perfected

Lest one would think he is speaking of his resurrection, he is not. He is speaking of the three days left in God's timetable at his first coming. For the next two days he will be calling out and curing a people, healing them and preparing them. One the third day, the Day of the Lord, the Sabbath day he will be complete his plan will be complete, he will be Lord of the Sabbath.

The third (3rd) day since Christ is the seventh (7th) day

The third day is upon us dear reader. Simply watch Jerusalem. For nearly two thousand years Jerusalem was of no importance to the world, ruled by the Ottomans and Muslims and various rulers. Then of a sudden toward the end of the sixth "6th Day" all of a sudden Britain is granted all of that Land in the Balfour treaty (*do you have any idea who the British people are? I'll write that book at a later date*) Britain restored the Jewish people to The Land. Since that date, all of the nations of the world are turning their attention to that small and insignificant piece of land? Why, because the headquarters of earths new King shall soon be set up there. Because, God has a promise to honor with Abraham and his descendents.

Notice how the once insignificant nation of Iran is rising as the biblical **King of the South**. Notice how that Egypt who was once a neutral friend of Israel under President Mubarak; they were a buffer zone between Israel and Iran; notice how that now that country is ruled by the Muslim Brotherhood, that buffer zone is gone. Danger is everywhere!

Notice the nations are crumbling, notice Germany rising! I shall not turn this into a prophecy book. However, the sixth (6th) day is closing swiftly as the nations hold their fingers on the nuclear weapons button to retaliate against any other nation. Droughts are plaguing the land, the sixth (6th) is lining up perfectly, exactly as the scriptures tell us they shall. Faith is hardly found on the earth, the sixth (6th) day is closing dear reader. The Sabbath day of our Lord is upon us, a great rest shall soon come to us after great destruction. Are you labouring to rest? Are you preparing your garments to reign with Christ in his Day, the Day of the Lord?

John the Revelator was worshipping on the Sabbath day, the Lords day when he was carried away into the coming Lords Day, in a vision he saw the rest coming to Gods people during the Lords Day and glorious was the sight! Prepare today, lose the sway of this earth as you submit yourself to God today and labour to enter into his coming rest.

The Ministry of Satan

Chapter Twelve

*Declaring the end from the beginning . . . My counsel shall
stand, and I will do my pleasure*
ISAIAH 46:10

God dreamed a dream

Is the world unattended? Has everything been hopelessly taken over by evil, malevolence, vice and despot immorality? Is the masses of humanity simply one big train wreck waiting to happen like wild horses out of control? So it seems! Billions have lived and died since Adam without any hope; one hundred and fifty five billion (155,000,000,000) to be exact. Myriads and masses of people have lived and died without having ever heard the gospel, is there no hope for them? Is there no hope for the teeming multitudes today who hurriedly rush towards their graves without any knowledge of the plans of God? Looking at this picture causes one to truly doubt that there is any order in all of this chaos. It is hard for the carnal mind to truly see any pattern or blueprint or any plan in this cacophony of crisis. However, if you are going to be on this very special *Dream Team*, sharing the mind of God or the very dreams of God then you must overcome these carnal thoughts and realize without one shred of doubt that our God specializes in creating order out of chaos. Simply look at the chaotic universe and yet there is perfect order; the sun never fails to rise, the stars never fail to shine, the tides never fail to roll, the rivers never fail to flow; only our God can create order with nothing but chaos.

The two wills of god; *Secret & Revealed*

Very soon your eyes will behold as God in his sovereign power will simply incorporate the chaos of this world into his perfect will. **God has two wills**; he has his *revealed will* and his *secret will*. His *revealed will* is his Word; for in his Word he has given us *Plan A*, the plans that he would desire for us to live by. He has shown us how we should live our lives in the instructions given to us in *Plan A*. However, He knew before He ever created *Plan A* that man wouldn't live by *Plan A*; therefore, *Plan B* was created before *Plan A* ever was ever revealed to mankind; now wrap your mind around that startling revelation beloved! So what was his secret will? His secret will was his Plan B, it was the plan that would take all the mess ups of Plan A and make them all fit perfectly into his overall plan and make them all work together for our good. Just as a parent, you may have an ideal plan for your child's life. However, experience has taught you

THE ONLY WAY THAT GODS PLANS CAN FAIL IS IF GOD HIM-SELF CAN FAIL

that ideals hardly ever find existence in reality so with that knowledge you already have a secret plan unbeknownst to the child; you are ready for when he messes up your revealed will your ideal plans.

God is never taken by surprise, He is never learning anything knew, He is never trying to figure anything out, He is never taking counsel; His purposes has been from everlasting and they will come to pass perfectly. When He is finished with His divine building project, the salvation of his creation, everyone will see why he allowed chaos because only in the chaos do we appreciate his order. I challenge you to read *Psalms 72:1-20* if you desire to know how this story shall end. This story devised by carnal minds, sacrilegious professors of profundity and so-called understanding, they all speak of a world gone mad and seemingly out of control. However, God's finished work will universally declare his wisdom and power, all his dreams shall be accomplished.

Isaiah 14:24-27
. . . surely I have thought (dreamed) so shall it come to pass and as I have purposed so shall it stand . . . This is the purpose that is purposed upon the whole earth . . . For the Lord hath purposed who shall disannul it

Those scriptures give me so much hope that our sovereign Father needs no counselors. He has dreamed a dream and he is now finding a team that will join his dream and bring it to pass upon the earth. His purposes or his dreams shall stand upon the earth; do you have his dreams for this earth, for his people, for his creation or are you just "*having church*"?

bersome load. The king demanded that the architect erect a center column under the archway before the king would worship there. As the story goes, the king prevailed in his demands and he worshipped there until his death many years later. The king finally died and only then did the architect reveal a startling secret to everyone. He in fact did not obey the kings orders. He erected a false column indeed; he left about a half an inch between the top of the column and the archway, completely hidden was this empty space between the arch and the column to the naked eye. Surprisingly in all of that time his arch had not sunken even by a millimeter. Today as a testimony to the truth of this story, in this cathedral a piece of wood is placed in that half inch space for all tourist to see the perfection of this architects perfect archway. Just like this architect, God is so sure of his plan, he creation and his strategies that he needs no human support for it to happen, his plans will be fulfilled and you have been invited to be a partaker in that divine plan, in that divine orchestration; like the king in this story, you can worship there in that sure place of Gods perfection and purposeful plans until you die!

THE ARCHITECT

Located among the antiquities and relics of Spain you will find the beautiful *Escorial Cathedral*. The sovereign monarchs of the Spaniards are all buried at this cathedral. An amazing architectural story lives among the tales of the cathedral. When building this edifice, the architect wished to build a vast arch. The arch was so flat on the top and so brilliantly designed that the king feared to worship under such an arch for fear of the arch failing under such a flat and cum-

PLAN OF THE AGES

Why does God's holy Word say so little about eternity? Very little is mentioned about that essence that exist outside of time; is there a reason? God's Word deals with the issues of time more than eternity because God's working the plans of eternity in the "*ages of time*" through the vehicle of time right now and that is where he wishes our focus to be, on the plan of the ages.

Hebrews 1:1-2
God who at various times and in different ways spoke to us in times past to our fathers by his prophets . . .In these last days he has spoken to us in his Son whom he hat appointed heir of all things, by whom also he made the worlds

Something very interesting is revealed in the above verse: Jesus is heir of everything; of the universe, the galaxies and the *worlds without end*. However, He is not heir alone! You and I are heirs to the same thing, *worlds without end*. Notice that Paul says that "**by him also he made the worlds**" actually the word "*worlds*" is another KJV mistranslation. The Greek word for "*worlds*" is "*Aionas*" and that word means

EVERYTHING WAS CREATED FOR GOD'S PLEASURE

"*ages*" not *worlds*. So this verse should read that *Jesus Christ created the ages or he created time*! He created the plan of the ages, the divine architectural plan for his building. He stepped out of eternity and created time and in doing so he actually created PURPOSE. He that is heir of all things actually created the program, the ages and the plan for the redemption of all things that he is heir to!

Carnal and ludicrous minds have postulated the idea and set forth these disconcerting images of God and his world and his plan. They have believed that this world is running haphazardly through space like a wild horse without reins. They believe and use scare tactics that our planet is about to run into all the other planets and Christians buy into these charlatans and their wares of woe. They continue to create movies in Hollywood that somehow this is a mad

universe on a collision course with some gigantic asteroid. However, it's actually the mind of carnal man that is mad because if memory serves me correctly; the sun has never been late one time for his assigned job. The moon has never failed in her duties of the night. The tide has never failed to tow in her wet feet. For millions of years this *chaotic* universe has operated in perfect and divine order. I challenge you to look up, look into the dreams and mind of God and remember this well; the only way that Gods plan can fail is if God can fail and I believe that up to this date his track record is beyond reproach. God does not create what he cannot control. He is not the mad scientist creating a bunch of Frankenstein's that somehow get out of his control. You must have faith in his sovereignty and his plans for the ages. He created the ages, the epochs of time for a purpose, that he might control the chaos.

Unfortunately the whole of Christianity has bought from the peddler of prevarications, they've greedily bought the lies and distortions of gospel truth. They seem to preach a gospel that says that God basically got into the creation business about six thousand short years ago and He really didn't know what He was getting into. He created a bunch of things called humans and He really had no idea how that would turn out; but He hoped for the best. However, God is basically just getting fed up with the whole thing, the whole bunch that he created and He's basically decided that He's gonna close shop and get out of the creating business. He's supposedly gonna find a few of the good ones and whisk them off to an eternal wonderland and just forget about all the rest of them; why not just let Satan have what He gave his life for, let Satan win them all and then they say that God will be so angry that He lost all of them that He's just gonna boil them all for as long as he lives and find call that justice. I call that whole scenario madness, poppycock and almost blasphemy and yet that is the true mind-set that people have towards the plan of God in their hidden but often unspoken thoughts.

Really? Well, if that's the case then you have a God that changes! My God doesn't change! That's a weak God, that's a God who isn't in control of his own house. May I ask you a question? If God knew in the beginning that this was all going to be one big colossal failure and that the majority of his creation would be lost and that it was all just going to be thrown into a lake of fire then why did he even waste his time? **Oh no dear friend, he's gonna get it back!** You can buy into that pack of lies about the great God of creation if you so desire. However, in my converted mind I have a different dream, it came from the Holy Spirit and in that dream I see the future; I see a victorious God who *will have all men to be saved*. I see a God who doesn't plan to give one inch of his earth, his people or his sovereignty to Satan. At the end of this story when you see just how perfectly he planned it all you might just wish that you had never doubted his secret will.

I have attempted however crudely in this book to show you the beauty of this plan, the perfectness of this plan and the intricacies of this plan. You must get the dreams of God, the thoughts of God in your mind and you must never again believe for one moment that the chaos isn't in his plans of order. Let us look further at God's plans for you, his beloved and his chosen, his *Dream Team*. In the final chapter of this book entitled "*The Feast of Israel*" you will see maybe for the first time how exact and precise God's

plan really is. I can make you this one promise if you have never understood the Feast of Israel and their spiritual implications for your life today; you have missed out on the greatest revelation of truth concerning Gods plans for the ages that perhaps you have ever heard. When you read the final chapter of this book concerning those feast of God I do not believe you will ever see God in the same way. You will never see anything but his plans and their perfections.

BACK TO THE FUTURE

Before we can proceed to the plans for your future we must first go back. In showing you the beauty of God's plans for you we must all learn a valuable truth about someone that came along way before you did and until you understand why he was created then you can never understand why you were created. It is now time for you to finally and maybe for the firs time understand the true purpose of the creation of Satan. Believe me, until you get this dynamic revelation into your Spirit then nothing else in Gods plans will ever make sense to you. You cannot proceed in understanding His plan for the ages nor for yourself without understanding His plans for Satan or Lucifer. In previous chapters we learned about Satan's rebellion and how that Satan was given this earth before it was recreated and we learned how that Satan rebelled but what we have not learned is why he rebelled.

What you and I learned in Sunday School about Satan is not necessarily the truth. We were told that Satan basically got one up on God, he pulled a fast one and baffled God. Think about it! God created a good angel named Lucifer and God had great plans for Lucifer and then one day unbeknownst to God Lucifer rebelled and caught God by surprise basically. We've been taught that since that day that God and Lucifer have been in this age old conflict for the souls of men and that unfortunately Satan is winning that battle as well. Poor God. It looks like according to the modern churches thinking that Satan is always one step ahead of the great Yahweh.

Lucifer exposed

Was Lucifer created without God knowing exactly what he would do? Now, let us be minded of the facts and know that only God has this rather unique ability to see *the end from the beginning* and he alone is able to take all of the mess ups of man and cause all of those mess ups to work for his good. Just as certainly as he does that with man; he also saw all of Satan's future antics and although he would have preferred for Lucifer to remain among the faithful; he created Lucifer knowing full well what Lucifer would become and his plans were made accordingly. Know this well, God is not now nor ever has been in a legitimate war with Satan. Although he has allowed the appearance of war between the two, it is a hardly a war if the end result is already planned and known. However, for the sake of appearances then indeed there is a conflict between God and Lucifer. However, the conflict is pre-arranged it is in divine order and the conflict ended in the mind of God before it ever began. However, the religions of today actually teach that God created Lucifer perfect without any evil or chance of evil in him and that God was taken by absolute surprise at Lucifer's rebellion. Let us begin understanding the purposes of God in the earth

by concentrating on the following scripture;

Colossians 1:16-17
For by Him were ALL THINGS created, that are in heaven and that are on the earth, visible and invisible, whether they be thrones, or dominions, or principalities, or powers: ALL THINGS were created by him and for him and HE is before all things.

Once the Holy Spirit illuminates this scripture for you then you will never again for one second concentrate on the evil works of Satan or Lucifer; you will understand that ALL THINGS mentioned in this verse, *all things in heaven and earth*; that includes Satan himself. He was created by God and notice the words carefully FOR GOD! Everything in the spiritual realm and the earthly realm is under the direct control of the sovereignty of Almighty Yahweh. Perish the crude thoughts that somehow God made a mistake in creating Lucifer and that He has been trying to find a way to fix that mistake all of these years. Before this chapter ends you will never again for one second have any fear nor give any attention to the evil workings of Lucifer. Remember this truth and this principle as the above scripture so plainly states; Everything was created for the purposes of God! Why doesn't God get rid of Satan? Because, **Satan has a ministry to fulfill among the Sons of God on the earth and no one but him can fulfill that role**. God used Satan's own free will and placed the evil choices of Lucifer in his perfect will and uses those wrongs choices for his right purposes. Let's look at the origins or the beginnings of Satan. Was he really created without evil? Did he invent evil? Did he bring something into the earth that can escape the very control of God? If so, then he is also a creator and might actually find himself equal with

God, perish the thought!

Man and his churches teach us that Satan in his beginning was perfect and holy but that he later fell from that estate. However, Jesus gives us a different picture of Satan's beginnings;

John 8:44
Ye are of your father the devil, and the lust of your father ye will do. He was a murderer from the beginning and abode not in the truth because there is no truth in him. When he speaketh a lie he speaketh of his own for he is a liar and the father of it.

Not quite the way the church teaches it! We must begin by looking into the misty mornings and the fog enveloping evenings of yesteryears; before time or the ages began and understand those happenings before we can understand the plan of the ages. Satan was always a murderer, from his beginning! The reason he couldn't stay "*holy and perfect and in the truth*" is because the truth was never in him! That my friends is the words of Jesus Christ, not mine. Now let us look at the scriptural phrase "***abode not in the truth***." That phrase is the imperfect Greek tense of "ornkiw" and it means "*I keep my standing*". The *J.B. Phillips* translation of scripture presents the scripture in it's earliest meaning; "*He was always a murderer and has never dealt in truth, since the truth will have nothing to do with him. Whenever he tells a lie he speaks in character for he is a liar and the father of lies*".

In the grand drama of Gods plan for the ages, we each have a role, a part to play. This is a seven-act drama being played out over seven periods of time or seven thousand years. Adam and Eve had a part, Abraham had a part, Jesus had a part, you and I have a part and Satan has a part. To understand this we must go back even further into the mind and the dreams of God as he existed alone with only his thoughts before the creation.

ATTRIBUTES

The attributes of a person is basically the abilities or the potentials, the propensities and proclivities of a person. If you have the attributes of a doctor inside of your person then those internal and hidden qualities will never be manifested unless someone is sick. If you have the attributes of a teacher inside of you, that can only be revealed if someone needs to be taught. If you have the attributes of a great architect, those propensities will only be seen if someone needs a building. Without the need for your attributes from someone else then those attributes will remain unfulfilled and as a result you will always remain incomplete and the world will not benefit from the amazing abilities inside of you. In my mind is the attributes of a teacher and a writer. However, those attributes will benefit no one unless someone reads a book or someone ask me a question and desires to be taught. Until then those are wasted and unmanifested attributes.

So it is with the Eternal Yahweh *(Yahweh is the sacred Hebrew name of God)* inside of Him are invisible attributes as revealed in *Romans 1:20* when Paul tells us that "***the invisible things of Him from the creation of the world are clearly seen.***" Have you ever thought about that? The hidden attributes and qualities of God were hidden in his mind as dreams but now those hidden thoughts are revealed to us by his actions. Jesus was one of those thoughts in the mind of God. However, that thoughts or dream could not become visible or manifested until the fullness of time or at the time when it was needed.

Inside of God was the ability or the attributes to be a Healer, a Father, a Savior, a Deliverer, a Friend and a King. However, if there is no one to be a father to, if there is no one sick, if there is no one lost then those attributes would never be revealed. However, in his mind and in his plan he saw the creation of Lucifer and he saw Lucifer's future and he knew that Lucifer would be the one that would be instrumental in allowing the release of those hidden attributes that desired to come forth towards mankind. He saw that Lucifer would seduce Eve and that only when that happened would His ability to be a deliverer would shine forth and as Paul says *"be clearly seen."* He knew that from Lucifer's actions that mankind would suffer sickness and then he could heal those sicknesses for his own glory. Therefore, he created Lucifer with these thoughts in his mind. He also saw that his children would need to be developed, tried and tested before receiving their eternal life and he enveloped Satan's evil choices and planned to use Satan's evil for his own good purposes, for the trying of the Sons of God. Therefore when the first Son of God failed this trying and testing of Satan then the Holy Spirit led the second Adam to the same entity Satan to be tested and tried and proven; thus **the ministry of Satan in Gods master plan is clearly seen**. There is no true, legitimate war between God and Satan dear friend except a war that God is allowing for HIS PURPOSES and his purpose is to win that war once and for all and by doing so forever winning the love and allegiance of his creation. Oh the wonder of it!

There is however one attribute that cannot be found in the very nature of God, the attribute of evil. God is incapable of evil and yet God knew that if he would create a creature with free choice that eventually evil would find its way into his creation. Therefore, he in his sovereign will chose to control that evil through the entity called Satan. God will never create what he cannot control. He saw that Satan would choose evil and introduce it to mankind so he has devised a way to ensure that Satan remains under his control and as such evil is always under the direct control of God. Now, this is difficult for some people to comprehend when I preach this sermon because they just cannot fathom God being responsible for evil. They would rather give Satan the credit for creating evil. However, here is the real question. Who is responsible for the destruction caused by the atomic bomb in Hiroshima? The ones who launched the bomb or the one who created the bomb? How can you alleviate God from the creation of evil when he in fact did not have to create a being knowing that those beings would become evil. He could simply have chosen not to create such creatures and he could have kept evil from ever manifesting. However, he created an angel that was capable of becoming evil so therefore God is in himself the creator and the controller of evil. Why? Because it must be that way. Had evil created itself then evil could control itself and the end results of evil would be out of Gods predestined plan. It would actually take an evil God to allow evil to create and control itself. Who was essentially responsible for the devastation caused by Frankenstein? Was it Frankenstein himself or the scientist that created him knowing full well that such things could have happened? The question begs an answer.

We must not be afraid of the truth about God.

God reveals plainly in the scripture that he indeed created evil for a purpose and that even though man has chosen the way of evil, in the end God will use that evil, that very horrible evil to drive men into his open arms. When men have grown tired of the results of evil, when they have buried enough of their precious children, when they have watched enough loved ones die of sin and the result of evil, it is evil itself that shall be used to turn them to the goodness of the Lord and to genuine repentance.

In my own life I have experienced some very evil attacks from people who meant me harm They succeeded in their attacks and as a result I spent three years of my life in prison paying for the sins I had been involved with. At the time of my going to prison I was in a total pity party and wondering how God could allow these evil people to have such a victory party over my fall. However, it was that very evil, it was that very horrible event in my life that led to the writing of this book; that led to my repentance and my full turning towards the cross of Christ. Evil is always working together for good for those who truly love the Lord and for those whom he has called in this age.

Did God really create evil? Surely not! Let's look at the plethora of scriptural references that will vindicate this glorious truth. Always remember, **Satan is the least of your problems**; focus on the goodness of the Lord and the evils of Satan will grow strangely dim in the light of God's glorious face. Was there anyone anymore evil than Pharaoh? Was he not the equivalent of *Adolph Hilter* in his hatred of Israel? Was he not the epitome of evil and a cruel taskmaster towards Gods people? Was he not directly influenced by Satan as *Hitler* was? Of course he was;

DID GOD CREATE EVIL?

However, the Word of God makes a strange declaration about Pharaoh;

Romans 9:17
(Speaking of Pharaoh) Even for this same purpose have I not raised thee up, that I might show my power in thee and that my name might be declared throughout all the earth.

Did God not see the evil heart in Pharaoh before he was ever born? Did God not take advantage of that evil heart and use it for his glory? Did he himself not deliberately harden Pharaohs heart so that when he displayed his power it would be spread around the world how great our God is? Would the modern church not go crazy if the Prophet Amos walked into their church and preached this message *"**God created evil**"*? Imagine hearing your preacher preach a sermon entitled with those words. In modern so-called Christianity we are told that every good thing comes from God and all bad things come from the devil. Sadly they fail to realize that even though it comes from the Devil, Satan is powerless to send those bad things unless God has allowed it. In doubt? Ask Job, he might disagree with the modern church's wrong understanding of God. When we find the Angels of God presenting themselves to the Father in the Old Testament; who comes with them to report for duty? Why of course beloved, it is Satan himself before the throne of God waiting for permission to do his job. What is his job? He's the official *"Quality Inspection Agent"* of the spiritually conceived Sons of God on the earth. No product lever eaves an assembly line until it is has passed through the inspection of the *Quality Control agent.* You will never be approved for the Dream Team, for Gods government until Satan has inspected you, tried you, tested you, burned you, afflicted you and done his job as only he can.

Would you stay and listen to Amos preach the sermon entitled "God created evil"? Well, that's exactly the message he preached in his inspired book called the Book of Amos in the Old Testament. In his day there was great judgement coming among the children of Israel from the Lord; invading armies, drought, pestilence and famine. All of the other preachers were telling the people to begin rebuking the devil for all of this destruction, they were preaching the so-called truth about a good God and a bad devil. Then here comes that little Prophet with a true understanding of God. He understood that all the evil in that city had been allowed and sent by the Lord. Although the Lord didn't do the evil he sent it through the ministry of Satan.

Amos 3:6
. . .shall there be in evil in the city and the Lord has not done it?

Who sent the evil? God did. This is the very reason that Paul instructs us not to "**Lay hands on no man suddenly**." We must use the gift of discernment when we pray for someone's healing or blessings because if they have come under the judgements of God in their life, if they have come under the reaping for the seeds they have sown then you will be wasting everyone's time with your prayer *(we can always plead with God for mercy and perchance he will show mercy yet again)*. However, after you pray for them and nothing happens then they will all point a finger at your God and say *"He no longer heals"* or *"God is dead he is not in the healing business anymore."* However, if they have sin in their life, if they have put their hands against the holy things of God and

brought his judgement into their life they have no right to ask for healing nor do you have any right to petition God for their healing. Remember the words of Jesus *"healing is the children's bread"* What he was saying is that only those who are true children of God, walking in the laws of his kingdom and being transformed into the stature of Christ, healing belongs only to them.

DIVINE DISCIPLINE

There are times when God is dealing with you; maybe you've harbored bitterness in your heart against someone; maybe you've got unconfessed and continual sexual sins or other sins in your life; maybe you've robbed God of his tithe and his Sabbath and his laws; if so then you are walking under a closed heaven and he says that you worship him in vain. God blesses the commandment keepers; he owes the lawless Christian absolutely nothing. The Kingdom must be taken by violence and force, you must be in a continual war against your flesh to access the blessings of the Kingdom of God. God will send evil when evil is the only message that you can understand. I've stood at the sickbed of people that I knew had blatantly violated the laws of God, they had spoken horrible things about the servants of the Lord and now they seek God's healing power. People who may not be aware of the evil seeds sown in these peoples lives they will pray earnestly for hours and lay hands on this sick person and demand them to be healed. I sit back and my heart breaks at our ignorance of the ways of God. If bringing you to your knees is the only way to awaken you from your sinful lifestyle then God will send Satan to do exactly that and all of the prayers of every Christian in the world will not help you. Would you like scriptural proof of this? Paul mentioned "*The sin unto death*" and this has perplexed the church for centuries, what is the sin unto death? It is the sin that you have committed that God will not stop the consequences of. In his mercy he has allowed you to get by with your private sins for years and years; He has been longsuffering in his goodness; allowing his goodness to lead you to repentance. In all of those times when the consequences came he extended mercy when his people would pray for you He allowed their prayers to prevail for you as he was still working with you in his goodness. However, he tells us through His Apostle Paul that there will come a time when we are not supposed to pray for that man that God is dealing with in his judgement of correction. He tells us "*don't pray for that man*" he continues to say about this particular type of man who is living under divine discipline "*turn him over to Satan for the destruction or the death of his flesh that his soul might be saved*" You see, in my own life I have lived through this process of divine discipline; God extended so much mercy to me dear reader and I spurned that mercy for many years. Every time I would get in trouble he would deliver me and answer the prayers of his people for my deliverance. However, there came a day when he met me on my Damascus road and knocked me off of my horse and forbid anyone to pray for me or contact me or even care. Why? Because he was determined to allow Satan to destroy me to get me to the point of the death of me so that I could finally live! This is why I counsel parents against the temptation of bailing your children out of trouble that their seed sowing had brought unto them. Perhaps you are actually interrupting the very process designed by God to save their souls. This is why Christ instructs us to visit those in prison because it is in those prisons where God is actually

saving the souls of rebellious sons and daughters. It's a perfect place to plant the seeds of the Word into their lives and pray with them as God deals with their rebellion.

Would you like God's own Word to prove to you that he created evil? How can you argue with the plain Word? These are not my words, they come from a vindicated Prophets mouth by the name of Isaiah.

Isaiah 45:7
That they may know from the rising of the sun, and from the west, that there is none beside me. I am the Lord and there is none else. I form the light and create darkness: I make peace and create Evil. I the Lord do all these things.

Who created evil and destruction? Satan or God? In a futile attempt to explain away this clear and undeniable reality the modern preacher will say " *Surely, it can't mean that God creates evil or sin or sinners, devils or wrongdoing*" so in the unconverted minds they begin postulating prevarications, lies and vain imaginations so they say "*This must mean he creates calamities and storms and hurricanes and bad weather*" You see they are unable to fathom a God who is good and yet controls evil. But you see that's what makes God good because he in fact is the creator of and controller of evil rather than allowing anyone else to create it and control it. Allow me to prove to you that this word "*evil*" in this scripture doesn't mean *calamity* as some translations of the Bible has rendered this word *evil*. The original Hebrew word for evil in this verse is *"Ra"* which means wickedness, evil and sin. This exact same word is used over five hundred (500) times in the Old Testament to mean EVIL not calamities, not disasters but *evil*. For example;

Genesis 6:5
. . .and God saw that the thoughts of their heart were evil continually

For you own Bible study you can see the point proven with crystal clarity in *Numbers 32:13, Psalms 34:14-15* and over five hundred more references are available for your study. The point is that God created evil when he created Lucifer so that he could overcome it and destroy it when the story ends. Why does puny man try to relieve God of the responsibility of evil when God so willingly takes the responsibility in his own Word? Do you remember the young blind man mentioned in *John 9:2-3*? The question was asked why the evil of blindness had been allowed in this man. Jesus makes it clear that the evil was allowed for the glory of God. In the end of God would overcome the evil and he would receive all the glory, this is Gods purpose for evil and the creation thereof. The more evil the world gets the more wonderful the one-thousand year Sabbath day becomes, the more our hearts long for the good things of the Lord that are soon to come upon the earth.

————————————————

THE SERPENT

We should also note that the book of Revelation calls Satan, *that old serpent*! (REV 12:9) We know from this verse that Satan is represented by the symbolic and allegorical Genesis story of the serpent. Now notice carefully what God's Word reveals to us about the serpent.

Genesis 3:`1
Now the Serpent was more subtil than any beast of the field which the Lord God had made

Who made the serpent? God did! So, therefore who controls the serpent? God does! It is high time to lose our satanic focus and "*in all things just give thanks*" Satan is only working in your life because God has allowed him to do so, recognize that and quit rebuking the devil, just resist him by "*Submitting yourself to God*" and then the ministry of Satan will leave your life as he did Jesus on the Mt. of Temptation. There is only one way to get rid of Satan's working in your life, let him finish the job. As soon as he hears you giving praise in the midst of the furnace, as soon as he proves that you are who you say you are, as soon as he proves that you are indeed a bona fide spiritually conceived Son of God then his job will end for a season until your next level comes and he will flee from you for a little while. When you get ready to go to a new level in God you will meet new devils from God to determine that you are indeed worthy of the coming revelations and understanding of Kingdom mysteries. If you pass the test, if you decide as Jesus did to live by every Word of God rather than blaming God and rebuking the devil then those demons will leave you and a season of peace will enter into you life.

————————————————

THE DESTROYER

But why? Why did God create a serpent, an evil devil? Jesus said these words about Satan "*The thief cometh not but to kill, steal and destroy: I am come that you might have life and have life more abundantly.*" With those words in our minds we can now solve this eternal mystery in our mind and move on past all these why questions; With this revelation you will never be the same, in all thing you will see the wondrous plan of God coming to pass in your life. Now read carefully as the Word of God reveals the mystery of Satan and his ministry in the body of Christ. He has just identified Satan as a destroyer, now let's go the Old Testament for the icing on this cake;

Isaiah 54:16
. . I have created the waster to destroy

Could it be? Can God possibly be admitting here that he created the destroyer to do exactly that, destroy? Satan has been identified by Jesus as a destroyer and here God says he created Satan to destroy. Why? Because God cannot destroy, God is love and God is good and he is all things wonderful. Yet, there must be destruction, there must be consequences, there must be evil, there must be darkness if there's light. So, God created the very creature that would be what he could never be, evil! Now lets stare even deeper into the mystifying fog-filled windows of truths in this passage; let's read the verse in it's entirety now for even fuller meaning.

Isaiah 54:16
I have created the smith (Satan) that bloweth the coals in the fire and that bringeth forth an instrument for his work.

You will find here that Satan's creation was for the purpose of creating and making the furnace as hot as possible to bring forth an instrument of worth. If you will remember he did this very thing with three sons of Israel, *Shadrach, Meshach and Abednego.* Satan through the King heated the furnace seven times

hotter, the *Smith* was blowing upon the coals. Now watch closely as we reveal to you the ministry of Satan among the spiritually conceived Sons of God who are being converted in this lifetime.

I Peter 4:12
Beloved, think it not strange concerning the fiery trial which is to try you as some strange thing has happened unto you.

Peter is telling us that we should never think it strange when the *Smith* begins blowing in our lives and heating up the furnace. We should rejoice that we have been counted worthy to be tested. There are many in our world that God would never send Satan to try them. He sent Satan to Job to prove that Job was a righteous and perfect man. Each time he sends Satan to try you he has faith that the same will be proven in you at the end of the blowing of the coals of your life. Do you still not believe that Satan has a ministry in the lives of the spiritually conceived Sons of God?

Matt 4:1-3
Then was Jesus led up of the Spirit into the wilderness to be tempted (tested) of the Devil. And when the Tempter came to him, he said, If thou be the Son of God, command that these stones be made bread.

If thou be the Son of God! In other words Satan is saying: *"Look, my job here is to prove whether or not you are indeed a Son of God and I will know whether you are or not by your response to this test that I've been sent to give you. If at the end of this test you choose the Word of God over human reasoning then indeed it will be declared that you are of the same nature and charac-*

ter as your Father and my job will be done here and I'll go about my business"

Rev 2:10
Fear none of those things which thou shalt suffer: behold, Satan hath desired to have you, That he may test you, be thou faithful and I will give thee a crown of life.

When do you receive eternal life? Now or when you have overcome Satan's test and his ministry in this life, when you are declared to be a true converted Son of God? Satan desires to have you that he may test you and prove that you are not a Son of God. Every time he can prove that one of God's spiritually conceived children is in truth not walking in the Word, he's not truly being converted, then that person actually lends credence to Satan's argument that no one will truly obey God with a free will and therefore increasing the possibility of lessening his judgement that is soon coming from a righteous judge. This is why he desires to test you because by the millions he has tested them and they have proved his argument, they have been his evidence that man cannot obey God and therefore the angels should receive a lesser verdict of judgement. This is why God says of his children that one day we will judge angels; Our life, our ability to obey God in Satan's world will actually stand in judgement against him at the judgement, we will literally judge the fallen angels. Every time you love God when God seemingly doesn't love you, every time you obey a command that makes no sense to you mind you are in fact judging the angels.

THE NEED FOR OPPOSITES

No man can be trusted until he is exposed to his opposite. A man who lives in a home alone and is never exposed to a female can easily pass the test of sexual temptation. However, once he ventures into the flesh pool of females then all of a sudden what's inside of him will be brought to the fore by facing his opposite. No man can be declared strong until he has been tested for weakness. Neither can you be declared an overcomer until you've faced something created by God for you to come over and that something, that someone is Satan. No man can be a bona fide converted Son of God until he does just like the first and second Adam has done and faced the serpent in the wilderness of his life and come out victorious choosing the Word of God over human reasoning.

God is building a house, a spiritual house of Sons. Just as the *House of Windsor* is a living house, it's not a physical house of stones but a living and breathing house of flesh, so is the house of God. This house is being built of living stones, you and I. However, every stone needs a chisel and a hammer to shape it and to form it for use in the building. We must be hammered and chiseled and guess who was created to do that hammering? The Word will answer your question.

Isaiah 48:10
. . .I have chosen thee in the furnace of affliction.

The Smith, Satan himself is creating the crucible of our affliction, he is heating the fire with his evil and his mayhem. Could God stop him? Yes and he one day will but until that day he is using this evil power for his glory and for the perfecting of his sons. If you are a stone in this house of God you will be shaped in the furnace of affliction.

The boxer who is ever successful will be given a partner to spar with him, an opposite to test his strength. This partner will become a constant companion in his training in his preparation for the championships. All champions learn to respect their sparring partner even when it hurts. Satan is your sparring partner. Does he hate you? Yes! Why? Because you are about to take over his earthly throne and rule in his stead. However, he is a what's called a *"Vassal king."* Basically a vassal king has no true authority, only a throne and that throne is under the control of an empire that he answers to and that throne is vulnerable to a complete take over at anytime from the rightful conquering empire or kingdom. Anytime a foreign invader took over a land, they didn't always remove the king. They simply allowed the king to remain on his throne but he was under total control by the empire. His title was basically a joke because he was a king in name only and he was taxed heavily and allowed to remain on his throne as long as he stayed in line and in obedience. However, should he ever rise in rebellion and attempt to regain his authority he will be removed. Satan has been allowed to remain on earths throne as a *"Vassal King"* under complete control and for the glory of God. However, very soon he will enter the anti-Christ and attempt to circumvent the plan of his ruling sovereign, God himself, and when he does then the Lord Jesus will come and bind him and remove him from the throne that he has been preparing you and I to sit on. Oh the glorious end to this story is beyond the human minds capacity, only in the Spirit can you even began to glimpse into this glory.

AFTER THE AFFLICTION

Become like *David* dear friend and recognize the ministry of Satan, embrace it, submit to God and say these words along with the sweet singer of Israel;

Psalms 119:7
It is good for me that I have been afflicted, that I might learn thy statutes.

Thank God for the furnace, *the Smith*, the afflictions. The Prophets tell us that because of the afflictions of Satan upon the earth that the entire earth would seek after God so that he might heal their wounds.

Hosea 6:1
Come and let us return to the Lord: for he hath torn and he will heal us; he hath smitten and he will bind us up . . .after two days will he revive us; in the third day he will raise us up, and we shall live in his sight

Who afflicted Israel? Who smote them? It was God in control of the ministry of Satan that had smitten them. Please notice carefully what day they mention their revival, their resurrection! The Third Day! Please be aware that they were in the fourth day of God's timetable at that time. Prophetically Hosea proves for us yet again the truth of God's seven day time clock. We shall all be healed on the third day after this prophecy is given. For clarification, the third day after Hosea's prophecy is the seventh day of mans creation. *(For clarification please read the previous chapter under the heading 7,000 years)*

How do we stop this madness you ask? Why must there be all this evil in our lives? How do we cause God to refrain from allowing Satan to work evil and destruction in our lives? David in the above verse gives you the answer. The purpose of the affliction is to cause you to obey God's laws and his way of "give" rather than Satan's way of "get". David said that when he was afflicted, those afflictions caused him to obey God's laws. How I can identify with this truth. When I flew past Gods mercy and goodness at breakneck speed chasing after my dreams and money and fame and fortune and prideful endeavors; I ran headlong into the ministry of Satan. After he afflicted me, after I lost everything it caused me also to remember God's laws and today I am truly enjoying the GOD LIFE because of those afflictions. Thank God for Satan, thank God for *the Smith* who blows into our lives and proves that we are being changed! However, you can circumvent the continuos circle of life that so many of us find ourselves in; you want to stop the affliction? Obey! Remember that the laws of God plus the love of God equals the life of God. The abundant and blessed life only comes from the laws and the love of God. When both of those have been established in lives then you will see the divine chastisement leave your life. You will always have those little curve balls that life throws just as general interruptions. However, you will know the difference in the curve balls and the curses! So today take inventory of your life; study his commands are you diligently keeping them all? Jesus said "if you love me do what I've said." He didn't say just believe on me or in me but he said *"walk after me, follow me, do what I did"*.

Be warned it's much easier to write about it than it is to live it. The moment you make up your mind to obey the laws of God and Christ you will begin to notice even religious people looking at you funny as very few will understand your new calling. However, be faithful and determine that if God's Word says it, that settles it, just do it. Keep these principles in mind; if it's holy unto God, don't touch it, keep it holy. Remove your hands from his Tithe and you feet from his Sabbath. Where he has placed his presence he doesn't even want you to wear your shoes there just ask Moses. He has placed his presence in his Tithe, his Sabbath, His Body and Blood, his Baptism, his Ordinances, his Church and his Gospel which is the good news of his coming Kingdom.

The New Jerusalem

Chapter Thirteen

*And he carried me away in the Spirit to a great and high
mountain, and showed me that great city, the holy Jerusalem descending out of heaven from God*
REVELATION 21:10

Dual Dimensions

Heaven and the thoughts of that spiritual dimension that man has never seen has been the hope of millions of those who have professed their faith in Christ and rightly so. This book that I have been given a mandate to write is in no way removing the reality of heaven from the minds of believers nor is it intended to. **I believe in Heaven!** I believe in the beauty of Heaven! I believe that at this very moment the angels of God are enjoying that celestial dimension and I believe that it is more wonderful than the mind can conceive. However, I believe that it is coming to earth rather than us going to Heaven. Can I prove this? Absolutely. The scriptures never speak of nor focus on a place called Heaven as the goal and the destiny of mankind. Man was never created to have dominion over Heaven. The angels belong In heaven, man belongs on the earth and you will always be a man even when your born again and given your spiritual body; the only difference is you will be just like Christ. After Christ resurrection Peter still declares "***that man Jesus whom you have crucified***" Although Jesus will always be a man in form and structure we will no longer be flesh and blood men but rather men with totally spiritual compositions. With that said allow me to speak about the dimension of Heaven. **Is Heaven a place?** Is Heaven a planet? Is Heaven a physical location or is it actually a dimension? I will argue in this book that Heaven is not a place but rather a dimension. If you don't get a correct understanding of your future and eternal destiny in the work of God then you will not have a true vision of the purpose of your earthly life.

Can you hear *Elvis Presley* singing "*Blue Suede Shoes*" right now? Well, he is! Actually, all of his songs are playing all around you right now,;in another dimension. Radio waves, television waves and internet signals; all of these unseen dimensions are just as real as the visible dimension. However, you cannot hear Elvis on the dimension that you are designed to live in. He is actually singing at a much higher frequency than you ears are tuned for. So, if you want to "bring down" or "manifest" his voice out of that higher dimension then you must have a transmitter that will actually translate the higher sound, the higher dimension and bring it to your dimension or your comprehension and understanding. This transmitter is called a radio, a television or a computer; all of those are what we refer to as mediums or vehicles of translation from one dimension to another. The same truth applies to light. Light in it's purest form is absolutely invisible. Your body is not made of matter it is actually made of light. For light to be manifested to the naked eye it must be transposed down to a lower light source such as the sun. This is the exact reason why that God created the light in the creation account four days before he created the Sun. Go read your Bible, that truth will stare at you like a blazing medallion in winter cold. Light was created before the Sun because light doesn't need a source, it is the source of all things. This is why the scriptures tell us that God is light! The next time you visit your doctor for an X-ray, simply ask the technician to explain "invisible light" to you. The light of X-ray is brighter than you can comprehend and yet it's invisible. For the invisible to become visible it needs a transmitter, a vehicle or a physical contact.

God is Spirit; Satan is Spirit; Angels are Spirit;

Demons are Spirit; and they all live in the exact same location as you do but in another dimension. Radio and Television waves are sharing the same air you breath but on a total different level of comprehension. God is not on a far off planet called Heaven but rather he is in another realm of existence; outside of time just as radio waves are outside of time. A voice never dies; when you speak a word, that word lives forever in other dimensions. I am told that scientist have proven that if you had the correct device that you could listen to conversations from thousands of years ago as those voices live perpetually in eternity as endless flowing waves of sound.

THEOPHONIES

This is exactly how God has operated since the dawn of time. He uses a vehicle or a transmitter to "*come down*" to our level. That vehicle or transmitter is called a "*theophany*" or rather a "*temporary, non flesh-n-blood body.*" This is how God was able to appear to Abraham at his tent door or to Moses in a burning bush or to Jacob as an angel .He in fact uses these vehicles to appear to our eyes. This is why many people become confused about the scriptures that says "***No man has ever seen God***" and yet we have many scripture that tells us that "*God appeared*" to certain people. You must understand the truths I've just taught you to understand that there is absolutely no conflict in these seemingly contradictory scriptures. No man has ever seen the Spiritual composition of God or for lack of a better phrase, the Spirit God! No man has ever seen the Eternal Yahweh in his essence of Spirit, in his true composition. However, many men have seen God in his

transmitters or vehicles of "*temporary appearances*" this is the very reason that Jesus is called "***the express image of his person***" this is why Jesus could say "***When you have seen me you have seen the father***" because until you become spirits in the resurrection it will be absolutely impossible to ever see God in his spiritual composition; so you must now see him in his physical composition or manifestation which Jesus so perfectly was.

Is God a burning bush? No, but God can be seen in a burning bush. Is God a rock? No, but he was seen in a rock in the wilderness. Is God a pillar of fire or a cloud? No, but he was in all of those things. Is God an angel? No but God can be seen in an angel. Is God a man? No but God can be seen in a man such as Christ and his present day spiritually conceived sons if he so chooses to manifest in that theophany or temporary body or entity whatever form it might take.

WHY EVEN CREATE AN EARTH?

If God has a better place than the earth; then why did he even create the earth? We are told that when he created this planet that the angels of God rejoiced at the wonder of it. Now, if they indeed live in a place called Heaven and that place is so much superior to this planet and we are all wanting to escape this planet and go live over there in the supposedly better place; then what would they, the angels have been rejoicing over? Wouldn't they rather have been disappointed in such a place with less glory than the one they supposedly occupied? **The creation**

of Earth was simply the visible manifestation of the spiritual dimensions of God, called Heaven. Earth was the tangible place where the spiritual place became visible. I will dare say that God is more interested in the earth than he is in a distant planet called Heaven. He is more interested in the galaxies of the universe than he is in a mystical place called Heaven. Heaven is his throne room, Heaven is his atmosphere or his dimension of existence. The earth is his footstool, the place where reveals his thoughts. **His thoughts are in the Heavens, his actions are in the earth.** The throne room is where minds meet and decisions are made and plans are erected. However, the plans of the throne room must have feet, they must have expression and those expressions are revealed in the populace of the kings kingdom. Heaven is the spiritual dimension of God, Satan, the Angels, the Demons and this is why Satan still has access to the Heavens until he is finally judged and bound because the Heavens is simply the dimension that he must exist in. However, in the book of Revelation at the last trumpet he will be cast down from this lofty dimensions and by some supernatural act of God he will in fact be reduced to an existence of torment and that torment will be in his inability to have access to the heavenly dimensions.

Why has the Christian church been so focused on *"leaving this world"* and saying *"Goodbye world goodbye"* when this earth is our gift from God to us. Jesus said that you and I are destined to *"**inherit the earth**"* no mention of Heaven is ever made from Christ concerning our eternal destination. Have no fear, I will prove all of this with the scriptures in this chapter. However, before you become convinced that I am teaching that there is no Heaven, your wrong!

> ## His thoughts are in the Heavens; His actions are in the earth

It's not the idea of heaven that we have wrong, it's the location of heaven that we have misunderstood. You are not going anywhere! You are not *"flying away"* you are not going to say goodbye to this beautiful planet Earth, you are in fact going to rule this earth and possibly the entire universe of planets for the glory of God. This is the very reason why Jesus said that he would *"**judge those who have destroyed the earth**"* because the earth is the ultimate of his creative exploits. How could you ever find a place more beautiful than our home? Have you driven through her fields of golden grain lately while the evening sun kisses her hair? Have you sit atop the Smoky mountains in the sloping foothills of North Carolina and watched the beautiful and tantalizing displays of nature? Have you basked in the sights of the Alaskan northern lights with its alluring call on a blackened night? Have you walked the winding country lanes on a Mississippi back road with the unorganized sprays of wildflowers and weeping willows dotting the path? Have you planted your feet into the cool, cascading waters of a spring fed stream lately? Maybe you should because you live on the most wonderful of all of God's creations. Granted, man has destroyed much of her beauty, her streams, her oceans and her air and this is the very reason that Paul says that she is ***groaning and waiting to be delivered*** from this curse placed on her by mans sin. If the earth is to be destroyed and we're all going to be shipped away to Heaven on the galactic railway then why is God going to remove her curse, just leave her cursed if she's going to be destroyed and were all leaving? Because, she shall never be destroyed. Doesn't the scriptures say that *"**The heavens and earth shall pass away?**"* Yes, However, once I show you the original wording of those verses later in this chapter you will understand that it is another infamous KJV mistranslation; the earth is never going anywhere! Scriptures tell us that "**God establshed the earth forever.**" Now, once you receive your new, spiritual bodies you will be able to operate in the heavenly dimension but you will be on the earth or somewhere in Gods physical universe. You will be able to manifest in a fleshly body if you need to just as Jesus did when he ate with his disciples in his post resurrection. It is not Gods intention for man to be ruling and reigning in the spiritual dimension called Heaven; he and the angels have that part covered.

Remember when Jesus said that "**no man has ascended into heaven except the Son of Man who is in heaven**"?

That scripture has baffled the minds of the church for years. Jesus was on the earth and yet he says that he was In Heaven at the same time he was on the earth? If Heaven is a location rather than a spiritual condition or dimension then he was speaking as a mad man. What he was saying was that no man has ever ascended into the realms of the Spirit except Jesus because even though he was on the earth he was also in the Spirit at the same time. He had completely destroyed his flesh in obedience to God and as a result he was already in the spirit or the heavenlies. Going into the heavenlies is definitely an ascending process but not with wings; rather with will! A will to obey God, an uplifted will caused by uplifted eyes; not to a higher place but to a higher position and a higher understanding and a higher calling. If I tell you that "*you need to quit standing on top of*

me" does that mean you are literally on top of me? No, it means that your mind-set is above mine and you have risen to a higher place than me and you are using that to your advantage. We can all rise or ascend into the heavens even while on earth. Even Satan in his rebellion against God in the pre-genesis account understood that reaching the dimensions of God would require an ascendency as he ascended and tried to reach the secret to Gods authority and power, the throne. The throne is a symbol, please remember that. When we say that the Queen of England is reigning on her throne; truthfully she does not sit on a throne at all times. Her throne is her unseen power to rule. That unseen and unexplained essence of power and authority is represented by a symbol of a throne, a crown and a scepter. You

IT'S NOT THE IDEA OF HEAVEN THAT WE HAVE WRONG, IT'S THE LOCATION OF HEAVEN THAT WE HAVE MISUNDERSTOOD.

and I ascend into that very dimension of the throne room when we become loyal subjects of the throne in our prayer life, in our mediation of the scriptures, in our good works, in our genuine and living faith. Jesus taught us how to be on earth and in heaven at the same time. Heaven is a mentality, its a mind set, it's a spiritual experience even while living in a physical world. One day when you have won the crown your body will line up with your thoughts and with your mind and they will both become one substance, spirit!

I can hear the thoughts of many right now as they begin thinking of all the scriptures that supposedly teach about a place called Heaven where we are all going to be taken to. Doesn't the scriptures teach *"In my Fathers house are many mansion and I go away to prepare a place for you"*? Doesn't John describe a far off city with streets of Gold and gates of pearl? A short answer for both questions is NO! This chapter will leave you with clarity of thought on both of those scriptural references shortly. I was listening one night to a world wide television evangelist who is known around the world for his funny antics behind the pulpit. I truly love this dear brother and enjoy his sermons at times. However, he said something that stirred up my spiritual mind. He was speaking of the so-called rapture and the catching away of the saints into heaven and he said these words *"Jesus told me that he's just taking us to heaven for a supper and then he's bringing us all back"* and I thought, really? So, if he's bringing us all back then why take us in the first place? The truth is ladies and gentleman; he's not taking you anywhere; he's bringing all of his rewards with him and those rewards are soon coming to a planet near you, a planet called earth; *"Blessed are the meek for they shall inherit the earth."* If you have been able to hang on this long and if you have read this far, may I invite you to read the next chapter where I will show you in the scriptures exactly what this coming Heaven on earth will look like, oh the wonder of it! Before we began studying about this city called the *New Jerusalem* as mentioned in the book of Revelation and which has always been taught to be a description of the physical planet of Heaven; we must first dissect some of the words of Christ which has additionally been used to preached voluminous sermons about a distant place called Heaven that we are all escaping to. These words can be found in the book of St. John

in chapter fourteen (14). From these verses many songs have been written and much poetry and prose has been scribed about those mansions in heaven. How our hearts have all longed for one of those mansions of our own where can all retire for eternity, sit back relax and listen to the songbirds of heaven singing from our front porches. The fantasy as you will soon discover in the next chapter is really not as wonderful as the actual reality. However before we can discover just how wonderful tomorrows world is going to be from the scriptures we must first find out what Jesus was talking about when speaking of those mansions.

THE ORIGINAL SCRIPTURES HAD NO CHAPTERS AND VERSES, IT WAS ONE CONTINUOUS SCROLL WITHOUT DIVISIONS.

THOSE MANSIONS OF MYSTERY

Did Jesus truly say that in his *"fathers house were many mansions"*? No, he did not! Thankfully the majority of modern translations of the Bible has recognized this grievous errors by the KJV translators and have corrected this verse to it's original intent and wording. Much damage has been done to our thinking about Heaven because of this mistranslated verse and completely misinterpreted chapter. St. John chapter fourteen (14) as you will soon discover has absolutely nothing to do with the subject of Heaven. With proper exegesis of scripture, context and spiritual revelation you will see a wonderful truth that has nothing to do with a future home in the sky. Let's begin;

St. John 14:2
In my Father's house are many mansions: if it were not so I would have told you. I go to prepare

a place for you. I will come again and receive you unto myself that where I am there you may be also.

Again as always we must find the context of this teaching. Always remember that the original scriptures had no chapters and verses, it was one continuous scroll without divisions. Many time the divisions of verses and chapters causes us to not read the entire settings and that's how we come up with wrong understanding. So, let's go back one chapter and see exactly what is taking place in this story. In the preceding chapter Jesus is basically giving his farewell sermon to some very sad disciples. The setting is gloomy, mournful, confusing and they are pretty much without hope. Jesus came and turned their worlds upside down; he was supposed to set up an earthly kingdom and they were gonna be mighty rulers with him and now all their hopes are dashed as he is talking about dying and leaving them. Simon Peter ask Jesus *"Where are you going, we want to follow you to that place."* With that question Jesus is now going to explain to them the baptism of the Holy Spirit and the purpose for that baptism that they shall soon receive after His resurrection. This sermon he is giving here has nothing to do with Heaven; it has to do with the *Apostolic Church of God* and that church becoming the House of God and in all actuality the very dwelling place of God. Remember this; up until this point Jesus Christ was the only member of God's house or family; he was the only one that God himself dwelled in fully. Jesus Christ was the firstfruit, the fist begotten son but not the ONLY son; he was the only begotten son at that point in time. However, Jesus is about to teach them about a future point in time when he will return to them and they shall be conceived with the same seed that he had in him and they too shall become the dwelling place, the house or the family of God,

spiritually conceived sons, yet unborn.

Jesus tells Simon Peter in chapter thirteen (13) and verse thirty-six (36); *Where I am going, you cannot go the moment I go, you cannot go with me. I must be the sheaf of the firstfruit, I must go first as the sin offering and when I am accepted of my Father then I will come back to you at Pentecost and I will be in you (receive you unto me) and you shall be in me and together we shall be in the same place, in heavenly places together until such a time that you are changed and can join me there in your bodies.* Now let's read Jesus words again and see exactly what he was saying.

IN MY FATHERS HOUSE; vs2

Have you ever heard of the *House of Windsor* or the *House of Tudor* or the *House of Kennedy*? These are living houses, not houses of stone and clay. The word "House" is the synonym of family. So, Jesus was actually saying "**in the family of God, the family of my Father**"

THERE ARE MANY MANSIONS; vs2

The word "**mansion**" was never uttered by Jesus, this is a gross mistranslation of the scriptures. In the original Greek language you will find the word used by Jesus was the word "**dwelling**" not the word "**mansion**". Jesus said in his original language *"In the family of God or the God Family there are many places for him to dwell or inhabit or live"*

I GO TO PREPARE A PLACE FOR YOU; vs3

Jesus was the pioneer, the first to go to the Father and there was a purpose for his going; to reconcile man to God and in doing so allow God to once again dwell with his creation through the ministry of the Holy Spirit or the Spirit of Christ. Jesus had to go first and be accepted as the firstfruit sin offering and then he could return in the upper room and become one with the Apostles and receive them unto himself. His entire purpose in life was to open the doors to Gods eternal life to men.

WHERE I AM THERE YOU MAY BE ALSO
vs3

Where is Jesus? Sitting in heavenly places, in the bosom of his Father. Are you not now in that same exact place with Christ? So because he went to the Father you now have access to the Father and of a truth, where he is , there you are also!

WHERE I GO YOU KNOW AND THE WAY YOU KNOW
vs4

Jesus is not telling them about a location he's telling them about God, the great Spirit God, Yahweh. He's telling them that he is going to or returning to God and that the way to get to God is by faith and obedience, that's the way. He wasn't telling them "the way" as in giving directions; turn left and go straight. No he was telling them; "*I AM the way*!" Believe upon me, do what I did, imitate me and live my life and in doing so that is THE WAY to return to God. "*I lived that life*" he said, "*I obeyed his commands now you can forsake your sins, your transgressions of his laws and do the exact same thing, that's THE WAY to where I am going. I am going into the favor of the Father and because I have done this you can also; and my Father will come and make his dwelling in you just as he did in me. There are many people or dwelling places in his family and you can now be one of them.*"

THOMAS SAID; HOW CAN WE KNOW THE WAY AND JESUS SAID UNTO HIM; I AM THE WAY, THE TRUTH AND THE LIFE; NO MAN CAN COME UNTO ME BUT BY ME

vs 5-6

Please note very carefully how the tone of this chapter is all about coming into fellowship with the Father, there is not one mention of a place called Heaven in this chapter. What we have here is Jesus bringing us into the family of God and conceived children who shall soon follow him into the same position as Sons of God.

HAVE I BEEN SO LONG WITH YOU AND YET HAST THOU NOT KNOW ME . . .HE THAT HATH SEEN ME HAS SEEN THE FATHER
vs9

Jesus is continuing to teach them about connecting with his Father and finding their place in that family of God or in the God family. Here again he is stating that currently he was the only dwelling place of God in the family of God. However, soon he says that there will be many dwelling places (not mansions) but dwelling places. The Apostles would soon be the dwelling place of God, so would the *Apostolic Church of God* and all the members thereof.

BELIEVEST THOU NOT THAT I AM IN THE FATHER AND THE FATHER IS IN ME
vs10

Are you beginning to see dear reader? Jesus is again speaking in this verse about dwelling places, habitations for God to dwell in. Jesus is saying plainly and clearly so there can no argument about it; at that point in time the Father dwelt in him alone. He was the first MANSION in the Fathers family, the first clean house for God to dwell in. However, in those whom God is calling he shall also take his abode and make his dwelling place in many people or many mansions!

THE FATHER THAT DWELLETH IN ME HE

DOES THE WORKS
vs10

Again, Jesus was declaring that he alone was the dwelling place of God, the Father dwelled in him. However, because of his life and sacrifice the dream of God would soon come to pass at Pentecost, God would have many dwelling places and many new members on His *Dream Team.*

HE THAT BELIEVETH ON ME, THE WORKS THAT I DO SHALL HE DO ALSO; AND GREATER THAN THESE SHALL HE DO BECAUSE I GO TO MY FATHER
vs12

Jesus shows us the purpose of his leaving the earth. While he was here, he did wonderful works. However, those works were limited to the time and the space that he as one man could cover. However, very soon God's Dream Team would be enlarges, the Father House would have many mansions or dwelling places over all the earth and the works that Jesus did would be multiplied by the millions as those called in the church age would soon be doing the good works of Christ, keeping Gods laws, loving people, helping the hurting, healing the sick and declaring the good news of the Coming Kingdom of God. It should be noted here that when Jesus said "greater works than these shall ye do" the word WORKS was not in the original, it was added. The truth is that no one can do any greater works than Jesus did. He simply meant that his works would be done on a greater scale, a larger scale with a family of God doing those works rather than just one son doing them in one location.

IF YOU LOVE ME KEEP MY COMMANDMENTS

Now, the works that he was speaking of is clearly given to us in this verse. Unfortunately as a Pentecostal all of my life we used this scripture as evidence that we would be doing the same miracles and have the same power that he had. However, what he means by "*greater works than these shall ye do*" was the works of keeping God's commandments. How people long to have the power of God without keeping the works of God. Jesus is telling his disciples which works to keep; My Commandments.

AND I WILL PRAY THE FATHER AND HE WILL SEND YOU ANOTHER COMFORTER THAT HE MAY ABIDE WITH YOU FOREVER;
vs16

By now your eyes should be clearly open to the meaning of this chapter; the announcing of the Holy Spirit not a place called Heaven. Jesus says to them; if you will do my works and keep my commandments then God will fill you with the Holy Spirit, he will conceive in you a seed and in that seed is the potential for eternal life. He will come and dwell wit, you will be one of his mansions.

FOR THE SPIRIT OF TRUTH HE DWELLETH WITH YOU AND SHALL SOON BE IN YOU;
vs17

Anyone who doesn't understand that the Spirit of Christ is the Holy Spirit evidently has never read this verse. Jesus said that at that moment the Holy Spirit was walking WITH THEM but would soon be IN THEM.

Again, this entire sermon is about the coming of the Holy Spirit not about a place called Heaven.

I WILL NOT LEAVE YOU COMFORTLESS I WILL COME TO YOU
vs18

Who is coming to the disciples? Jesus is! He is coming in his spiritual form. If you think that the Holy Spirit is a third person of a Godhead rather than Jesus Christ himself then you should study the subject for a clearer understanding of the scriptures.

AT THAT DAY YOU SHALL KNOW THAT I AM IN MY FATHER AND YOU ARE IN ME AND I IN YOU
vs20

Who shall be in you? Another person beside Christ, a third person? Absolutely not but Christ himself shall be in you. The Spirit of Christ is the Holy Spirit. The Holy Spirit dwelled in Christ and we know from the scriptures that God was In Christ, so at the end of the day the Holy Spirit is the Spirit of God that was in Christ and now lives in you and because of this Spirit you are now one of the many mansions or dwelling places in the family of God or the God family.

HE THAT KEEPETH THE COMMANDMENTS, ONLY THAT PERSON LOVES ME AND THAT PERSON SHALL BE LOVED OF MY FATHER AND I WILL LOVE HIM AND REVEAL MY-SELF TO HIM
vs 21

How Jesus loves the commandment keepers and he promises to reveal who he is unto them by the infilling of the Holy Spirit.

IF A MAN LOVES ME HE WILL KEEP MY COMMANDMENTS AND MY FATHER WILL LOVE HIM AND WE WILL COME TO HIM AND MAKE OUR DWELLING WITH HIM

As we close this expose of John chapter 14; do you see once again the word dwelling in this scripture?

Jesus closes this sermon with the same thought about the coming of the Spirit to dwell in many mansions or many people in his family on earth.

I hope that by now it has been made abundantly clear to you that Jesus never one time preached about mansions in Heaven. He never promised to bring us to Heaven. You should be so thankful that God is revealing these truths to you. I realize that I could present a million scriptural proofs and it will never be enough to convince the one who prefers tradition over instead of truth.

What about those streets of God? What about the gates of pearl? Doesn't the Bible teach about the place called Heaven that we are flying away to? Actually it does not. However before we get to the next chapter where I can explain to you the beauty of God's real Heaven on earth let me first explain to you the meanings of the picture of Heaven that we have always held in our minds. Let us turn now to the book of Revelation and study on the New Jerusalem; I believe that your eyes will soon open and you will be blessed beyond measure by this wonderful truth; it's much greater than the traditional man-made fantasy.

The New Jerusalem

Rev 21:2
And I John saw the holy city, New Jerusalem coming down from God out of heaven prepared as a bride adorned for her husband.

Do you believe that this chapter where this city of Jerusalem is being described is in fact the literal planet of Heaven? If you do, don't feel bad; I felt the same way for nearly forty years of my life. I loved to preach about those golden streets and gates of pearl, oh how it endeared the heart and made glad the soul. However, I soon realized that all upcoming vacations to places like Maui, Disney World, the Smoky Mountains and various other places did the exact same thing; they provided emotional responses from the carnal mind. The same is true about our understanding of Heaven. The truth is this chapter is not describing a literal city! It is describing a people! Before I explain that you from the scriptures why don't you read this chapter very closely and you will see even in verse two (2) that this New Jerusalem is coming down to the earth! There is no one going up to New Jerusalem, it is in fact headed towards the earth. Why? Because all of Gods plans for man are centered upon the earth, why is that so foreign to our minds? Also before we proceed please note the context that this entire chapter begins with "The Bride of Christ." Beginning even in verse two we are being given hints as to this upcoming revelation of truth.

Never forget that this book of Revelation was never written for the world, it was written for and to The Overcomers, the Bride of Christ, the bondservants of Jesus Christ. Therefore it is written in symbols and coded in idealisms and metaphors. Without a spiritual mind to "***hear what the Spirit is actually saying to the Church***" you will make the same mistake of the carnal mind and read these pages as a carnal person reads a novel, at face value. However, these symbols in the Book of Revelation interpret themselves and need no private interpretation. Every symbol, their meanings are given to those who will simply take the time to find them. If we can read this book at face value then there would be no need

to *"hear what the Spirit is saying."* There is a message beyond the message, there is a meaning beyond the meaning and it is your job to find it. For example; When John sees *"A lamb standing on Mt. Zion"* the carnal mind accepts that and keeps reading. However, the spiritual mind sees the Lord Jesus Christ, not a four legged lamb also we don't see a literal mountain; why? Because we know from the Word that mountains are always symbols for kingdoms and governments. Therefore, this lamb standing on the mountain is our King, the Lord Jesus Christ standing amidst the 144,000 other lambs, His government His Dream Team, His ruling and royal family that follows him wherever he goes; the ones who have kept his testimony and his commandments.

Rev 21:3

Behold the tabernacle of God is with men; and he will dwell with them; and they shall be his people and God himself shall be with them and be their God.

Where is the dwelling place of God going to be when this age ends? With men! Where do men live? On the earth. He will be their God on earth, not in Heaven! Is that not as plain as the nose on your face? God shall come to man; man is not going to God.

Rev 21: 4

...and God shall wipe away all tears and there shall be no more death, neither sorrow nor crying, there shall be no more pain for the former things have passed away . . .He that sat upon the throne Behold I make all things new. . . It is done!

Did you notice that set of scriptures? When God comes to earth what does he do when he dwells with men? He sets everything right that was wrong under Satan's government. He wipes away tears, pain, death, sorrow, hunger and fills the earth with righteousness. He actually makes all things new! New, just like it was in the garden of Eden. Also of special importance is verse six (6) where he declares "*it is done.*" What does that mean? That means that the seven (7) days have ended! The weeks is over and now time is no more! The time table of God is over and eternity has begun. The work and the plan of the ages has ended exactly as God said it would. Satan is defeated and Jesus is Lord over all the earth. This is the very reason why so few people understand my meaning of speaking against *"the finished work of the cross"* message; I do that because the work was not finished at the cross! It is finished at the end of the seventh day at the end of the Lords Day. What was finished at the cross you ask? The suffering was over but the work still had two more days to go. However in this verse that we just read the entire week has ended, it is done!

Rev 21: 6b
I will give unto him that is athirst of the fountain of water of life freely.

Now we have stumbled upon a great and mysterious scripture that I will not be able to deal with until the last chapter of this book. However, suffice it to say that God is not through giving salvation when this church age has ended! If He is then how is He going to do it after "*It is done*" and the end has come? The only thing left to take place when He comes to earth after the millennium is the "Great White Throne" judgement where all the dead shall be raised . . .is it possible that at that point all of those who never had a chance at salvation will receive the chance then? According to the above verse, that's a fact. I will explain that entire process in the

last chapter of my book entitled "The Feast of Israel" a most compelling chapter where the entire plan of the ages will be revealed as crystal before your eyes.

Rev 21:7
He that overcometh shall inherit everything.

The context is again made clear this verse. This whole chapter is to and about the overcoming Bride of Christ who has overcome in this mortal lifetime and counted worthy to rule and reign with Christ. What are the overcomers to inherit? Simply remember the words of Christ to find out "*Blessed are the meek for they shall inherit the earth*" Who are the meek? The Overcoming Bride, and what is she going to inherit? Why beloved, it's the Earth, not Heaven! However, it's safe to say that you will inherit a heavenly existence if you realize that heaven is simply a re-created earth! So as we begin diving into the depths of this chapter, keep in mind who this chapter is about; these Overcomers, the collective Bride!

Now, if you'll pardon a non-sequitar I'm going to skip ahead a few verses to make a point and then I'll come back to the order of sequence.

Rev 21:10
And he carried me away in the spirit to a great and high mountain and shewed me that great city, the holy Jerusalem descending out of heaven from God.

In every debate that I have been invited to about this subject, all of the opponents go straight to this verse to prove that Heaven is a literal city or planet. They go on to read all the following verses that describes the beauty of this literal planet. Although I will never understand why they don't point out that if this is a literal city; it is still coming down from Heaven to the earth. However, I will digress and get back to the point at hand. So, do you believe that this is a literal city? Let's find out by using that amazing Bible study principle of; Context! Surely you must agree that up until this verse we have been reading about a people, a group of overcomers that God is now dwelling in. So, is it probable that John is going to completely change the subject in midstream? Actually John makes it abundantly clear what these symbols he's about to see in a spiritual vision actually represents. He will tell you in his own words who this New Jerusalem is, this great city; he does that in verse nine (9) the verse immediately preceding this current verse that we are studying, verse ten (10)

Rev 21: 9
. . .Come up higher and I will shew you THE BRIDE, the Lamb's wife.

Could anything be any clearer and explained in more detail than this? Does John leave any doubt in anyone's mind what these symbols are indicative of? He says plainly that he has been talking about the Bride in previous verses and now he's going to describe to you the allegorical symbols of the Bride herself. What did Jesus say he would do with his church? He said he would "build" his church. He was a carpenter and understand architect and indeed this is exactly what he has done in this vision, He has built His church and that building is glorious beyond compare. John plainly states that the Angel of the Lord said to him *"Let me show you the Church of Jesus Christ"* that great city, the building of God that he built through the seven (7) days of time; beginning with the Prophets and ending it with the Apostles.

Does the scriptures identify this great city that John saw? It does and it does so perfectly!

Hebrews 12:22 & 23
But ye are come unto Mt Zion and unto THE CITY of the living God, the heavenly Jerusalem and to an innumerable company of angels. . .to the general assembly and the church of the firstborn, which are written in heaven and to God the judge of all and to the spirits of just men made perfect.

Wow would be a proper word right now! What city did John say he saw? The New Jerusalem or in other words as Paul wrote, the Spiritual Jerusalem. We already have the natural Jerusalem but we also have the spiritual or new Jerusalem. Who is considered that great city? The Church of God, she is Mt. Zion, she is New Jerusalem, she is The New Temple, the New City, the New Name, the New Stones and John is seeing the beauty of Gods building in symbology. The meaning of each of those symbols shall soon be abundantly clear to your converted mind. Would you like more scriptural proof that New Jerusalem is the Church of God?

Galatians 4:24-26
Which things are an allegory! (for those who dont believe in allegorical interpretation, even the apostles understood the allegories of scripture) Which things are an allegory (a word picture) for these are the two covenants, the one from Mt. Sanai . . .For this Hagar is Mt. Sanai which answereth to Jerusalem which now is . . .Jerusalem which is above is free, which is the mother of us all

Did the writer just tell us that spiritual or new Jerusalem . . . now is? Beloved if you are an overcomer and if your being converted in this life then you are a proud member of that New Jerusalem church which now is. It doesn't say "shall be" but rather the New Jerusalem is in the spiritual realms right now and we are working on the earth or coming "down from the spiritual" as we work in our mortal bodies on this earth for the purposes of God. So when John sees the Church coming down from heaven to the earth what is he seeing? He is seeing a people who have been tried in the fire and they live in the spirit and they "*come down from those heavenly places*" to work among and serve humanity. Just as Jesus came down from heaven and worked among men. Just as Jesus was in heaven even while he was on earth, so are you and I in the spirit at all times while coming down and working the works of Christ on earth. Oh the riches of his wisdom!

Rev 21:11
Having the glory of God and her light was like unto a stone most precious, even like a jasper stone, clear as crystal.

It wouldn't hurt to notice his referencing this supposed literal city with the pronoun of "her." If this is a neutral and natural city shouldn't the pronoun be "it." However, this truly is a "she" it's the Bride of Christ, the *Apostolic Church of God.* Notice she has the glory of God. This again proves that this is the bride and not a city. We find scriptural references in Romans 8:18 about the "***glory that shall be revealed in us***" after we have endured the ministry of Satan, been tried in the fire and been found worthy of the government of God. This bride that John saw was filled with the glory that was promised unto her. I Corinthians 11:7 also shows us more context; Here the woman is mentioned as being the *"glory of the man"*. Paul is teaching about the womans need to

walk in submission to her husband and thus the reason why she shouldn't have short hair because it's a symbol of that submission. He goes on to teach that in that submission she is literally giving glory or honour to her husband in that physical symbol and in giving glory to her husband she is automatically giving glory to his head which is Christ. So with that understanding we know that brides literally walk in the glory of their husbands. Here, the Bride of Christ is walking in the "glory of God, her husband". Of course because of that, her light, her testimony, her example is now going to shine throughout the whole earth. When seeing another vision of the bride in Revelation 12:1, John sees her as a woman clothed with the sun, so again more scriptural proof that this is the bride of Christ and not a literal city. Jesus said of his church that we were the lights of the world. John now sees that aspect of Gods church in this vision.

Rev 21:12
And had a great wall and high, and had twelve gates, and at the gates twelve angels, and names written theron, which are the names of the twelve tribes of the children of Israel.

What is this wall that John is seeing, what does this symbol represent in Gods church? Christ is a builder and He builds His church and protects His church. A wall is protection, a wall is security, a wall is a promise of safety. Jesus Christ is the wall of his church. He has given us His protection and His safety. Notice his words in Matt 16:18 "***I will build my Church and the gates of hell shall not prevail against it***" Nothing shall overcome my church, she is safe from even death. In symbol John is seeing a fortified city of refuge.

Isaiah 49:16
I have graven thee upon the palms of my hands, your walls are continually before me.

Just as natural Jerusalem has walls that Isaiah is referencing here, so the spiritual or new Jerusalem has walls. He is our strong tower, he is our refuge and our strength.

Twelve Gates,

John keeps seeing Gods numerology in this vision, that divine number of twelve. Twelve is the number of Divine Government, it indicates that everything is under perfect order and controlled by God. Twelve is the doubling of six and six is the number of man. Twelve tells us that God has man under his sovereign control and care. There is a reason that He created twelve zodiacial houses to rule the natural heavens. There is a reason that twenty-four elders sit before him *(12 Patriarchs from the Old Covenant and 12 Apostles from the New Covenant)* There is a reason he chose twelve tribes of Israel and twelve Apostles. Twelve is divine in its origin and here John the revelator sees twelve gates into the body of Christ. What is a gate? An entrance, you can't get in any other way than through the gate. The only entrance into the kingdom of God is through these twelve gates. Verse 27 of this same chapter tells us about a group that "in no wise enter" into this kingdom. It is those who never bowed down in obedience, they never came under the government of twelve. Notice in Matthew 16:19, He gave the Apostles keys to the kingdom, how many apostles? Twelve! Their message, their gospel is the only entrance, it is the twelve entrances into the kingdom of God. They alone have the keys to the gates of the city. If you believe and live their message in its entirety then you can indeed walk through the gate, they will open for you be-

cause you too will have the key to enter the resurrection power needed to enter into his Kingdom! The Apostles and their doctrine are opening and closing this kingdom to any man who comes. You must enter into God's bride through their authority and their message.

Twelve Angels

Who are these twelve angels at the gates? What is an angel? A Messenger. These are not heavenly angels, these are the very same ones who hold the keys to the gates, the original messengers to the church, the Apostles.

Twelve Tribes

Allow the forthcoming scripture from the gospels to prove to you just who these angels are at the twelve gates with the twelve keys. These twelve Apostoles were not sent to the gentiles, they were sent to "the lost sheep of the house of Israel" God called Paul to the gentiles primarily.

Luke 22: 29
(speaking to the Apostles) *That you may eat and drink at my table in my kingdom and sit on thrones judging the twelve tribes of Israel*

If you don't understand who these twelve tribes of Israel are that these Apostles will be ruling over in the coming kingdom then you have been robbed of a great insight.[1] You must find out who these twelve tribes really are. For those who think that Israel is just the Jews, you are mistaken. The Jews have natural, full blood brothers that have completely lost their identity among the nations of the world. These Apostles will be ruling over the twelve tribes of Israel

1 *You may request my book: America and Great Britain in prophecy*

which includes natural Israel and the "grafted in" Israel, the Church of God. So, the fact that John sees, twelve gates, twelve angels and twelve tribes means that he sees one church made up of all the tribes of Israel; all in one city behind one wall and governed by the gospel of the Apostles. Notice the names written on these twelve gates, it's the names of the tribes of Israel. What does this prove to us? This City is Israel, the Church of God, it's so plain that God wrote their names on the gates in this vision to make it plain to us who this is.

Rev 21:14
And the wall of the city had twelve foundations and in them the names of the twelve apostles of the Lamb.

Upon what foundation is the Apostolic Church of God built upon? Beloved, the foundation of the Apostles. In this verse who names are in the very foundation of this vision? Does this not show you how perfectly this vision is of the Church of Jesus Christ and not a literal, physical city? The foundation of the church Paul said is built upon the Apostles and the Prophets. Jesus Christ is not the foundation of the church, he's the cornerstone that ties the foundation together. He takes the twelve representatives of the Old Covenant and the Old Church in the wilderness and he ties them together with the twelve representatives of the New Church and the New Covenant and he stands between them both and causes them to fit into a perfect foundation. His church is built upon the cooperation between the two witnesses, both the old and the new testaments or covenants. By taking twelve from the Old Covenant and twelve from the Ne Covenant he now has twenty-four elders who represent the churches of both covenants who have now been included in

one number, the number 24. To prove this simply add those two numbers together, 2 + 4 and you once again come up with six (6) which is the number of man. Gods church in both Covenants is a church of men, governed by men, served by men and filled with men or mankind.

Rev 21:15
And he that talked with me had a golden reed to measure the city and the gates thereof and the wall thereof.

Now we come to one of the most amazing aspects of this entire vision. The measurements mentioned in these two verses are skipped over so easily by the casual reader but contained in these measurements are more of the perfect workings of God in his symbols, patterns and in his numbers. First you will notice that this city lieth foursquare; in other words this church is built from the North, South, East and West. She is made up of men from all four corners of the earth, she is a foursquare church. She is perfectly square, she measures up to the "full stature of Christ" she measures up to the foundation and the walls. She is lining up perfectly with the Apostles and Prophets and with the cornerstone, her Lord Jesus Christ. Judgement or Inspection begins in the family of God. There is a measuring that is taking place in each of our lives to see whether or not we are growing up into Christ as Paul tells us we must do. Are we becoming so much like him that the foundations are measuring up with the walls, our life is measuring up with his life, our ways are measuring up with his ways. Indeed before you will receive any rewards in Gods kingdom there will be a mighty measuring. There will be an inspection of your works, your actions and every idle word spoken by you. As you increase in your measure, you increase in your authority in the kingdom of God.

Rev 21:16

And the city lieth foursquare and the length is as large as the breadth: and he measured the city with the reed, twelve thousand furlongs. The length and the breadth and the height of it are equal.

Please take special note as to the measurement of this bride. Her height, her breadth and her width are equal. Plainly spoken, her faith and her works match up. She is not out of balance in any of her doctrines. She is perfectly rounded. Her faith is just as important to her as her works and her works are just as important as her faith. She is walking in a scriptural balance and as a result please notice her exact measurement, 12,000 furlongs. Do you see anything familiar in that number? Oh I do, I see that divine number of twelve again. This is a church that has equaled out not only her faith and works but also her carnal and spiritual nature. Absolutely, she has mastered the flesh and come under the complete governance of the number twelve so much that is now identified as being in the measuremen t of 12. Not only is she measured as twelve but 12,000 which is 12 with a multiple of 3 10's. 10x10x10 is 1,000 so now we have a fully god governed church who has also been measured with the number 3 which is the number of the Spirit while 4 is the number of carnality. In all of Gods workings he never works in 4's. The number four always represents the worldly mind-set, the thinking of carnal knowledge and understanding, the ways of the mind. When you recognize that 4 multiplied by 3 equals 12 then you will understand that when the carnal number of 4 is overpowered by 3 then you have a fully conquered church, conquered by the spiritual mind rather than the carnal mind and this is why this church is measured not only with 12 but also with 3 zeros, she has

measured up to the mind of the Spirit of God.

Rev 21:17

And he measured the wall thereof, a hundred and forty four cubits, according to the measure of the man that is the measure of the angel.

I'll not be ashamed to tell you; when the Holy Spirit of God gave me this revelation without ever having heard any of these things from any other man, I was overwhelmed in my mind for many months and am still amazed at the perfection of these numbers and these symbols. For example, look at this verse, notice a very intriguing number pops us in relation to the Bride of Christ, 144. Read the verse again and notice that all of the 12's are totaling up to 144. Now, if you will remember and I shall not get into my revelation of the 144,000 in this book *(Order my book: The 144,000 for a detailed explanation)* However, suffice it to say, there is no irony here, this is not just chance numbers, these are all divine numbers in Gods numerology of the Bible. So, here we have the church being measured up to 144. Take a moment and find out the square root of 144 and you will one again find the divine number of twelve (12)! Twelve (12) multiplied by twelve (12) or in other words twelve (12) to the absolute highest power that you can take it to is 144,000 or 144. Anytime you see 144, you are seeing a number that represents a group of people under absolute obedience and operating fully in the divine government of God. Twelve is the number of Divine Government and those who have fully submitted to that government are being measured here as the 144. This number 144 is the "***measure of a man***" but not just any man. Please read the verse carefully, this 144 is the number of the man that is "of the angel" or "belongs to the angel"." The word "of" there is the word "ek" in Greek which means "out of or from" The man who has measured up to the 144 measure is the man who is fully owned by the angel and literally flows from the angel. Who is the angel? Oh the precious Word will interpret itself for you.

Rev 8:3

And another angel came and stood at the altar having a golden censer and there was given to him much incense that he should offer it with the prayers of all the saints upon the golden altar which was before the thone.

The Angel of Yahweh throughout the Old Testament was the Lord Jesus Christ and in this verse, he alone intercedes for the saints before the throne of God. The Angel is Christ. As you and I measure into his full statute of 12 and walk in the spirit of 3 then we are indeed the man who is "of the angel."

R*ev 21:18*

And the construction of the wall was of jasper and the city was pure gold, like unto clear glass.

Now you will begin to see the mentioning of gold when John speaks of this city, this new Jerusalem. Of course he is speaking of the symbol of Gold and what that symbol always represents in the Word of God. You will remember that the ark of the Covenant has the covered in pure Gold, why because the holiness of God is always represented with this symbol, gold. Scriptures tell us that when God has tried the church in the furnace of afflictions that we shall then come forth as pure gold. All of the instruments of the house of God which you and I are that house, all the instruments must be purified and sanctified and cleansed by the fire of God. John saw a holy church, a church of pure gold. Earlier in this book of Revelation in chapter 3:18 "I counsel thee buy of me gold tried in the fire . . .that thou mayest be clothed"

God wants his church adorned in the tapestries of gold. We cannot qualify for the golden city until we have become golden ourselves. Why did he say that this gold was like clear glass? Because beloved, glass is nothing more than sand that has been burned in the fire. The Church of Jesus Christ is that beautiful sea of crystal before the throne of God, she has been burned in the fire and become as glass when it has been formed from the burning of the sand. When God through the ministry of Satan has tried his church she will shine forth in her glory as the golden city of God.

Rev 21:19

And the foundations of the wall of the city were garnished with all manner of precious stones: the first foundation was jasper ; the second sapphire; the third a chalcedony; the fourth, an emeralds; the fifth, sardonyx the sixth; sardius; the seventh, crysolyte; the eighth, beryl; the ninth, a topaz; the tenth, a crysopasus; the eleventh, a jacinth; the twelvth, an amethyst.

What a wonder as I began diving into the spiritual meaning of this verse. All of these precious stones are identically mentioned in Ezekiel 28:13 as the very same stones that Satan once wore in his garments in the heavenlies. Evidently all of those stones were taken from him and given to the bride as her wedding stones. Ah, each stone has a meaning and each stone is also mentioned one other place in the scriptures, in the breastplate of the High Priest of Israel as recorded in Exodus 28:15-30. You will be amazed to find the exact same twelve stones in the Church of the Old Testament and now here they are adoring the Church of the New Testament? Coincidence? I think not, I think I see a pattern in these stones. Upon God's holy church, these stones originally worn by Satan himself are given to adorn the Bride

The World Tomorrow

Chapter Fourteen

*Eye hath not seen neither hath ear heard what the Father
has prepared for those who love him.*

THE GARDEN OF EDEN

THE PIONEERS OF OUR SPECIES; ADAM AND EVE WERE THE TWO MOST BLESSED HUMANS THAT EVER LIVED. They lived on a perfect earth with a perfect environment, perfect health and perfect harmony among even the animals. They never worked by the sweat of their brow, they had absolutely no stress as all of their needs were supplied by the abundance of the earth. They never feared storms as the earth never saw rain storms but rather each day there was a beautiful mist of water that watered the grounds much like the modern yards of the wealthy, and as a result the most beautiful manicured gardens are easily maintained no matter the lack of rain. Adam and Eve had abundant and healthy food;

THAT'S EXACTLY WHAT THE EARTH WAS IN IT'S BEGINNING. . . HEAVENLY

their lives were heavenly. Their existence was heavenly as they enjoyed the pristine and crystallized waterfalls, the descending sunsets, the northern lights, the tranquil weather and even the beautiful lions and horses that walked among them with no fear. There was no murder in their world, there was no theft, there was no sexual immorality, a broken home couldn't be found, hospitals had no purpose, mothers didn't die when children were young from the ravages of cancer, fathers didn't send their sons to war. Each day they spent in fellowship with their Father as they learned His laws, His ways and His mind. They literally ruled the earth, they were the King and Queen of this planet. Whatever their desires were it was always met as they were literally the divinely created son and daughter of God. Now, may I tell you the strangest thing you have ever heard? Many people who read this book seem to think that Heaven is better than what I just described to you. However, that's absolutely impossible as God created the earth and said it was **very good**. This earth was Gods ultimate creation in the visible and manifest world. Now, here's the question that demands an answer from you. If you could live in such a place, a world without war, disease, sickness, death, orphans, murder, stress, pain, heartache. . .Would you call that place heavenly? That's exactly what this earth was in its genesis, Heaven! I state emphatically as I shall prove in this chapter that this planet shall soon be released from the curse placed on her by Adams sin and she shall be completely restored to her Edenistic qualities and you have an invitation from God himself, the Almighty Yahweh to live eternally in this wonderful world tomorrow. When God created this earth, His word says He *"established it forever."*

THE END OF THE WORLD

There shall never be an *"end of the world"* as we so often fear and preach. Actually, there will be an end of the "age" or there shall be an end of calculated time. However, the earth, the planets and all of God's vast universe wasn't created to be obliterated and destroyed and brought to an end. The host of Heaven has existed possibly billions of years and there's never been one second of chaos but rather perfect order and perfect timing.

Actually, it is this perfect timing and uniformity that proves the absurdity of the atheist, it proves the illogicality of the ignorant when they pour out from convoluted minds their vials of vomit and call is reasonable thinking, they call it education. Reasonable thinking demands that you consider the facts and here is the facts, I shall illustrate the facts with the following story.

Having bought the most perfect individual time-piece available, Mr. Herbert Armstrong recounts his discovery in his book "*Does God Exist.*" He tells that his perfect watch known as the *railroad watch* to his amazement did not keep perfect time and had to be adjusted by a second or two every week. This adjustment was made according to the master clock of his city, the master clock of any town is always found at Western Union. However, even the master clock of the town doesn't keep perfect time; once or twice a week it must be adjusted by a second or two to be in accordance with the national clock located in Washington D.C. at the Naval observatory. However, that great national clock is not accurate either and it must be adjusted in a similar fashion. What is it measured by? By none other than the master clock of the universe that has never been off by even a millisecond, the heavenly bodies which are studied by the astronomers; the sun has never risen one second past its due date; winter has never lasted a day longer than its scheduled time; the stars have never failed to flicker and light up the darkened path of weary travelers. Now, to the enlightened thinkers among us who deny the existence of a Creator; if you truly pride yourself on deep thinking you must think

about the perfection of the ultimate design, the universe. You in fact present the idea of a design with no designer, a creation with no creator, shall you soon postulate the idea of a child with no human seed?

I should like to present this scenario to the wisest among us; the freethinker, the non religionist, the enlightened ones. Would you believe me if I told you that in fact this perfect watch that Mr. Armstrong purchased, known for it's preciseness and perfection was actually not made in a factory after all? In fact, it was not designed, nor was it planned or put together by skilled time technicians at all, the truth is it just sort of happened over time, it evolved on it's own. The iron ore just eventually ascended from the depths of the earth, refined itself, formed and shaped itself. The silicon came from the earth over a few million years and turned into glass by some sort of big bang. All of the delicate little mechanisms, the cogs, the wheels just assembled themselves by some unforeseen force of nature, wound themselves up and started keeping time. Do you believe my story? Of course you don't and you question why we dont believe yours? Perish these thoughts of ludicrousness! Rather than a freethinker these blinded people are simply non thinkers, rather than enlightened they are walking in the penumbra of psychotic imbalance.

Is there anyone reading this book right now that wouldn't desire to live in God's Eden? Yet when these truths are explained people have such a hard time fathoming a "*Heaven on Earth*" and yet they fail to realize that's exactly what earth was in it's beginning, Heavenly.

In this chapter you will learn amazing biblical truths that will transition your entire paradigm and radically change your entire mind-set concerning the true destiny of the Sons of God. Sadly, many people do not want the truth, they prefer myths and madness rather than God's holy Word, for reasons I shall never understand.

What will our ministry be in this wonderful coming reign of Jesus Christ and what will the earth be like and who shall be living during this time and where shall the government be established? Countless questions will be answered shortly as together we study the scriptures.

ALL WRONGS PUT TO RIGHTS

Everything that is wrong with the earth today shall soon be changed and made right: According to Pauls writing's this blessed planet is in tears, in anguish, in bitter pain *(metaphorically of course)* awaiting the time of deliverance when her doctors shall arrive and heal her. Who shall these doctors be? The sons of God who make up the royal and ruling family of God, the actual God family *(isn't it ironic how semantics offend us, the God family is the exact same thing as the family of God, how we always fear the unknown or the nontraditional)*; they shall have power, they shall be the leaves that bring healing to the nations (Rev 22:2); in them shall be the river of life that pours forth and heals the waters or the nations or the earth.

Romans 8:22
For we know that the whole creation groaneth and trevaileth in pain together until now.

If we are going to be removed from the earth and delivered to the planet of Heaven and telling this world good-bye then why would the earth be awaiting it's deliverance? If destruction is her lot then why does Paul teach about the time when

> ### ALL OF THESE CALAMITIES OF LIFE THAT I'VE MENTIONED HAS ALL BEEN CAUSED BY ONE THING;
> ---
> ### HUMAN LEADERSHIP!

"the creation itself shall be delivered from the bondage of corruption"? This corruption spoken of is the curse of sin and it's wages, death. Paul knows full well the future ministry of the sons of God, he understand that our inheritance, the inheritance of the meek is "***the earth***" and as a result it will be you and I that brings the needed deliverance from corruption when we are resurrected and chosen to rule this planet at the side of Christ.

All of the following turpitudes shall soon be eradicated.

- GREED
- PREJUDICE
- CORRUPTION
- FINANCIAL INEQUALITY
- SICKNESS
- BROKEN FAMILIES
- WAR AND DEATH.

All of these calamities of life that I've mentioned has all been caused by one thing; Human leadership! Human leaders are selfish and operate under Satan's sway of selfishness and "*me first*" they all live by the "*way of get*" rather then the "*way of give.*" In order for all of these ills to be removed from the earth first Satan must be bound; his invisible influence must be destroyed from the earth and then secondly all human leadership must be removed and replaced by the rulership of truly born again sons of God who have conquered their humanity and been translated into the spiritual family of God by their resurrection. All of these necessary changes will take place as told in the book of Revelation and the book of Daniel. First, Satan will be bound during this one thousand year reign of Christ and as a result his mental sway over the nations will be destroyed and then we read

Daniel 2:44
"In the days of those kings (governments) the God of Heaven will set up a kingdom (government). It will crush and put an end to all these man made governments and of this government there shall never be an end.

My Lord, if that doesn't give you spiritual stimulation and cause you to leap for joy in anticipation of this great Day of the Lord, you should be concerned about your spiritual well-being. We just read in Daniel that all human governments or kings will be replaced by the spiritual and heavenly kingdom of God. Remember that the word *government* is not just a platitude or just a mystical word; it's a literal kingdom that consist of literal government officials who shall reign and rule over a literal earthly government that replaces all human government. Only with the removal of human government can Heaven come to earth because as Paul makes clear in his Apostolic teaching *"Flesh and Blood cannot inherit the kingdom of God"* Are you still flesh and blood? Then at this moment in Gods plan it is not time for you to inherit the government of God, that can only happen when you are no longer flesh and blood

but when you've been raised a spirit body. The sons of God, you and I , who overcame in this life will be the trusted members of that future government which replace all the governments of this earth, oh what joy that brings to the converted Spirit of the conceived Sons of God who are waiting their full adoption at the resurrection. This replacing of human government with heavenly government will take care of the first problem mentioned earlier, Greed. The reason that God can be assured that greed will never threaten his Kingdom is this: His government of spiritually born sons, they overcame greed in their earthly walk. They grew so strong in the Spirit that they overcame that evil influence in their life and at the judgement they will counted worthy to rule when God looks inside of their heart and sees if the motive of greed was fully overcome. Did you put others ahead of you? Did you visit the fatherless and the widows? Did you allow yourself to be walked on? Did you take the wrong even when everyone knew you were right? All you were doing was practicing for your new job in Gods government.

Psalms 37:10
Just a little while longer and the wicked shall be no more.

Psalms 37:28
Jehovah is a lover of justice and he will not leave his loyal ones. To time indefinite they will certainly be guarded.

The above verse states clearly that God loves justice. For the millions of people on this planet who cannot find justice, God has a plan for them. God will bring true justice to the earth in His kingdom. Man will no longer be judged prematurely by feeble judges who cannot by human ability see the intent of the heart, the motives. However, Jesus will know with those eyes of fire what you truly intended to do or be. He will judge you fairly, not as men judge you.

Satan's bound

Before any legitimate government can take over and have true authority over the people; the current ruler, the current head of state must be removed by force or by agreement. God is a legalist, he created the laws that govern nature, society and physics. One of those laws is the laws of authority. At this moment in time, this earth is Satan's. Jesus recognizes this, sadly the church doesn't. Jesus tells his tormentors that he is allowing himself to be crucified because he understands the times He understood that this is the age of darkness (Luke 22:53) He acknowledged Satan's right to rule among men when Satan told him on the mountain of temptation that the kingdoms of this world had been given unto him by God. This is the very reason that men are deceived and cannot receive salvation without a very special gift of grace bringing the conviction power of God upon them. Satan's influence is over the mind just as Christ desires for his influence to be. How does Satan control the minds of the masses? The scriptures teach us the technique that Satan uses; he controls the emotions and the minds by exerting his thoughts, his selfishness into the human race by having tainted the bloodline of the perfect sons of God and more importantly by controlling the air. One of the official titles of his monarchy is "*Prince of the power of the*

air." Just as Prince Charles is the "*Prince of Wales*" that simply denotes Wales as one of his realms of authority. With Satan, not only has he authority of the flesh which he inculcated with his vile DNA and traits but he has also has authority over the air which controls the minds of the masses, their thoughts and their emotions. He can sway the thoughts and emotions of entire nations. Simply remember in your mind, the hatred that filled the Germans or the sexual promiscuity of the French or the greed of the Americans. This is all within his authority and his supernatural power. Ephesians 2:2 demands your attention as it will fully explain the ways of Satan's power and why he must be bound from exerting his power of mental control in order for the Lords Day to be accomplished, in order for the masses to "change their minds" about Christ and all of them accept him as Lord. Do you remember how easy it was for you to accept Christ and yet so difficult for your neighbor or relative? Sadly, for them they did not receive the grace or the call to receive Christ in this age but in the next age, the final age, all men shall receive what you received; deception shall be removed from all men.

Ephesians 2:2
Wherein in times past ye walked according to the course of this world, according to the prince of the power of the air, the spirit that now worketh in the children of disobedience.

Ephesians 2:3
Among who also we all had our conversation in times past in the lust of the flesh; fulfilling the desires of the flesh and the mind; and were by nature the children of wrath (Satan) even as others.

This passage is loaded with a cornucopia of revelation and wonder. First, how thankful we should be for the words *"in times past."* What a joy for the elect to be able to say those words. However, millions around you cannot give the same testimony for they are still living in the NOW what you were living "in times past."

ZOMBIES AMONG THE LIVING

You walked in the zombie march, in perfect step with the other masses of blinded and dead humanity headed for the death chamber laughing all the way. You walked according to the *"course of this world."* According to "the King who has influence over the atmospheric region." How are moods controlled? Have you ever hear someone say *"there's just something in the air"* when they were depressed or happy? It's always blamed on the air and rightly so for in the atmospheric region is where the sound waves are carried and on those sound waves, on those frequencies is music, videos, voices and countless opinions and Satan influences and has authority over this region of earth. Only those who have had their minds changed and converted and brought under subjection to the Word of God can counter those strong atmospheric changes which brings, depression, doubt, anger and various other emotions. Verse three (3) again demonstrates the areas of Satan's influence, the flesh and the mind. Here is the job of the Overcomer; take dominion away from Satan over your flesh and your mind and you now qualify for the Kingdom of God.

For those living in this church age this changing of the mind must be done against the odds. The odds are stacked against you; you are a stranger among this worlds populace; you don't walk according to their course; you don't believe all that their entertainers try to throw at you; You don't believe all their newscast; You don't fit into all their molds; You don't enjoy their games; You don't like their songs; You don't dress like them; You are out of sync with them and as a result you are no longer a zombi, you are no longer dead to sin. However, it's a sad state when the zombies call the living, strange.

So, you've been called to overcome and prepare now for the day when these zombies will have an awakening. The one who has held them in deception will be bound outside of the earths atmosphere and his influence will cease and all men, all flesh will receive the Holy Spirit which will give them all new hearts and new minds and they shall all bow down and confess Christ. After the thousand year of Gods Sabbath rest Satan will be allowed to bring his influence back to earth to test all of those who were given the gift of the Holy Spirit so freely, to test their experience and see if they can now live the same life you lived before them and if they can Overcome; upon doing so Satan's ministry will end and he will be banished along with those who failed his final testing.

THE TRUE GOSPEL OF CHRIST

All preachers claim to be preaching the gospel of Jesus Christ but in actuality they are preaching the gospel "about" Jesus Christ rather then the actual message Jesus preached. In our days we hear the man Christ Jesus preached about, we hear about his life, his death, his story, his miracles, his death, his resurrection but very seldom do we hear his gospel or his message. He didn't tell us to preach about Him, we're commanded to preach WHAT HE PREACHED. Now, what did Jesus preach? Did He preach about Heaven? Did He preach about retiring for eternity in some distant place? Did He preach about how to live you best life now? Did He preach about how to get rich, stay rich and always be rich? Did he preach that His kingdom had already come and was now filling the hearts of believers? Did he preach about the importance of being Spirit filled and speaking in tongues? Did he preach about the rapture of the church? No, an emphatic No! The message Jesus preached had one over-riding them, the coming Kingdom on earth. For proof of this statement let's look at Marks writing;

Mark 1:1
The beginning of the gospel (message) of Jesus Christ . . Now after that John was put into prison, Jesus came into Galilee preaching..... The GOSPEL OF THE KINGDOM OF GOD and saying, the time if fulfilled and the Kingdom of God is at hand, repent ye and believe the gospel. Mark 1:14-15

What gospel or good news message are we commanded to preach? The soon coming Kingdom or government of God to the earth. This is what he sent out seventy men preaching and he commanded them to preach one message and one message only, The Kingdom of God (Luke 10:9). He sent the Apostles to preach only one message, The Kingdom of God. (Luke 9:1-2). I am completely convinced that before this revelation that I truly had no idea of my purpose for preaching. Sadly, I felt my job was to win the lost by preaching to them about Heaven and Hell, I was clueless to the true gospel of the soon coming

Kingdom. Now, I realize that my true job as a true minister in God's true church is to train, teach and equip the members of his Dream Team for their role in His future government, his soon coming world wide second harvest of souls, a revival of unimaginable proportions; and to prepare them now to qualify for those places of authority in the Kingdom of God. Again, the minister is not called to win the lost he is called to teach the church. God himself will draw all men unto him in the appointed times and when he does one of his children will be there to bring the gospel of the Kingdom to that person at just the right time. Right now God is building a *Dream Team* and he is equipping them and calling them into higher living, overcoming lifestyles and he is purging them. At this moment He is not saving the world as is quite evident by simply looking around. All that God is saving at this moment in time as will be proven in the next and final chapter is the elect, the predestined Bride who shall bring the nations to Him during the millennium reign. This will be the children that the bride produces for her groom during their millennium honeymoon. Oh the majesty of it all! You must read the final chapter of my book to fully understand why God is not calling all men to repentance in our day, only a few for a very specific purpose, only those who he has predestined to be in His government of Overcomers. Doesn't the scriptures say that "*Today is THE day of salvation*"? No it does not; the next chapter will prove to you the error in that translation.

Before Jesus was ascended into Heaven what was the very last subject that he once again dealt with before he left? Why of course, the Kingdom of God that would soon come to the earth (Acts 1:3). The Apostle Paul preached on the Kingdom of God (Acts 19:8; 20:25;28:23,31) and do you realize that God Almighty pronounced a curse on any man or angel that preached any other gospel that wasn't concerning the coming Kingdom of God to the earth. (GALATIANS 1:8-9). Remember this well, the Kingdom age comes after the Church age, we are NOT in the Kingdom of God right now, we are currently in the Church of God and very soon the Church of God after her purging, training and schooling will be promoted into her position as the rulers of the Kingdom of God, Daniel said that the Kingdom was given to the saints.

THE MORE YOUR HUNGER, THE MORE HE WILL FEED YOU

Dear saint of God you must become fully convinced in your own mind after reading the plethora of scriptures presented in this book of the importance of understanding the coming Kingdom of God to the earth. Without this understanding you are missing the greatest revelation that gives you the true understanding of your purpose in this life. Jesus Christ when he returns in your lifetime He is not coming as Saviour; He did that on his first of a two part series. He is coming as King of all Kings and guess what he will be doing, ruling this earth! Do you really fathom this? How can you even think for a second that Heaven is your destiny when it's plain that the earth is where he is setting up his kingdom? You can read in Revelation 19:11-16 that He is coming to RULE ALL NATIONS. Then concurrently Daniel verifies this fact again in his writing when he says that Christ kingdom will consume all of the worlds governments. Additionally we read in Revelation 11:15 that the kingdoms of the world are become the kingdoms of our Lord and of His Christ and He shall reign forever and ever! How long will

his reign be? Forever! Who will be reigning with Him? You! And how long will you be reigning? Forever! So, when will you have time to go to Heaven? You Wont! Now, do you see the picture? Heaven is coming Here! There will be millions of years of creative work among the universe and the galaxies for the sons of God to be part of. Remember, our family business is the business of creation; we are creators with God and in our new bodies we shall inherit our place along side Jesus Christ; when "all things" the entire universe will be given to us to rule and reign forever and ever.

The reason that so many people cannot understand this thought is because they fail to realize that the Kingdom of God is a literal government and that shall ruler over literal people on a literal earth. Mark these facts well and your mind will began perceiving the beauty of this marvelous truth. Just as the Chaldean empire and the Roman empire were literal governments, so is the Christian empire! When Jesus stood before Pilate he was asked by Pilate *"Are you a King"* and Jesus stated his entire life purpose and the entirety of his gospel in these words *"**For this purpose was I born"*** (JOHN 18:36,37) Jesus continues to explain to Pilate that He indeed had a government or a Kingdom but that His kingdom was not for this age or this period of time. Jesus knew full well unlike many preachers today that His kingdom had an appointed time or an appointed day and that until that time was fulfilled that his Kingdom would remain an intangible, invisible Kingdom.

PRACTICALLY, HOW DOES THE CHANGE IN GOVERNMENTS TAKE PLACE?

The inevitable question that comes to the mind is, How? How is this literal kingdom going to come in a moment and make everything better? How is Utopia going to take over the earth? Your Bible has all the answers, sadly no one has ever taken the time to teach them to you. You are about to read some of the most amazing scriptures that with unfolding majesty will open the eyes of your understanding and cause you to hunger for even more truth; the more your hunger, the more He will feed you! To understand how all of this will be accomplished is to remember that just like God implemented stages of development in the re-creation of the earth and in his dealings with man over six-thousand (6,000) years he will also bring His kingdom in incrementally, step by step.

Before we can understand the works of Christ in his future earthly kingdom we must understand where He is now and what He is doing. He is actually in that spiritual dimension called Heaven and he is waiting for His throne and Kingdom to be given unto him. Remember at this moment He has not yet been given His kingdom, He is serving in the role of High Priest, not King of Kings, that's a future role that he will play. Remember, in his parable about the nobleman in Luke 19, the nobleman goes to the father and stays gone a long time in order to receive his kingdom. Also, in Daniel the Kingdom is not given to Christ until the second coming. The price has been paid, the qualifications have been met and

as soon as His government is prepared to rule then he will return with His government to Mt. Zion and take over the nations of the world.

The Psalmst David said He is waiting until all his enemies become his footstool. In the book of Acts we see that Jesus is waiting for the **"restitution of all things."** (ACTS 3:19-21). Interestingly enough the word **restoration** means *"returning to a former condition"* Jesus is waiting for the time when he will come and restore all things. Now, if Heaven is the goal then why even waste His time restoring the earth? Why even bring Utopia back if we are leaving the earth? Do you see the absurdity of this entire "escaping and flying away" message? Sadly, while we're flying away to Christ, he will be coming this way, that sort of defeats the purpose doesn't it? When he comes to set up his Kingdom it will be the restitution of ALL THINGS. Peace, prosperity, joy and liberty and justice will all be restored to the earth.

NO FLESH SAVED

Why is there a certain time that he must return? Because if Christ does not return man will completely anniahlate himself with weapons of mass destruction. The purpose of Christ next coming is to keep a portion of humanity *(a remnant)* alive before every human is destroyed by the inventions of men. If Christ does not return to restore all thing then men would be obliterated and there would be **"no flesh saved or kept alive."** (MATT 24:22) At the very moment in the soon coming World War III between the Muslim countries and the Christian nations there will come a point when the nations of the world who have stockpiled these weapons of death for many years will be forced to begin obliterating mankind in death and destruction that your mind cannot fathom. The deaths in World War II will pale in comparison to the deaths of this next war with hundreds of thousands killed at one time. At the very moment when nearly two-thirds of humanity has been obliterated and the rest of the world is begging for deliverance from someone, from somewhere, that deliverance will come in the eastern skies.

He will appear as King of all these fighting kings on the earth. When he first appears he will be treading the winepress of his wrath and he shall rule with a "rod of iron." (Rev 19:15; 12:5). Have you ever taken time to question what that means? What is a rod of iron? A demonstration of power and military might. He is coming to stop the greed, the human suffering, the poverty, the diseases, the pain, the tears; He will intervene because we called for him. He will shorten those days for the elects sake, you and I! He will literally step into earths affairs because the elect would be destroyed if he didn't. *(As a an interesting side note; if we have been in a secret rapture before all this happens then why would he need to shorten the days for our sakes)* There wouldn't be a man of His creation left. The nations will be begging for food, for help, for pity and no one will hear them. His coming will usher in world peace. It is no accident that in every beauty pageant, in every newscast everyone is simply wanting world peace. There's a hunger in the hearts of men for peace and this desire is placed there by God for only the prince of Peace can bring man his true hearts desire.

Even though Christ is coming to restore the earth and help mankind and even though he's coming for our salvation and as our God; just like children, the wicked will not recognize it as such. It would be interesting to note here the findings of a recent article in a leading weekly newspaper here in America. They stated "*the once optimistic hope of Americans for a well ordered and stable world is fading. Rather than improving as once predicted, conditions are worsening. The prevailing feeling is that these conditions are to the point of being unable to be solved except for a strong hand from someplace.*" Did you read that last line" ***A strong hand from someplace***"! The nations are shaking, the people are worried, there is an undercurrent of fear that things are about to explode on the world markets and in the worlds militaries. The silent volcano of human greed is churning and bubbling in the inferno of egos and in the minds of maniacs. Ladies and gentleman, that "*strong hand from somewhere*" is waiting for the moment when he must ***"shorten the day."*** What days? The six days of man! That allotted time of man, the six days or the six thousand years that are slated to expire during this century and the Word says that God will not allow the full length of those days to be completed because if he did there would be no flesh left alive or saved on the planet. So, for those who are waiting for the completion of the sixth day to serve the Lord, you fail to realize that before that sixth day is completed He's going to shorten the work for the elects sake.

When Christ returns to save the nations, man will be true to his rebellious nature and once again reject Christ initially. Just as a child will get angry when a parent is trying to intervene for the child's own good, the child is too selfish to see the intent of the parents, all he sees is the Strong Hand of authority and resents that authority. The nations will be the same way, they will resent Christ! (Rev 11:15, 11:18). We read where military forces will attempt to fight him as they will assume him to be some type of alien invader; the very reason why Satan has inspired Hollywood to make so many space alien movies to condition the minds of men about the possibility of alien invasion. These governments of men will actually attempt to tell the people that they are in fact being attacked when Christ returns and they will rise and fight against Him. . .feel free to read it in your own Bible (REV 17:14) This third World War will be centered around Jerusalem. If you do not believe this, simply listen to the news lately. All news events and talks of war are centered around Jerusalem. Jerusalem disappeared off of the map of world interest for nearly a thousand years under the Ottoman and Muslim rule, then in this century reappears to prominence. Coincidence? Of all the nations of the world, why Jerusalem? That insignificant piece of land should not be so desperately desired. It has no wealth, it has no oil, it has no gold and yet it's the most desired real estate in the world and the next world war will be centered around Jerusalem. . . .feel free to read it in your own Bible (ZECHARIAH 14:1-2) Now notice that in supernatural power and with a "rod of Iron" Christ will demonstrate to the world the magnanimity of His power as he destroys those nations that rise against him in Zechariah 14:3. In this second coming He is not coming as the little lamb but rather the roaring Lion. With the opening of His mouth the nations will tremble, the earth will convulse and he will totally annihilate his enemies, they will become His footstool (REVELATION 17:14). The he shall stand with his government that he just previously resurrected from the graves, they met Him in the air as he now joins with them and sets His feet on the Mount of Olives and prepares to set up His government after destroying the human governments. (ZECHARIAH 14:4) Remember when Jesus stressed to us to "*pray for the peace of Jerusalem*"? That command always baffled me

because Jerusalem cannot have peach until her Messiah comes. With that understood we see now what Christ was really trying to tell us. When you pray for the peace of Jerusalem you are actually praying for the hastening of the second coming.

THE ROD OF IRON & CHRIST RIGHT TO RULE

There is worldwide crisis in leadership! Why can't leaders lead? Why cant great empires such as the British, the Roman, The Grecian empires all last forever? Why is it a law of reciprocity that they all fail? Why is it a fact that America must fall? Because of the inability of leaders to rule in righteousness! Beneath the cloaked layers of political niceness there is a very selfish nature in leaders who seek the top for their own purposes. Their inability to live and rule with righteousness leads to the fall of all human ruled empires. Remember the words of sacred scriptures "***Righteousness exalteth a nation***" when a nation is led by true and righteous character it could be a utopian nation but at last there is none righteous. The gospel that I preach, the good news that I serve as witness of is this: Lift up your eyes unto the hills from whence cometh your help because our redemption is drawing near, a righteous King is coming with ten thousand of his saints who have all learned the ways of righteousness while living on the earth and we shall all be governed by true righteousness. (ISAIH 11:1-5)

For Christ to rule he must have the legitimate authority to do so. For him to rule over men he must have first been a man. For him to bind Satan he must have first conquered Satan. For him to judge the flesh he must have first conquered the flesh. For him to judge disobedience he must have first been obedient. He qualifies in all these areas. Finally, for him to end death he must have first conquered death. The only way to replace a king is to remove a king! His authority is earned; he came to our world the first time and earned his stripes, he earned his position of Lion by first becoming the lamb. His authority will be absolute and without question.

Isaiah 11:4
He shall strike the earth with the rod of his mouth, and with the breath of his lips He shall slay the wicked.

When Christ returns you will see the Lion. He will never take another strip nor another slap in his face. His having done those things will give him the legitimate authority to rule with force now. The same thing applies to you and I. As we take the wrong in this life as were ridiculed in this life we are earning our right to rule just as Christ did. We can rule because we first served, we served humanity in this period of our existence. Notice carefully the following verse and you will see that this rod of iron isn't only given to Christ.

Rev 2:26-27
He who overcomes will I give power over the nations. . .He shall rule them with a "rod of iron".

This is the secret as to why we must overcome hatred, revenge, malice and bitterness in this life because when a person has authority to use a rod of iron and that authority is mixed with unrighteousness then evil comes forth. For you to be given this rod of iron to rule the nations with Christ, your

character must be the same as his. Never one time will you enjoy using this rod but as Christ servant you will not hesitate to bring order and peace to a chaotic world , you will help Christ in quashing all rebellion. For a perfect example of authority in the wrong hands, in the hands of unrighteousness; a tyrannical Father who has harbors hatred for a step child and uses his authority for the venting of his own anger, the child can have no justice with such authority. Imagine the national leader like Adolf Hitler who has authority but ungodly character, the results speak for themselves. Before granted authority in God's kingdom there must be a complete obedience to His every Word. The motives of the heart must be examined to ensure that His future government will never be rebelled against again. Once your temporary character is changed, your eternal character will always remain what it became in this life.

How did God prepare David to rule and reign? He made him a shepard first. David was not taught to rule as a tyrant but rather as a lover of the flock. This is why God despises tyrannical pastors who abuse the flock because the Pastors are the examples of the Shepard Kings that he is raising up in the church age to reign on the throne of Christ. Before Christ could carry the title of *King of Kings* he first carried the title *Chief Shepard* (I Peter 5:4) Those in the government of God will have such a love for the governed that the nations will be healed by the love and care of these Shepard Kings who also function as priest in God's kingdom.

THE TERROR OF THE LORD

Unfortunately, the only language that man understands is power. Sadly, Christ must speak to the masses in that language. Before he can heal them he must hurt them; before he can bind them he must break them. You will see what happens when the armies of the earth gather against him in Rev 17. But we find how he will overcome these armies in the following verse.

Zechariah 14:12
And this will be the plague wherewith the Lord will smite all the people (armies) that have fought against Jerusalem their flesh shall consume away while they stand upon their feet, and their eyes shall consume away in their holes, and their tongue shall consume away in their mouth.

Something so terrible will happen for Christ to prove his power and authority over these armies that while they are standing on their feet with the opening of his mouth their flesh will fall off of their bones. Rebellion against Gods ways and Gods laws must be immediately put down for the new government to ascend the throne of world power. At this moment the nations will finally realize the effects of six-thousand years of sin, it's results and their inability to rule themselves. They will recognize the authority of Christ to rule, they will confess him and they will call him Lord. This will be the greatest revival in world history.

THE BIG MEETUP IN THE SKY

I've been going to Camp meetings and Conven-

tions all my life. There is just something that lives in the memory and never dies about good and godly fellowship among the Bride of Christ. Our meetings are filled with love, anticipation and joy. The music, the voices, the sermons, the altars all find permanent rooms in our houses of memory. The greatest camp meeting of all is upon the church and is to happen very soon. This camp meeting will take place in the air and will never end! We know according to the angels at Jesus ascension it was promised that he would return in clouds just like he left in clouds. In the book of I Thessalonians 4:14-17 we are told that just as He is returning in clouds, the resurrected saints will rise to meet him in those clouds that He is returning on. Those who are still alive will be changed in their DNA structure instantly to be transformed into a spiritual body. While this body will have a human form it will be completely different in it's DNA structure. It will be able to live eternally with no need for blood, air, food or water. While the new Spiritual body can enjoy the taste of food if it so desires as Jesus ate fish after receiving His new body; it will not depend on any of these things for life, the body will be an eternal body. In that body we shall rise with the saints who are in the grave and all together we shall meet the Lord in the air (I Thessalonians 4:17). *(If there is a secret pre trib rapture then whats the point in having a resurrection).*

This meeting will take place in the second heaven, not the third Heaven. This will happen before the natural eyes of the entire world, a sky filled with saints who are all wearing the white robes which denote their status in God's government. Then Christ will do battle with the armies of the world. Then he shall judge His saints and give them all their rewards, their positions and their duties in the Kingdom of God and then everyone shall go to work bringing in the largest harvest of souls that the world has ever seen. According to Zechariah 14:4-5 we shall then descend from the clouds and take possession of the Mount of Olives, Mt. Zion and Jerusalem. These immortal saints (you and I) shall now rule the nations of billions of mortal humans that we will bring unto salvation, at that moment the church age has ended and the kingdom age will have begun. The binding of Satan will happen simultaneously during all of these simultaneous events.

What about human nature

What will then happen to the instilled human nature at Christ appearing? Old habits will not be automatically removed. However, without deception men will be free to make the only choice, the right choice. So, with Christ coming the very first thing that His government must do is re-educating the masses. All government when they take over a nation they begin first with the schools, re-educating the minds. In the same manner Christ's government will be a government of teachers. Without a deceived mind we will be able to teach all men the ways of God and about His laws and as a result bringing all men to voluntary repentance. Many might wonder, why will men choose Christ then if they didn't now? If you are standing in the garden with a blindfold on and I tell you to move you will possibly not move because you are blinded to the snake at your feet. Even if I scream and beg you to move you may in rebellion decide not to move since you don't see the danger, you don't know about the snake. However, if I remove the blinder what must I do to get you to move at the first sight of the snake? I could simply

take your hand and you would voluntarily move. So it will be with repentance. Once the blinders are gone and man sees how wonderful life is under the government of the immortals all we will have to do is take them by the hand and lead them to the truth.

From the moment of Christ supernatural takeover until the binding of Satan, Gods law shall go froth from Jerusalem and cover the whole earth (ISAIAH 2:3) During this time the curse of the 6,000 years will be ended and all of mankind will no longer be barred from the tree of life in God's Eden. Christ and His team of ministers, His government will begin calling all men to repentance and the rivers of the Holy Spirit (the Sons of God) shall flow out of the New Jerusalem (Zech 14:8). A brand new civilization shall now grip the earth. For the most beautiful scriptural account of this new civilization read these following scriptures;

Isaiah 2:2-4
And it shall come to pass in the last days, that the mountain (government) of the Lord's House (His Sons) shall be established in the tops of the mountains (world governments) and shall be exalted above all the hills (earthly kingdoms) and all nations shall flow unto it. And many people shall go and say, Come ye, and let us go up unto the mountain of the Lord (his government) to the house of the God of Jacob; and he will teach us of his ways, and we shall walk in his paths, for out of Zion (Gods family of sons, his government) shall go forth the law and the word of the Lord from Jerusalem.

In the next verses should you continue to read you will find the results of these nations learning to live by the Ten Commandments, the laws of God. All wars shall cease to the point that all weapons will be broken down and used for peaceful purposes such as farming and manufacturing. There will finally be world peace, so much so that even the animals will be free from the atmospheric control of Satan, they will lose their anger and their desire to kill.

Isaiah 11:6-9
The wolf shall also dwell with the lamb, and the leopard shall also lie down with the kid; and the calf and the fatling and the young lion together; and a little child shall lead them. And the cow and the bear shall feed; their young ones shall lie down together (can you imagine this kind of peace?) And the Lion shall eat straw like the ox (no more killing the prey) . . .they shall not hurt nor destroy in all of my holy mountain.

This will be a world of solved problems. This will be a world like humanity has never known, this will be Heaven! There will be no illiteracy, everyone will be taught the laws of God by the resurrected sons of God who are training right now as you read this book to take their place in that government of teachers and preachers and priest and kings. There will be no poverty anymore, no famine and no starvation. Crime will be decreasing rapidly as people learn the laws of God and as he pours out His Spirit upon the entire population. People will live in honesty, integrity, chastity, kindness and happiness.

TOPOGRAPHICAL CHANGES

Not only will human nature be changed but the earth itself will undergo major changes as it's healed of so many diseases that have plagued it since Adams

fall. Imagine for a moment that the earth no longer had any deserts. All of the worlds hunger problems could be solved if not for places like the Saharaa desert with thousands of miles of total wasteland. Imagine if all the Arizona deserts were beautiful farmland providing food for the nations. Jesus Christ with his supernatural power is going to cause all the deserts of earth to cease being a wasteland and they shall all blossom like a rose, they shall have life.

Isaiah 35:6-7
Then shall the lame man leap as a hart, and the tongue of the dumb sing: for in the wilderness shall waters break out and streams in the desert. And the parched ground shall become a pool and the thirsty land springs of water; in the habitation of jackals where each lay shall be grass with reeds and rushes.

Did you have any idea that your Bible said these things? Did you ever consider what they actually meant? These scriptures are all foretelling the coming Kingdom of God on the earth.

Isaiah 35:1-2
The wilderness and solitary place shall be glad for them; and the desert shall rejoice and blossom as the rose. It shall blossom abundantly and rejoice even with joy and singing.

This power to change the earths agricultural landscape will be given to all the sons of God. Not only the land but we shall authority to heal all diseases that still lingers from Satans years of governing the earth. Every crippled shall walk at our touch, every blind eye shall open at our command. Also, the wealth of the world that is hidden beneath the sea shall be reclaimed by the sons of God. The oceans will be reduced in size allowing for the wealth beneath the sea to be discovered. Also, the land reclaimed from the sea will provide for more prosperity.

Isaiah 11:15
And the Lord shall utterly destroy the tongue of the Egyptian sea and with his mighty wind will shake his hand over the river and shall smite it into seven streams and make men go over dryshod.

A HIGHLY ORGANIZED GOVERNMENT

God created government among even His angels with a hierarchy. God is all about government and our obedience to authority. There's a reason for this; because His government will one day rule the earth. Once He has established His rule with a rod of iron he will then begin educating the world in His laws and His ways. It is important to understand that he will not be ruling the nations alone just as He doesn't rule the heavens alone, he uses his angels.

His Kingdom will include those who have positions of authority over one city, five cities, ten cities, nations and land masses. For that government to function perfectly all human traits of greed and selfishness must be removed entirely. This can only happen with born again Sons of God who passed their test while in this life. This will be a government of church and state being totally united. As a matter of fact we are shown that during this millennium reign everyone will be honoring God's Sabbaths, especially the weekly sabbath. My question to the so-called Christian churches, if God loved His sabbath in the Old Testament and we are going to be keeping His Sabbath for all eternity then why doesn't He care about His sabbath in our day? Why would He discontinue what shall continue forever?

Another thing that shall continue during the millenium will be the keeping of God's Holy Days and His festivals. I will dare say that you are about to arrive at the climatic chapter of this book where you will be taught one of the most amazing revelation of my lifetime, the Feast of Israel. Until you understand the following lesson and the meaning of the Feast of Israel then you are quite possibly clueless as I was as to Gods total plan for the ages. In the wonderful world tomorrow, in the Kingdom of God you and I will be keeping all of Gods Sabbaths as Isaiah, Jeremiah, Micah, Daniel and Ezekiel all describe. However, the Feast of Israel will be taught to everyone during the Lords Day and everyone will keep these Feast. So, it is incumbent upon you to understand what you will be doing in the Lords Day by beginning to learn their meanings and even practice their keeping in this age that we now live in.

The Forgotten Feast of Israel

Chapter Fifteen

*Verily. . ."My Sabbaths" ye shall keep and it shall be
a sign between me and you throughout your generations,
that you may know that I am the Lord that doth
separate (sanctify) you.*

Exodus 31:13

CONGRATULATIONS

Because of our discomfort with leaving the comfort of tradition and walking into areas of new understanding; I am not surprised when many readers will not have continued their study of this book long enough to arrive at this great culmination chapter. However, should you fail to read this final chapter then many of the truths I have presented in this writing will still be lingering in the dust filled and antiquated room of misunderstanding. This is what I like to consider "The Great Chapter" because only within these final pages of study will all the pieces of this scriptural puzzle make perfect and spiritual sense. I am firmly convinced that any believer who does not have the full understanding of the *Feast of Israel* also has not the understanding of God's total redemptive plan for humanity. I was ignorant of these truths all of my Christian life until the holy spirit of God revealed the meanings of these feast by using the writings of other great men of God and also by divine inspiration. Try as I might, I could not make the Word of God fit together as it should in my mind until this master key of understanding was given which is needed for the complete plan of Gods program for the ages. This chapter will bring all the fragments of truth that are scattered in various pieces among many great denominations and sects into one whole picture of beauty; they will manifest perfectly in your mind. You will be fully convinced of Gods' perfection and His plan for the ages when you have finished this chapter, at least that is the authors hope.

The Feast of Israel, what are they? Why do they matter in our day? What's the big deal? The answers will amaze you! The New Testament without the Old Testament is a great misnomer. There is no such thing as a New Testament Christian because according to the words of Paul, the entire Word of God is for our instruction and our learning. For the reasons that I shall never understand the modern church has placed at enmity with each other; both the Old and New Testaments. Rather than realizing that the Old Testament is the only scripture used in the early church we choose to ignore the pages of the Pentateuch, the Law and the Prophets and in so doing we do a great disservice to the Body of Christ. You should begin today with a thorough study of the Old Testament and listen to the truths in those ancient, God breathed writings. In the early Apostolic church these alone were referred to by Christ and the Apostles as the Holy Scriptures. Not one word of the Old Testament has been abrogated. Only the specific instructions concerning the temple, the sacrifices and the oral law of the elders have been modified; not done away with but modified.

When the legislature of a state amends a law, it does not abrogate or do away with the law, it simply modifies that certain law for the changes pressed upon it by the circumstances of the times and the changes in society. In days gone by the interstate speed limit was fifty-five (55) but that law has been modified as the circumstances change. However, we would be fool-hearty to say that the speed limit law has been done away with. Gods eternal laws that have existed before the creation of man has never nor will thy ever be done away with. Fall in love with this law, fall in love with the safeguards that the master has given to mankind and in so doing you will fall in love with the good way, the old paths and you will ultimately receive the reward of eternal life.

In those dust covered and forgotten pages of the Old Testament lies the unknown and often over-looked mysteries of the seven feast *(appointments)* that God commanded His people to celebrate and to honor on an annual basis. Undoubtedly, those carnal minded Israelites had no idea why God was commanding these feast. To those among the natural church of Israel, the keeping of these feast probably made very little sense to their way of thinking. If they had any understanding of the feast it was simply a natural understanding as it related to their specific race and nation of people. However, I am certain that they had no idea that they were acting out in a type or a shadow what was to come upon the nations of the world.

THE HAPPENINGS OF THE NATURAL REALM ARE MERE SYMBOLS OF THE GREATER TRUTHS BEING PLAYED OUT IN THE SPIRITUAL DIMENSION

Just as the stars in the heavens preached the redemptive plans of God before the Bible was ever written, in the same way these Feast of Israel, as they were faithfully observed, they were also preaching and revealing Gods awesome plan for the ages. The happenings of the natural realm are mere symbols of the greater truths being played out in the spiritual dimension.

Actually, no one else in the world kept Israels' feast nor her Holy Days. These Feast indeed separated the children of Israel from the children of Satan otherwise known as the Gentiles; the various nations of the world. These feast or Holy Days was their identifying traditions that caused them to be unique and holy unto God. They were forbidden to keep the holidays that had their source from the heathens and the pagans; because God was going to reveal to you and I His great plans for the ages in the keeping of these Feast. While the mysteries of these feast might have been hidden in times past; they are now about to be revealed before your reading eyes!

I contend that once you see Gods plan for the ages hidden in these Holy Day the majority if not all of your questions about the timing of His return will begin to be answered.

If you will notice in this book I have made mention several times that God is indeed not calling to salvation the entire world at this time. I have made mention of the fact that the dead who have died without hearing the gospel will get their adequate chance. I have made mention of the fact that God is not calling everyone to repentance in our day and if your mind is still unsettled about those issues then you come to a clear understanding as you read about these forgotten feast of Israel; never again will you wonder. Before we continue; you need to ask yourself this question, Why was God so serious about the keeping of His Sabbaths or His Holy Days? He declares death to any man who didn't keep them, they would be *"cut off from the church of natural Israel."* Why is this? There must have been a reason that God wanted these days honored forever; they must contain a message that His true church would be able to understand in the keeping of His Holy Days. This message is not plain on parchments of paper, they are not revealed to the carnal mind but it is made crystal clear on human hearts filled with the Spirit of God which is the spirit of truth and understanding. God never intended for His Bride to be ignorant of His plans. He hides his plan from the world but reveals them to the Bride. His word states plainly that He *"does nothing without revealing is first to His prophets."*

The Seven Feast

- Feast of Passover
- Feast of Unleavened Bread
- Feast of Pentecost or Firstfruit
- Feast of Trumpets
- Day of Atonement
- Feast of Tabernacles
- Feast of The Last Great Day

Feast of Passover

All Bible scholars and commentators agree that Christ and the early Apostolic Church of God kept all of the feast of Israel without any second thought. Not keeping the feast was unthinkable in the New Testament church as we can easily prove from Pauls many references to his desire to *"keep this feast."* He always seemingly planned his missionary journeys around the timing of the festivals and feast. There is a very good reason for this; he understood the validity of these feast and their correlation to the New Testament church, he understood not only their natural meanings but also their christological and eschatological meanings. *"**In the early Christian church the custom of celebrating the festivals together with the whole of the Jewish people was never questioned, so that it needed no special mention.**" (The New International Dictionary of New Testament Theology, Volume 1, page 628)*

The teachings of Christ gave these wonderful festivals new meaning in the hearts of that early *Apostolic Church of God* and in certain places he specifically modified and updated some of these festivals to better illustrate the true purpose of the feast. One must read no further than the *Encyclopedia Britannica* for the very proof of these statements; *"**The sanctity of special times such as Christmas and Easter was an idea absent from the early Christian church; they continued to observe the Jewish festivals of Leviticus 23, though in a new spirit, as commemorations of events which those festivals foreshadowed**" (Volume 8, page 828 , 11th edition)*

These early believers, unlike the modern church had a great reverence for the commands of God and very special regards for his creation of these special appointments as found in *Leviticus 23:1-4*. You will find in these verses of scripture that these are not considered the "feast of the Jews or of Moses" but rather they are considered Gods' feast, they are copyrighted by Him and belong exclusively to Him and His children forever as very special get-togethers and times of intense fellowship.

As you open your own Bibles now and begin to study these life changing truths with me you will begin this journey through the seven annual feast of God in the book of Leviticus where you will find the very first feast that God instituted.

Leviticus 23:5
In the fourteenth day of the first month at even is the Lords Passover.

The very first of the seven festivals to be observed

each year is the Feast of Passover. God instituted this feast at the beginning of the exodus from the land of Egypt as recorded in the book of Exodus 12:1-27. Now, as promised we will begin to journey into the meaning of these festivals especially as it relates to Gods plan for the ages.

This feast of Passover is the very beginning of the series of feast for a reason; because is represents and reveals to us the very first step in Gods plan for the salvation and redemption of Gods' greatest creation, mankind. This festival of Passover not only looks back and remembers the delivering of Israels' first-born sons from the curse of death but it also looked forward to the great sacrifice of Jesus Christ, our Passover lamb.

Please study the following scriptures for a better understanding; *I Corinthians 5:7, I Peter 1:18-19.*

What is the just punishment for your sins? Do you realize that you were born in the state of a fallen man and born a sinner in utter depravity? Do you understand that you were born in the land of Egypt as a slave to the control and the sickness of sin without any hope of freedom? Your addictions and your fleshly desires ruled you, they were your Pharaoh; your taskmaster. You bowed down to your alcohol, drugs, pornography, bitterness and hate and you said *"Yes Sir Master"* to all of their demands. Each and every time the master of nicotine commanded you to "light up" you said *"Yes Sir Master"*; every time a woman or man gave you attention and your flesh began to lust as a dog does, you said *"Yes Sir Master"*; just as those natural Israelites were born slaves and just as they served a Pharaoh, you once served sin. As a slave to sin, the price for that sin must be paid and according to Holy Writ, that certain penalty is noth-

ing less than death.

As we celebrate the feast of Passover we are in fact celebrating and remembering the above mentioned truths; we celebrate our freedom from the life of sin and bondage, our exodus from the stronghold of addictions and lawlessness. Each year as we celebrate this appointment with God, called Passover, it helps our continued understanding, it keeps before our minds the beautiful reality of our first step; our beginning on the path from Egypt to our promised land of rest, the coming Kingdom of God.

As we continue to read the scriptures in this study we will find that God commanded that this feast of Passover be kept forever![1]. Of course, our Lord Jesus Christ was obedient to every word of His father and He continued to celebrate this feast every year as our example to doing the same[2]. Before His crucifixion, the Lord Jesus Christ made a few modifications to this annual feast of Passover that the church mistakenly calls "Communion"; this is a term instituted by the Catholic Church and not the Word of God. God calls this feast, Passover[3]. What changes did Jesus make to the Passover feast? Very few indeed, he simply modified this annual feast by changing the elements of the Feast to more closely represent His body and His blood, the true meaning of Passover. Rather than shedding the blood of a lamb and roasting its body; the ritual was simplified to the elements of wine and unleavened bread. Then, He commanded His disciples to continue keeping this annual Feast as a constant reminder of the Passover Lamb providing freedom from the curse of death to all that believe upon Him[4].

1 *Exodus 12:23-24*
2 *John 2:13, 23*
3 *Matthew 26:17-20*
4 *Luke 22:19-20*

Shortly after His resurrection He called His disciples together and told them to *"go and teach all believers around the world to continue keeping all the commands of Christ"*[1] I have shown you in the previous scriptures that the annual keeping of the feast of Passover is a clear command of our Lord. . Lest someone think that we make these claims without Apostolic authority; please read the words of the Apostle to the Gentiles, Paul himself[2]. It is clearly seen in Pauls writing that the early years of the *Apostolic Church of God* were filled with the annual observance of Passover, the Lords supper. Unlike the modern church, those early believers were clueless of any festival called Easter or Christmas, the records of history show that they kept only the original feast that God commanded.

ACCEPTING CHRIST INTO YOUR HEART IS NOT ENOUGH!

Finally, allow the scriptures to show you that this annual Feast of Passover will continue to be kept throughout eternity as the sainted millions remember the glorious victory wrought by Christ, our elder brother on the mount called Calvary[3]. Today only the true *Apostolic Church of God* keeps this annual feast but in the coming kingdom age, the entire world will join in with us[4] as together we celebrate this beginning of our salvation experience as represented in the annual Feast of Passover.

———————————————

FEAST OF UNLEAVENED BREAD

1 *Matthew 28:19-20*
2 *1 Corinthians 5:7-8 ; 11:23-26*
3 *Matthew 26:29, Luke 22:15-16.*
4 Isaiah 66:23

Next

we approach the second feast in Gods plan for the ages. This feast reveals to us the "next step" on the path of salvation the next chapter in Gods story of redemption. Passover is indicative of our initial leaving from Egypt, making a decision to follow Christ, to be converted, it's the perfect anti-type of true repentance. However, accepting Christ and repentance is NOT enough! You must now began running this race towards the prize which is eternal life in the Kingdom of God. Now, you must begin training for your place on *The Dream Team.*

Now that you have repented, confessed and acknowledged your need for a saviour; now that you have been forgiven by God for all previous sins as symbolized in the Feast of Passover; it is now time to actually forsake sin. The forsaking of sin is the message being preached to us quite loudly as we celebrate the annual feast of Unleavened Bread. God grants us grace at the feast of Passover, at our initial repentance. However, he now empowers us by the Holy Ghost to begin the process of forsaking our lifestyles of lawlessness, which is sin. We must now strive to put all sin away from us, we must begin pressing towards the Overcomers path as we choose to travel down the road less traveled, that narrow path of sanctification and holiness. Passover is wonderful and Oh how we thank God for it but without our participating with God in the Feast of Unleavened Bread then Passover was a waste of time for all involved. God did not bring you out of sin to be nonchalant about your remaining there. At Passover, God did His part. He gave a pardon, full and free. He paid a debt He did not owe. As we celebrate this second feast or appointment with God each year, we do so to be constantly reminded of our part of the agreement; the forsaking of all sinful lifestyles. God gave His church this second feast to keep before our forgetful minds the constant reminder to not only keep the Passover; to not only receive the pardon from death but to also LEAVE the place where we were once bound. Christ accepts you "*Just as I am*" However, He only remains with you as you become "*Just as He is*." The purpose of your redemption is for your deliverance from the slavery of sin and it's dominion over you.

As we search the scriptures about this second feast we find that God commanded His children to keep this feast immediately after Passover[1]. Just like the Feast of Passover, this second feast of Unleavened Bread was commanded to be kept forever! Just as we use the natural elements of wine and bread in the previous annual feast; during the Feast of Unleavened Bread, we also use a natural means to impress upon our natural minds the vital and life giving spiritual truths represented by these natural symbols.

> AS YOU REFUSE TO CONFESS AND RISE ABOVE SIN; YOU ARE MAKING A MOCKERY OF THE CROSS OF CHRIST

During this seven day feast we are instructed by God to celebrate this feast by removing all natural products from our homes that contain yeast which is the symbol of sin. In removing these items from our home it's a most wonderful opportunity for us to be reminded annually and a time to teach our children the dire consequences of sin and our responsibility to rise above the flesh and the leavening of Satan. We have such a wonderful opportunity during this feast to use these natural actions such as simply removing natural leaven from our homes to teach us the profound truths that we so often forget about sin and its tendency to spread as a malignant disease through our bodies until it ends in death.

As you read *Exodus 12:15-19; 13:7* you will see how serious God is about this annual appointment with Him as together with the Holy church we focus our attention on the lessons provided in this annual feast.

I just love how the Old Testament and the New Testament are always in agreement. We know from Pauls writing that the early church also kept this annual festival. He continues to teach us in his writings about the importance of removing sin from our lives on a daily basis and quite ironically he also compares our sin to leaven[2]. Leaven puffs up and so does sin. Sin left unconfessed will become your worst nightmare. Sin left unhealed will disease not only your mind and your body but everyone that you love and hold dear will suffer from your selfishness of sin. As you refuse to confess and rise about your sins you are making a mockery of the cross of Christ. As you claim to follow Him and yet remain in Egypt you commit sacrilege of the highest order. You cannot rightfully celebrate Passover without entering into the long and winding journey through the Feast of Unleavened Bread. God hates sin and you must hate it with the same passion.

Unleavened bread contains no leaven and therefore indicates the absence of sin. Our lives must become as unleavened as this natural unleavened bread used as a symbol in this feast; as we abrogate sin, as we abhor sin and we eradicate the very last vestiges of it from our lives. We must not only be delivered from Egypt but that cursed land must be delivered from

1 *Exodus 12:14-17, Leviticus 23:5-6*

2 *I Corinthians 5:8*

us. Our passions must not smell like Egypt, our looks must not remind us of Egypt, our language must not be indicative of that filthy land. Look back at Egypt, what did you lose there? All I see when I look back is a life filled with shame and embarrassment. Yet, so many Christians wish to celebrate Passover (communion) each year while living in Egypt, drinking the blood and eating the body while mocking those very elements by the lives they live. One cannot adequately celebrate the crucified Christ until they have been crucified with him as a living sacrifice.

This annual appointment with God is to serve as our constant reminder to put all sin, all breaking of Gods laws away from us as we move on from the elementary doctrines of Christ and move unto perfection; completeness in the full stature of Jesus Christ.

Feast of Pentecost, Weeks or Firstfruit

Again why does God give us the command to keep these annual appointments with Him? He wishes to use these simple celebrations, these natural illustrations to reveal to us the continuity of His eternal plan for the church and the world. The keeping of these feast could be compared to your employers continuing education classes; for the purpose of keeping employees in constant remembrance of company policies, plans and strategies. Many employees dread these events because most of the time it's the same thing they heard last time. However, repetition is the best teacher and these annual feast serve as the continuing education of Gods Apostolic Church. It is during these annual events that the truth which lies behind the symbols are revealed to us over and over again and it gives us constant assurance that our God has everything in perfect control, on a perfect path and in perfect timing.

This third feast is one of the least understood of them all and sadly so because contained within this simple feast are some of the most prolific truths that the church has ever known. When you think of the word "Firstfruit" or "First born" what do those terms indicate? In order for something to be "first" there must be others yet to come. If I tell you that *"I was here first"* then you can safely assume that others are here also, correct? This third feast of Pentecost was originally called the feast of Firstfruit and for very obvious reasons.

Without the knowledge of the mysteries hidden behind this Feast of Firstfruit it is not hard to understand why most churches believe that every person who dies "unsaved" before Christ returns can never receive salvation. They believe that Christ came the first time for the purpose of desperately trying to save the world in some last ditch effort to try and rectify the damage done by Satan. They seem to think that some sort of contest is going on between Christ and Satan for the souls of men; if they are correct in their assumptions then the score is not looking very promising for Christ. I wish to say magisterially that there is absolutely no contest going on between Christ and Satan and no matter what the mirage may look like, Satan has never nor will he ever have "one up" on our King. This annual feast of Firstfruit reveals to us that in fact one day God will redeem the majority of His creation. He will not walk away into eternity with perhaps five percent of His created beings and walk away content with

His defeat and wonder for all eternity how he could have lostso many. He will not simply allow Satan to bring the majority of His created beings into the clutches of eternal death. However, at this juncture; at this moment in Gods time clock, at this act in the seven act play; God is not calling the world to salvation; He is only calling the Firstfruit, the elect, the Church of God. One day He will indeed call in the "other" fruit, the final harvest, the larger harvest but today He is only calling those who will make up the first harvest. Let us begin studying the scriptures as this vital master key of truth helps you to unlock the treasures of an understanding that perhaps before now you have never known. The truth of this matter will amaze you and you begin to see the hidden mysteries of these festivals the so perfectly show Gods plan for the ages in regards to the redemption of His created beings.

As we read *Leviticus 23:15-17, 20* ; we find Gods specific instructions concerning this third annual feast. In those scriptures we find that this feast is also to be kept forever! We must stop and understand that all of these feast were scheduled around the agricultural events of Israels annual harvest seasons. God uses these two natural barley and wheat harvest which came forth in the spring and the autumn, to demonstrate to us his *"two spiritual harvest."* One day God will gather into his barn a very large harvest of soul;, the majority of His creation will be gleaned into His kingdom from the clutches of Satan. However, today His focus is not on that large autumn harvest but rather His focus is on that small spring harvest, often called that *"little flock"* in the Bible.

God intended for the spring harvest to represent the church which is being called out as a firstfruit company of believers. We are in fact called by God,

the *"firstfruit of salvation"*[1]. This firstfruit harves; this early spring harvest of souls marks the small beginning of His final harvest which shall be called to him during the Millennium reign of Christ and also at the second resurrection.

Now, let's study in detail the specifications of this great feast called Firstfruit. Here is exactly how the first harvest, also called the spring harvest proceeded. First, on the morning of the first day of the week (Sunday) during the Feast of Unleavened Bread a sheaf or one stalk of fresh cut barley was prepared and brought to the priest. The priest would then wave this first grain or this first sheaf from this early first springtime harvest as a wave offering to be accepted of the Lord, Yahweh. This particular offering was referred to as the "wavesheaf offering" and this offering represented the "first" of the firstfruit harvest. In simpler terms; when the early spring harvest was ready to be harvested it could not be harvested until the first stalk was taken from the spring harvest and waved before the Lord as a dedication of the entire harvest being represented in the first of the firstfruit. Once the "irst of the firstfruit" harvest had been waved before Yahweh then the spring harvest could begin of this relatively small crop compared to the much anticipated autumn harvest later in the year. Beginning with this day of the waving of the offering the gleaning began and continued until 50 days later when this harvesting would culminate in the feast of firstfruit when Israel gathered to celebrate and give thanks for their early harvest. This feast of firstfruit was held 50 days after the feast of unleavened bread and thus the reason we now call it the feast of Pentecost because the word Pentecost simply means 50.

_____

1 James 1:18

So, what is the connection with this wave offering and our Lord Jesus Christ? Remember, the first harvest was completely represented in that very first stalk of barley that was waved during the feast of unleavened bread. Who was the very first to be resurrected from the dead into Gods family or into the God family? We find the answer in Acts 26:23; we are plainly told that Jesus Christ was the first to rise from the dead. Again, if He is designated as the first then this can only mean He is not the only one that's going to rise from the dead. His being recognized as the first only reiterates the obvious. . .there must be more to come. With His designation as "first of the firstfruit" as noted in *I Corinthians 15:20.23* and *Colossians 1:18* . . .who do you rightfully imagine the firstfruit will be? If we can safely assume that His being the "first of the firstfuit" can only mean that there is more to come after Him in the resurrection. Can we not also assume that if we are the firstfruit then there must be another harvest to come after we have been harvested?[1]

Let us proceed deeper into this marvelous truth. Please note that Jesus Christ was resurrected towards the closing hours of Saturday, the Sabbath and then later on the first day of the week (Sunday) He ascended to His father to be waved before Yahweh and to be accepted as the representative of the entire first harvest[2]. The resurrection happened at the exact same time as the wavesheaf offering was presented to the priest in the Old Testament, on the first day of the week during the feast of Unleavened bread. Remember, Jesus died during the Passover which immediately precedes and leads into the seven day feast of unleavened bread. So while Christ lay in the tomb the feast of Unleavened Bread was being celebrated in Israel. On the first day of the week during this festival, Jesus Christ, the first of the firstfruit, the first sheaf of the first harvest of souls was waved before Yahweh and accepted. He was now the first resurrected Son of God, not the first begotten or the first created Son of God but rather the first resurrected, spiritually born Son of God and as such He was the first harvested product of Gods master plan for the ages. Jesus Christ was now the firstborn from the dead, the firstborn of many brethren, the very firstborn Son of God, the first human to overcome temptation and to complete the process of salvation of being completely born again.

Now, we must consider a very important element of this great mystery. Jesus Christ needed power to overcome sin! Jesus Christ was a man, His godliness had been abdicated for His manliness. He did no spiritual works in the entirety of His life until a very special even took place, the infilling of the Holy Ghost. The very blood brothers of Christ, His entire family refused to recognize Him as anyone special; they called Him mad on a few occasions. Apparently He never seemed to impress upon them who lived with Him daily that he was anything more than a man. He in fact did no miracles and no spiritual work until he finds Himself in the river of Jordon[3]. In the following verse it will be made abundantly clear to you that Jesus was a man just like you and I who depended completely upon and desperately needed the baptism of the Holy Spirit before He could began His ministry.

John 14:10
Believest thou not that I am in the Father and the Father is in me? The words I speak to you I speak not of myself: <u>BUT THE FATHER THAT DWELLETH IN ME HE DOETH THE WORKS.</u>

1 *James 1:18, Romans 8:23*
2 *John 20:17*

3 *John 5:30, 8:28*

Who does the works? Not the man Christ Jesus, He was just like you and I, helpless without God. Who did the works that Jesus was able to do? Something dwelled in Him that gave Him the power to overcome, the power to heal, the power to cast out devils and this power was not His power it was the power of the Holy Ghost which is the Father as He indwells each spiritually begotten Son of God. The Holy Ghost is not a separate person from the Father. If Jesus credits all these wonderful works to the Father and we know that He didnt do all these works until the "Holy Spirit" settled upon Him in baptism then who is doing the works? The Holy Spirit or the Father? Absolutely, it's the Father because the Father is the Holy Spirit; the Holy Spirit is in fact as the scriptures teach us the very Spirit of God or the Spirit of the Father or the very essence, life, breath, the very substance of the Father. This substance, this essence filled the man Christ Jesus and as the scriptures teach Jesus was filled with the Holy Ghost and power. He was totally dependent upon His father for everything. He walked on the water only because His father graced Him to do so. As He trusted in God He was able to walk upon the water. He walked on water as a man not as a God; He used the very same source that Peter used to walk on the water, faith in the Father, the Holy Ghost. Jesus is God because Jesus learned obedience and at His ressurection was declared to be Very God[1]

The first of the firstfruit promised those of us who shall make up that first small harvest that we needed that same spiritual help that He had; in fact He promised us that same spiritual help[2]. When you read the verses in John chapter 14 please note that Christ has promised them a Comforter. Now, slide down to verse twenty-six (26) and we learn that this Comforter is indeed the Holy Ghost and this Holy Ghost when it comes would tell them the exact same things that Christ had already taught them. The reason for this? Because Christ said repeatedly that He only taught what He heard His Father say; His Father was the Holy Ghost. One must only read the account of the Immaculate Conception to identify who the Father of Jesus is "***For the Holy Ghost shall conceive in you***"[3] that's the words spoken to Mary by the angel. The reason the Holy Ghost will speak the same words as Jesus spoke is because Jesus only spoke what His Father, the Holy Ghost was speaking so therefore their words would be identical.

Up until this point the Holy Ghost had been "With" the disciples because it had dwelled in Christ and Christ was "with" them. However, the administration of the plan now changes and the Holy Ghost will no longer be "with" them but it shall soon be "in" them; the exact same Holy Ghost that dwelled in Christ now dwells in the church. We find that the church received this wonderful promise exactly fifty (50) days after Jesus, the "first of the firstfruit" was waved before Yahweh. The first harvest was now empowered to begin building the church of Jesus Christ. On this wonderful day of Pentecost, the firstfruit were established in the earth as a sure guarantee to the Father that very soon at the first resurrection this first harvest would come to full fruition and from this first harvest will eventually come an even larger and greater harvest, the second harvest.

Many people have no problem experiencing Passover (the forgiveness of sins) they even venture into the feast of Unleavened Bread (the forsaking of sin, sanctification) but they fail to proceed and

1 Romans 1:4
2 John 14:16
3 Matt 1:18-20

celebrate the feast of Firstfruit or Pentecost; they fail to receive power which comes from the indwelling presence of Jesus Christ. If you have not received the Holy Spirit today then you are in fact missing out on this tremendous Feast of Firstfruit. This gift is freely given upon true repentance which results from true and living faith in Jesus Christ. That faith then produces it natural results; works; and then you follow Christ in obedience to the watery grave of baptism where you call on and confess the name of the Lord Jesus Christ publically and following that obedience and by the ministry of the laying on of hands you are guaranteed to receive the Holy Ghost; this is the promise of God to all who obey Him.

Now, that you have left Egypt, (Passover) forsaken a lifestyle of sin (Unleavened Bread) you really should celebrate this third Feast of Firstfruit and allow the baptism of the Holy Spirit to place you into this first harvest called the Church of the Lord Jesus Christ. You are placed into this first harvest upon receiving the Holy Ghost. So, annually we as the *Apostolic Church of God* gather to wave our physical symbols of wheat before the Lord as we remember the resurrection of our Lord and as we are reminded of our resurrection, what a glorious reminder. Only in keeping this annual feast are we constantly aware of the hope that lieth within us, the hope of the resurrection of life.

FEAST OF TRUMPETS

As glorious as the Feast of Firstfruit is; without the feast of trumpets it's only a wish rather than a true hope. The firstfruit harvest

of believers cannot be reaped without those believers being completely born again as spiritual beings. This born again experience will not happen until the second coming of the Lord Jesus Christ and as we celebrate each year the Feast of Trumpets this is what our celebration is in fact reminding us of on a consistent basis; the second coming of Christ.

This festival and all of the ones we will discuss from here on out are unlike all the previous ones; they have not yet been fulfilled. The prior feast we've discussed have found their fulfillment in Christ and in the Day of Pentecost. So therefore those feast are commemorative feast, in remembrance of past events. However, all of the feast have not yet found their fulfillment and they are in fact shadows of things still to come. This feast of Trumpets not only foreshadows and foretells the coming of Christ to resurrect and change the firstfruits, it also foretells the terrible times of war and destruction that lie just ahead in Gods time line as revealed in these feast. The feast of Trumpets that we celebrate annually by the physical blowing of trumpets serves as a wonderful time of anticipation as we remembers Gods promise to protect us from the horrors that shall soon come upon the clueless world.

To understand the feast you must read its origins as recorded in the book of *Leviticus 23:23-25*. Please make a special note that this feast begins the final autumn feast which we celebrate each year. All the previous feast took place in the early part of the year in the spring. Those spring festivals have all been fulfilled in our lives. However, these upcoming feast we celebrate in anticipation of their fulfillment not in remembrance as we do the spring feast. The feast of Trumpets is to begin in the seventh month, towards the end of the year. As a scriptural numerologist I pay particular attention to any sevens that I see in scripture as this is the number of completion, it's Gods signature. In this seventh month we will find the remaining four feast. All of the upcoming, yet unfulfilled feast are all set to take place in the seventh month, the time of completion and fulfillment. The festival that begins on the first day of this seventh month, the Feast of Trumpets is actually the beginning of the end on Gods time line and in Gods plan for the ages.

Whenever a trumpet sounded in ancient Israel, great fear fell upon the people because this sound was normally associated with war and destruction. This Feast of Trumpets is actually celebrated each year in our congregations with the blowing of several different types of trumpets. This simple and symbolic ritual keeps before our eyes the truth of the wrath of God upon ungodly men. This festival reminds us to be ready for these cataclysmic events that will begin as the seven angels begin to sound these seven trumpets and especially when the Lord Jesus Christ descends from heaven with a shout and the voice of a trumpet.

We know from the teachings of Christ Himself that His kingdom would be established, His second coming would happen during a time of great world war[1]. There is a very good reason why Jesus must return. Man, in our quest for global domination; as a result of our evil hearts, we have devised weapons of mass destruction such as our forbears have never known nor even dreamed of. For the first time in the history of our species we could totally anniahlate our very existence on earth with the push of a few buttons and the entering of a few codes. The destruction of all flesh would be completed in a matter of hours

around the world if in fact Satans diabolical plan of mass destruction takes place, everyone would die. Should Jesus not return at the very moment that He will return then in fact we would destroy our own selves[2] According to the scriptures in Matthew 24 the final trumpet, the last trump, the seventh trumpet when it sounds will save all flesh from complete extinction by that glorious appearing, the blessed hope of the saints.

Unfortunately, the modern church with itching ears have been lulled into complacency and absolute deception with the theory of a rapture when we shall all somehow escape the tribulation. However, nothing could be father from the truth. While we shall have supernatural protection during those evil days; we shall not be exempt from troubles and trials. If those early martyrs suffered for the cause of Christ how do we consider ourselves more privileged than they? However, the scripture plainly states that while we wait here on earth, we shall know Gods sovereign protection[3]. In fact the only reason that Christ will intervene during this time of trouble on the earth, this World War III is simply for the sake of "*the elect*" which is the Church, the firstfruit harvest. He will cut time short and rescue mankind from nuclear annihilation[4].

Each year as the true Church of God celebrates this feast we not only keep this appointment in anticipation of the second coming of Christ but also as a continual reminder that God has promised to protect His little flock during these horrible times of wrath to be visited upon the earth. Once the persecution has ended and at that very dramatic point when the nations are engaged in a global religious

---

1 *Matthew 24:3, 6-8*

2 Matthew 24:21-22
3 *Revelations 3:10, 12:14*
4 *Matthew 24:22*

war of mass devstation then our Lord at the moment of our utter destruction as a species will intervene and call forth His *Dream Team*, His family of tried and proven brothers and as they rise to meet Him in the air, they will then descend with Him as the 144,00 upon the Mount of Olives and together rule the nations with Him. These are the glorious events that annually we as a church celebrate. We choose to keep these truths before our eyes and in our consciousness in the forms of these feast and this is the very reason God commands us to keep them forever; in doing so we keep these truths before our eyes. When Satan tries to convince the chosen people of God that our God has lost control; our God is grasping at straws trying to think of some way to counter Satans plan; our God is asleep at the wheel; the world is in chaos . . . Whatever his lies are we are assured in the keeping of the annual Feast of Trumpets that our God, Yahweh, is a sovereign ruler with an absolutely well timed plan for Satans final defeat and for the soon coming final harvest when Jesus Christ will offer as an offering to His father, the nations of the world that was lost in the garden of Eden! Who wouldn't want to join with Gods true church in the keeping of such annual celebrations of truth? We, the saints of the most high God can be assured that as we come together each year in constant celebration of these truths we have a very special destiny tied to the Feast of Trumpets. Not only are we celebrating our promised resurrection but also our promised potential as rulers in the government of God;

Revelation 20:6
. . .they shall be priest of God and of Christ and
they shall reign with Him a thousand years

I invite you to experience more than Passover, Unleavened Bread and Pentecost . . .strive to arrive

at this great Feast of Trumpets . . .this will be the great rendezvous of the Church both the Old Testament church and the New Testament church. It is so wonderful each year to arrive at our meeting location and in perfect unity with Gods true saints rejoice together at our future role in Gods government on this restored earth, this heavenly earth.

FEAST OF ATONEMENT

The fifth festival celebrated each year by the *Apostolic Church of God* is one of my favorites. This feast is a true celebration of the saints as we join together to be reminded each year of the final demise of our arch enemy, Satan himself. Lest we grow weary in our minds by Satans daily attacks, lest we fail to remember that he indeed has a short time; we joyfully celebrate the day of atonement. After the feast of Trumpets, the second coming of Christ, immediately Satan, the God of this world will be dealt with.

Please be reminded that at Christ first coming He did not come to remove Satan from his legally given realm of authority. Jesus came to be obedient to His father, to earn His position as the first born Son of God in the resurrection, to pass the test of temptations, to obey every word of Gods eternal laws. Just as Christ passed His first test, just as sure as He cried "it is finished" and accomplished His first goal; He shall do the same at His second coming. The Lamb will return as a Lion, not for peace and not for suffering but to receive His promised kingdom and there cannot be two Kings in a kingdom; so one of these kings must be deposed. This is the true purpose of Christ second coming; to finish what he started, to destroy the works of Satan; to end His tyrannical rule over the hearts of men created in the very image of God. Pauls tells us that Satan is still the current world ruler[1]. However, immediately following the feast of Trumpets when the second coming occurs and the members of the government of Gods new and glorious kingdom is resurrected to eternal life; then immediately after the marriage supper Satan will then be imprisoned for one thousand years during the 7th day of the Kingdom of God on earth.

What does this mean? Remember, Satan as ruler of the airwaves; he controls the population through the atmosphere where his dominion is located. He saturates the minds of men with conflicting emotions of hate and lust and greed and envy. He causes men to be unable to see the truth of Gods Word unless of course they are called by the Holy Spirit and chosen or elected, then the scales are removed supernaturally by the Holy Ghost. However, for the rest of humanity; they are completely deceived[2]. Only when he is bound and his influences stymied will the nations of the world who were not called in this day; only then will all men be able to truly hear the gospel. Only then will the eyes of the blind be open to the marvellous truths that you and I can now so plainly see by the gift of grace. You and I have come to God under Satans government. While living as an exiled colony of Gods kingdom under the control of a fallen government ruled by the forces of evil; we have remained faithful to the laws of God in a lawless world. This is the very reason for this special group of believers; there is great position awaiting in Gods future world-ruling government. However, one day men will hear the gospel without being deceived. Satans power over the minds of humanity will be broken and then every "*eye will see, every tongue shall*

1 *II Corinthians 4:4*
2 *Rev 12:9*
Shane Vaughn

confess" because they will no longer be held in Satans sway. This all happens on the Day of Atonement which we celebrate annually with a great revival style atmosphere of praise and celebration and we gleefully anticipate the victory of our God over the forces of darkness. All of humanity living in the coming 7th day will finally be made - at one- with God and His resurrected sons, the royal family of eternity, the ultimate *Dream Team*.

To better understand the mysteries contained in this feast let us study it's true purposes from the scriptures. We find this feast described in the book of *Leviticus 23:27; 16:29-31*. I strongly encourage you to read all scriptural references to determine these truths for yourself. Here we find that this annual celebration or feast or appointment was to occur nine (9) days after the Feast of Trumpets. I absolutely love to see Gods perfect plan being revealed in the timing and unfolding of these often misunderstood festivals. The modern church has robbed herself completely of these annual celebration from the modern preacher who has completely distorted some of Pauls writings concerning annual festivals[3]. On this Feast of At-one-ment Gods church is commanded to appear before Him in a holy convocation and to do no work on this day, it is what we refer to as a High Sabbath[4]. This is the only feast where we are required to fast; all other annual feast are celebrations which involve feasting. However, on this particular day there is a reminder before our eyes of the results of Satans six-thousand (6,000) years of ruling and that result is the awful consequences of sin. As we fast at this Feast of Atonement we are both celebrating Satans defeat and also recognizing the horrors of his rule and such an acknowledgment causes us to mourn

3 *Order my book; Gods Holy Day for a better explanation and deeper study of Pauls writings concerning the Holy Days*
4 *Leviticus 23:27*

for the loss of millions who have died as his slaves in this fallen world. Also, we must remember that the thought of "Atonement" gives us an interesting word play of etymology. Literally when the word is broken down we can see that finally at this coming feast man will truly and finally be set At-One-ment with God our Heavenly Father. However, this grand reunion cannot truly happen until the progenitor of sin is restrained and our fellowship with God will be unhindered unlike it was in the garden of Eden.

In the Old Testament God has plainly revealed to spiritual minds how this Feast of Atonement on that future day will be carried out. We find this mystery revealed to us in the entire 16th chapter of Leviticus. In this chapter, the Levitical priesthood have been instructed by God how the Day of Atonement should be symbolized: The priesthood was to make a special offering once a year for the sins of the entire nation of Israel[1]. Before this offering could be made two goats were brought before the priest and lots were cast to determine which one would be the sin offering and which one would be the "Azazel Goat" sometimes mistakenly called the Scapegoat[2]. One of these goats of course represented Christ, the sin offering that would remove the sins from the nation. However, many people fail to recognize who the second goat represents. Read closely in verse ten (10) and you will see that this second goat was to be banished. Our English word "*Scapegoat*" is absolutely a wrong translation of the original Hebrew word from which it derives. Most Bibles have corrected this error and now state in the margins that rather then scapegoat this should be known as the Azazel goat. The word Azazel among those desert dwellers

of Sinai always referred to Satan, the Devil.

Now, note carefully something most interesting in this symbology; once the goat representing Christ was killed and the sins removed from the people; those sins didn't just evaporate into the unknown; they actually had to be placed on a responsible party and in this story that would be the Azazel goat. Although the sin offering removed the past sins from the people; he couldn't carry responsibility for the sin. You will note that in verses 21-22 of this same chapter in Leviticus that once the sins had been transferred to the responsible part, the Azazel goat, he was then removed from the camp and taken into the wilderness which is always the symbol for sins and temptations.

These types have been and shall be fulfilled in the persons of Christ and Lucifer. While Jesus took the penalty for our sins, he suffered the "*curse of the law*" which is death; He is not responsible for the origins of sin, He is not the source of sin and therefore is not ultimately responsible. The real cause of sin is a person, Lucifer[3]. As seen in the symbols of Atonement, all the sins originated by Satan will ultimately wind right back up on his head as he will finally bear the responsibility. Although Jesus paid the penalty, true justice will not have been served if the responsible party doesn't pay the final price and bear the ultimate responsibility. He shall bear a great punishment for all eternity because he is an eternal creature with eternal life inherit within him and he cannot die so therefore he must suffer eternal torment, his only just reward.

Rev 20:1-2
And I saw the angel come down from heaven having the key to the bottomless pit in his hand and a great chain in his hand.

---

1 *Leviticus 16: 29-34*
2 *Leviticus 16:7-8 - Most Bible translators have corrected the word "scapegoat" to "Azazel goat"*

3 *John 8:42-44*

And he laid hold on the Dragon, that old serpent, which is the Devil, and Satan and bound him a thousand years.

Notice where Satan will be cast . . . into the great abyss or bottomless pit. What is this? This is the same in typology as the ancient wilderness as mentioned in the book of Leviticus. Both places; the wilderness and bottomless pit are metaphors for the unknown, a place to be feared. The Azazel goat was to be cast into the exact same type of place as the bottomless pit, into the wilderness where he would be forgotten. When Satan is bound just like the Azazel goat he will no longer be able to broadcast his thoughts into the mind sets of humanity and thus continuing his deception; his purpose will have ended.

Also, it should excite the spiritually begotten child of God to notice another intricate detail revealed in the feast of Atonement. The Azazel goat in the Old Testament was bound by what's called in the King James version "*a fit man*"[1]. When this part of that Old Testament symbology is fulfilled very soon after the second coming, there will be another "*fit man*" referred to as an angel in the book of Revelation and this "*fit man*" will bind Satan and lead him away into the wilderness, the unknown area called the bottomless pit.

The fifth step in Gods plan for the ages will have been fulfilled then because at this event people will then begin to realize their sins and without Satans deception they will desire to repent and in this last day Gods spirit will then fall on all flesh as prophesied by Joel, the true outpouring on all flesh will happen after Satan is bound. Only then will people be "At One" with Christ at this beautiful feast of "At-One-Ment."

I personally invite you to find some of Gods people who annually keep this coming event in the forfronts of our minds as we joyfully keep this feast of Atonement. You should be reminded on a regular basis that Satan is a defeated with a definite end. Is there any other holiday that your keeping which portrays such a wonderful message? Then perhaps God is calling you to join others in rejoicing in the annual festivals. Are we advocating the keeping of these feast as necessary for salvation? Absolutely not. However, we do conclude that these feast will help you on your journey in keeping the truths of Gods plan ever before your eyes. Why do many Christians continue to celebrate Christmas, the birth of Christ? Isn't one time enough? No! In the constant annual remembrance our focus is kept in a right direction, a constant reminder of Christ birth. Gods holy festivals are designed to help your faith, to keep your hope alive. Rather than the holidays of pagans and men who have no hope in God perhaps you might consider celebrating Gods Holy Days, His feast and appointments. In doing so your faith will arise to a new level, you will look forward all year to the celebrations that Yahweh instituted rather then the meaningless holidays of pagans and men.

FEAST OF TABERNACLES

The sixth event on Gods calender, the sixth festival or appointment is one of extreme importance. You should pray diligently for God to personally reveal to you the depths of

1 *Leviticus 16:21*

this particular feast. Only with a true understanding of these yet to be fulfilled feast of Israel can you see Gods hand working in the kingdoms of men.

The Feast of Tabernacles occurs only five days after the feast of Atonement. So, it occurs shortly after Satan and his evil influences over the minds of men has been bound. You can find the details of this feast for your own personal study in *Leviticus 23:34 and also Deuteronomy 16: 13-15.* This particular festival is a seven day feast just like the feast of Unleavened Bread. You will notice in verse 35 of Leviticus 23 that God commanded this feast to be kept by his true followers forever! This feast is also known as the *Feast of Ingathering* because it is associated with the two annual harvest in Israel. While the Feast of Firstfruit was the early and small spring time harvest and as it represents the small little flock called The Church . . .the Feast of Tabernacles is held during the late autumn harvest where the large harvest is gathered in, representing a much larger harvest than the small church gathered in the first harvest[1].

In order to get a true feel of the celebratory nature of this particular feast of God you need to spend some time studying Deuteronomy 16: 14-15. They are told to "***rejoice in their feast.***" This was to be a time of dancing and joy and merriment. Everyone including the servants and the strangers were to participate in this free for all celebration. Again they are told "***Thou shalt surely rejoice***" . . .Laugh, Play, Sing, Dance, Rejoice, all of those words indicate the festivities that the inhabitants of earth shall know when Satan has been bound and the Kingdom of God is being established upon the earth and the **Dream Team** begins to bring forth the plans of God throughout humanity. An old song of the church re-

minds us *"What rejoicing there will be when the saints shall rise."*

As we study more about this 6th feast which will transpire during the 7th day of Gods plan for the ages, we read about the food that is to be enjoyed during this feast[2]. In this verse we see God telling them and us that during the celebration of this feast we are to enjoy everything, all the bounty of the earth. Why? Because every year as the church gathers for this seven day conference, we all spend this week in total feasting and celebration and rejoicing as we anticipate the coming fulfillment when God shall use us to help Him gather in the much larger harvest of souls, the greatest revival the world has ever known, this shall all occur during the golden age of Gods kingdom on earth. During the Millennium under the righteous rule of Christ and His glorious sons the earth shall rejoice, she shall give forth abundantly of her crops, every man shall know the ways of God, the laws of God, every man shall be filled with the Holy Spirit and given a great gift of enjoying the earth as Adam and Eve did, in its Edenistic qualities. Every year as a church we celebrate this coming celebration as we worship the Lord in song and dancing and joyful fellowship and banqueting. This wonderful world tomorrow will be a literal utopia and you and I shall serve the nations of the world during this time if we have been counted worthy of the kingdom of God by our living and active faith which drives us into complete obedience to the Masters will, His commands.

As you continue to read more about this particular feast you will find it was also called the Feast of Booths; *Leviticus 23:40-42.* During this feast all the Israelites moved from their permanent homes

1 *Leviticus 23:39*

2 Duet 14:26

and pitched temporary dwellings or booths for the duration of this feast. Why did they do this? Because in moving into temporary dwellings they and we are reminded of the temporary nature of this fleshly body that we currently live in. We are reminded that during this coming Feast of Tabernacles during the Millennium we shall all be released from the holds of the flesh and live in our new Spirit bodies. We also know that by reading *Micah 4:1-2* that during this time the nations of the world will come to us for instructions in the ways of God. According to *Isaiah 11:9 and Jeremiah 31:34* the whole world will finally be gathered in as the final harvest of God. Before God could acquire this large autumn harvest he first called for the early spring harvest, you and I. Oh the glory and the majesty of Gods ways.

FEAST OF THE LAST GREAT DAY

After the One Thousand years foreshadowed by the annual feast of Tabernacles have ended then the great finale of Gods plans will finally be shown to the world. Only those who understand these wonderful feast and their meanings have any idea of how God plans to deal with the billions who have died without having a chance to hear the gospel. Of all the subjects that I discuss with theologians and ministers, this subject always produces a mixed bag of answers of which none make any sense. It wasn't until I began to understand this final feast of Israel that finally I understood Gods plans for those that He did not call to salvation in this our day. .He is a fair and just God and He will never allow anyone to die eternally with-

out a chance. However, He is also a Holy God and He will never allow anyone to come to Him through any other means than the gospel of Jesus Christ and believing in the same. So, this presents the world of theology with a great conundrum.

Perhaps you have an answer to the age old question; What happens to all of those billions who have lived and died without the luck of a missionary reaching them? What about those who live around you that the Holy Spirit has not drawn them to repentance, they are completely blinded to truth. What effects you and produces a response falls off of them like water on a ducks back. Are these people lost forever? What about the aborted children? What about those who died before ever hearing the gospel in any form? Is the destiny of all these people an eternal death, separated from God? What is your answer to this question? It begs an answer rather than a preconceived idea that in the end makes absolutely no sense. Learned men of great wisdom have answered this same question for me with the following answers:

- *Well, God has a special plan for those people.*

- *Well, anyone can look at nature and know there's a God and therefore they are without excuse.*

- *Well, God in His mercy will allow them to be saved without accepting Christ.*

The reason that none of the above "canned answers" will work is because they are based upon mans reasoning rather than the plain dictates of the Word of God. The answer to this age old and daunting questions is gloriously revealed to spiritually understanding minds in this last, seventh and final feast of

Israel, the Feast of the Last Great Day.

I can't help but wonder why we have come to believe that God will be satisfied with just a little handful of His created beings. Do we really surmise that God created a people that He was absolutely unable to bring to salvation? Are to accept that this amazing and august God will walk off into eternity accepting the loss of His created being and wonder for all eternity how Satan won and what more could God have done to keep from losing His own creation. Of the 155,000,000 that have lived and died without the gospel, we seem to think that God is just going to say "Oh well, I tried" and relinquish their souls to His archenemy? We misinterpret the words of Jesus when he talks about "few there be that find it" as he taught on eternal life. What people fail to understand is that during the age of the church there is indeed very few who will find eternal life but during the kingdom age, eternal life will find each and everyone that at one time died without having heard the gospel. As Joel prophesied " In that Day, God will pour out His Spirit upon ALL FLESH" *(Order my book: Was This really That for a better understanding of the happenings at Pentecost)* God created mankind and claimed that crowning achievement as His own masterpiece and I dare conclude that He has absolutely no intentions of accepting defeat and relinquishing 90% of His handiwork to the belching flames of hell. Scripture plainly tells us that God has one desire, to see all men saved!

II Peter 3:9
The Lord is not willing that any should perish . . .but that all men should come to repentance.

I Time 2:4
God our Saviour. . .who would have ALL MEN to be saved and to come to the knowledge of the truth.

Try as I might, I cannot fathom the great Creator as not seeing His desires come to pass. According to the Word of God, His desire is that ALL MEN be set free from Satans control so that they may hear the glorious message of truth and be brought unto salvation. So, is it any stretch of the imagination that in fact He has designed a perfect plan as revealed in these Feast of Israel to bring to pass His eternal plan for the majority of men to be saved and returned unto God, their Creator. You can believe on thing, God didn't create a plan for salvation and then only granting this plan to those lucky enough to have someone "reach them: with this plan and then all others not so lucky will simply be out of luck. On the other hand according the Word of God, no person, no one will ever be saved without accepting Jesus Christ as the sacrifice for their sins by faith.

This feast of the Last Great Day reveals to us so perfectly how that God will in fact give every man born to woman the opportunity to hear the glorious message of Christ. All of those that He did not personally call to salvation in the church age, all of those who died before Calvary, all of those who were completely blinded on purpose such as natural Israel; they must all get their chance. But when? But how? But where? All these answers God has beautifully revealed in this final feast. Just as the week is not complete without Gods seventh day Sabbath, neither is the plan of God complete without this seventh feast. Gods justice, love and mercy is grandly presented in this final and seventh feast. Let us study this feast a little deeper.

What was the last and final feast and how was it celebrated? We must turn to *Leviticus 23: 36,39.* Immediately following the Feast of Tabernacles or the Millennium reign of a thousand years we find in the above scriptures evidence of yet another feast, completely separate and yet at the same perfectly united, it is referred to as the 8th day. This 8th day transpires after the 7th day of the Feast of Tabernacles and of course 8 is always the number of new beginnings and its at this point that John the Revelator sees a "*New heaven and a New earth*" . . .coincidence? This 8th day being mentioned is in fact "the last day of the feast" making it plain that this celebration ends the plan for the ages of time and it ushers us into the new day of eternity. Notice carefully that Jesus Himself kept this 8th day festival as proven in *John 7:37*. This festival is a perfect type of The Great White Throne Judgement which will occur at the 2nd resurrection of those who didn't die in the faith, they are referred to as "the rest of the dead." These events are described for your further study in the book of Revelation 20:5 - 12. At this point all mortals who were not in the elect, or members of this chosen Dream Team, they shall rise again to mortal life whereas the church rises in the first resurrection to eternal life. In the first resurrection the judgement will not be for eternal life but rather it will be a judgment of rewards for the works of Christians done in this lifetime. However, the second judgement, the Great White Throne Judgement will be for God to judge the souls of men to eternal life or eternal death. If you read the scriptures you will notice here that this judgement will be a place where decisions are made according to the works of these people who have never heard the gospel and if you will notice, not only will the Book of Life be there but also other will books will be there for the judgement. It just so happens that the original Greek word for "*books*" is "*biblia*" which is the exact same word used for the English word "*Bible*". We have reasons to believe that the actual books that will be opened at this final judgement will in fact be the very Word of God. The gospel will be presented from these books and every man and woman and child will be then judged by their response to the gospel presented to them during this time of judgement.

The Beginning

My personal thanks for reading my books
I look forward to hearing from you

SHANE VAUGHN
Facebook: shanevaughn38
E-mail brothervaughn@gmail.com

Phone: 903-508-9376

Address
318 Friendship Church Rd
Columbia, Ms 39429

OTHER WRITINGS AVAILABLE BY
SHANE VAughn

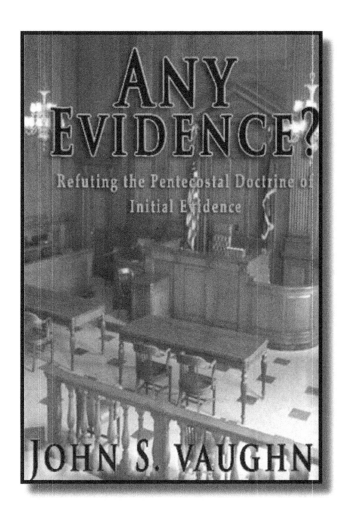

The doctrine of *Initial evidence* as established by the Pentecostal church; is it a provable doctrine? Is speaking in tongues the initial proof that someone has recieved the Holy Spirit? Is speaking in tonugues required for salvation as the Pentecostals teach?

OTHER WRITINGS AVAILABLE BY
SHANE VAughn

A full commentary on the book of Hebrews. In this book you will find answers to many questions cocerning eternal security, the promised rest of the believers and the danger of losing the hope of salvation.

OTHER WRITINGS AVAILABLE BY
SHANE VAUGHN

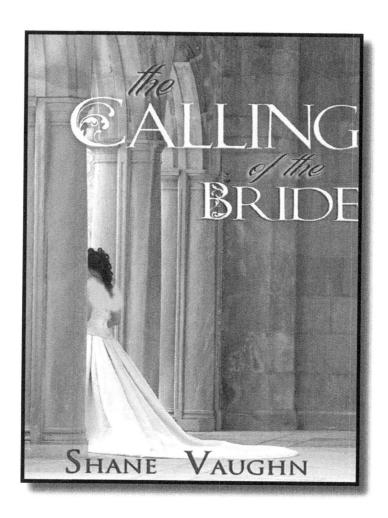

Does God work alone on the earth? In this book you will find your true and ultimate purpose as a member of the Bride of Christ. Perhaps until reading this book you have never completely understood your true potential while living on earth. There is a reason that you've been called into the Bride.

The Beginning